BLOOD THEOLOGY

The unsettling language of blood has been invoked throughout the history of Christianity. But until now there has been no truly sustained treatment of how Christians use blood to think with. Eugene F. Rogers, Jr. discusses in his much-anticipated new book the sheer, surprising strangeness of Christian blood-talk, exploring the many and varied ways in which it offers a language where Christians cooperate, sacrifice, grow, and disagree. He asks too how it is that blood-talk dominates when other explanations would do, and how blood seeps into places where it seems hardly to belong. Reaching beyond academic disputes to consider how religious debates fuel civil ones, he shows that it is not only theologians or clergy who engage in blood-talk, but also lawmakers, judges, generals, doctors, and voters at large. Religious arguments have significant societal consequences, Rogers contends; and for that reason secular citizens must do their best to understand them.

Eugene F. Rogers, Jr. is Professor of Religious Studies and of Women's, Gender, and Sexuality Studies at the University of North Carolina at Greensboro. He is the author of six books, including *Aquinas and the Supreme Court* (2013) and *Sexuality and the Christian Body* (2003), which was named "essential reading" by *The Christian Century* among books published in the past 25 years. His next book is *Elements of Christian Thought* (2021). His next book is *Elements of Christian Thought* (2021).

"This book offers an exhilarating reflection on what it is to think about, with, and for the sake of blood; and to so think – as it has long been thought – within the Christian tradition, but not only the Christian. Eugene Rogers' theological reflections are at all times in fruitful dialogue with those of other faiths and of other disciplines, most notably Judaism and anthropology, from which he learns and deepens his thinking. Rogers does not present a systematic reflection on blood. Rather he repeats blood's contradictions through a series of fragments: chapters that address various sites of blood's use, its spilling into social thought, into different cultural domains. Rewarding its readers with ever-deepening insight, the book is a singular and powerful work of theology that will enthral and provoke."

Gerard Loughlin, *Professor of Theology and Religion, Durham University, author of* Alien Sex: The Body and Desire in Cinema and Theology *and editor of* Queer Theology: Rethinking the Christian Body

"This book is sure to be both popular and important. The author is a distinguished theologian and philosopher. The topic is both fundamental to, yet neglected by, Christian theology, although 'blood' studies are big elsewhere in the academy, such as in anthropology and sociology. There is no other extended study of the Christian symbolics of blood – or certainly not by someone who brings together at a high level theology (Patristic, medieval, and modern), social theory, post-modern philosophy, and biblical studies. 'Blood' (real and symbolic) is something which, as the author points out, seeps into almost all historical theological topics: death, sacrifice, Eucharist, childbirth, and creation. It is also to the fore in many contemporary concerns of the churches: debates over killing animals and eating meat, torture, and – controversially – same-sex relations, racism, and (somewhat unexpectedly) creationism. A good book on the Christian symbolics of blood will be important to historians, social theorists, social scientists and the like, as well as to theologians and, indeed, church authorities as they struggle with some of the issues above. In sum, this is an original and important book by one of this generation's most innovative theologians."

Janet Soskice, *William K. Warren Distinguished Research Professor of Catholic Theology, Duke University, and Professor of Philosophical Theology, University of Cambridge; author of* The Kindness of God: Metaphor, Gender and Religious Language *and of* Sisters of Sinai: How Two Lady Adventurers Found the Hidden Gospels

BLOOD THEOLOGY

Seeing Red in Body- and God-Talk

EUGENE F. ROGERS, JR.
University of North Carolina at Greensboro

CAMBRIDGE
UNIVERSITY PRESS

University Printing House, Cambridge CB2 8BS, United Kingdom

One Liberty Plaza, 20th Floor, New York, NY 10006, USA

477 Williamstown Road, Port Melbourne, VIC 3207, Australia

314–321, 3rd Floor, Plot 3, Splendor Forum, Jasola District Centre, New Delhi – 110025, India

79 Anson Road, #06–04/06, Singapore 079906

Cambridge University Press is part of the University of Cambridge.

It furthers the University's mission by disseminating knowledge in the pursuit of education, learning, and research at the highest international levels of excellence.

www.cambridge.org
Information on this title: www.cambridge.org/9781108843287
DOI: 10.1017/9781108909983

© Eugene F. Rogers, Jr. 2021

This publication is in copyright. Subject to statutory exception and to the provisions of relevant collective licensing agreements, no reproduction of any part may take place without the written permission of Cambridge University Press.

First published 2021

Printed in the United Kingdom by TJ Books Limited, Padstow Cornwall

A catalogue record for this publication is available from the British Library.

Library of Congress Cataloging-in-Publication Data
NAMES: Rogers, Eugene F., Jr. (Eugene Fernand), author.
TITLE: Blood theology : seeing red in body- and God-talk / Eugene F. Rogers, Jr., University of North Carolina, Greensboro.
DESCRIPTION: Cambridge, United Kingdom ; New York, NY, USA : Cambridge University Press, 2021. | Includes bibliographical references and index.
IDENTIFIERS: LCCN 2020041191 (print) | LCCN 2020041192 (ebook) | ISBN 9781108843287 (hardback) | ISBN 9781108824187 (paperback) | ISBN 9781108909983 (ebook)
SUBJECTS: LCSH: Blood – Religious aspects – Christianity.
CLASSIFICATION: LCC BR115.B57 R64 2021 (print) | LCC BR115.B57 (ebook) | DDC 234–dc23
LC record available at https://lccn.loc.gov/2020041191
LC ebook record available at https://lccn.loc.gov/2020041192

ISBN 978-1-108-84328-7 Hardback

Cambridge University Press has no responsibility for the persistence or accuracy of URLs for external or third-party internet websites referred to in this publication and does not guarantee that any content on such websites is, or will remain, accurate or appropriate.

For Carol, Michael, and Margarito

CONTENTS

Acknowledgments		*page* ix

PART I WHY WE SEE RED

1	How Blood Marks the Bounds of the Christian Body: Overtures and Refrains	3

PART II BLOOD SEEPS IN WHERE IT HARDLY SEEMS TO BELONG: BLOOD UNNECESSARY AND INEXHAUSTIBLE

2	Blood after Isaac: And God Said "Na"	39
3	Blood after Leviticus: Separation and Sacrifice	51
4	Blood after the Last Supper: Jesus and the Gender of Blood	83

PART III BLOOD MAKES A LANGUAGE IN WHICH TO CONDUCT DISPUTES: FAMILY, TRUTH, AND TRIBE

5	Bridegrooms of Blood: Same-Sex Desire and the Blood of Christ	117
6	Red in Tooth and Claw: Creationism, Evolution, and the Blood of Christ	131
7	Blood Purity and Human Sacrifice: Castilians Meet Aztecs in War	161

viii CONTENTS

PART IV THE BLOOD OF GOD AT THE HEART OF THINGS:
CAUSALITY SACRAMENTAL AND COSMIC

8 How the Eucharist "Causes" Salvation:
The Physiology of the Eucharist, or Virtue and Blood Chemistry   185

9 The Blood of Christ and the Christology of Things:
Why Things Became Human   201

Appendix – Review of Gil Anidjar's *Blood: A Critique of Christianity*   217

Sources Cited or Consulted   226

Scripture Index   237

Subject Index   240

ACKNOWLEDGMENTS

This book has richly benefited from the support of several granting agencies: The Tantur Institute for Ecumenical Studies in Jerusalem, a foundation of Notre Dame University, lent me a beautiful office in an empty library from December 2009 to July 2010. The Center of Theological Inquiry, supported by the Templeton Foundation, invited me to join their team on Evolution and Human Nature in Princeton for the academic year 2012–13. The Human Distinctiveness Project, administered by Notre Dame and funded by the Templeton Foundation, invited me to what I called "Evolution Summer Camp" in the summer of 2015 and, together with the Lady Davis Fellowship Trust, supported me at the Hebrew University of Jerusalem for the academic year 2015–16, where the research team on Poetics and Christian Performance at the Israel Institute for Advanced Studies found me an office on their hall and a place at their table. Finally, the Department of Religious Studies at the University of Virginia hosted a daylong workshop with faculty and students who had read the entire manuscript.

Longer and shorter passages have benefited from the insights of editors and anonymous reviewers for the following publications which are used with permission:

"Sociology and Theology of Creationist Objections to Evolution: How Blood Bounds the Christian Body," *Zygon* 49 (2014): 540–53.

"The Binding of Isaac as a Trickster Narrative: And God Said 'Na,'" *Journal of Textual Reasoning* 8 (2014) at https://pages.shanti.virginia.edu/JTR/volume-8-number-1/ (ca. 11 printed pages).

"The Genre of this Book," review essay on *Blood: A Critique of Christianity* by Gil Anidjar in *The Theology Syndicate* 2:1 (February 2015): 145–54.

"Tanner's Non-Competitive Account and the Blood of Christ: Where Eucharistic Theology Meets the Evolution of Ritual," in Hilda

Koster and Rosemary Carbine, eds., *The Gift of Theology: The Contribution of Kathryn Tanner* (Minneapolis, MN: Fortress Press, 2015), 139–57.

"The Fire in the Wine: How Can the Blood of Christ Carry the Holy Spirit," in Myk Habets, ed., *Third Article Theology* (Philadelphia: Fortress Press, 2016), 251–64.

"Blood," in Adam Johnson, ed., *Companion to the Atonement* (Edinburgh: T. & T. Clark, an imprint of Bloomsbury Publishing PLC, 2017), 403–6.

"The Blood of Christ and the Christology of Things, or Why Things Became Human," in Stephen Wright, ed., *The Promise of Robert Jenson's Theology* (Minneapolis, MN: Fortress, 2017), 159–75.

It is a pleasant task to think back over the colleagues, students, and friends who have accompanied me on this project:

Ro Chan Hong, who first sent me to Borneo.

Colleagues on the Episcopal panel tasked to write a theology of same-sex relationships, where blood kept coming up, sometimes without my knowing at whose instigation, and sometimes in productive disagreement: Ellen Charry, John Goldingay, George Sumner, Daniel Westberg, Deirdre Good, Cynthia Kittredge, and especially (in very different ways) Grant LeMarquand and Willis Jenkins.

Father Michael McGarry, CSP, the rector who welcomed me at Tantur; later rectors Timothy Lowe and Russell McDougal; Issa Daboub who ran reception; the librarians, Carole Mickel Tabash, Sahar Hazboun, and Jacqueline Mazoyer, who welcomed me at a later time; the cook, Abed; the Vice-Rector, Sister Bridget Tighe, F.M.D.M.; and among the scholars who passed through, Ellen Cherry, David Burrell, and Eleonore Stump. Others from that time included Omar Othman, who began to teach me Palestinian Arabic; Avivah Zornberg; John Gager; Steven Kepnes; Adam Cohen and Linda Safran; Yonatan Livneh, who sometimes found me books even though he didn't have to; Hillel Newman, Aryeh Kofsky, and Lorenzo Perrone, whom we persuaded to eat dinner as often as we could and who wanted me to read all four volumes of the acts of *Sangue e antropologia nella liturgia* of the Pia Unione Preziosissimo Sangue.

Colleagues at Princeton and the Center for Theological Inquiry, including Will Storrar and Robin Lovin; Celia Deane-Drummond and Dominic Johnson, who led the group; Nicola Hoggard Creegan, Markus Muehling, Agustín Fuentes, Rich Sosis, Jan-Olav Henriksen, Aku Olavi Visala, Hillary Lenfesty, Jeffrey Schloss, and Robert Song. Others in the Princeton orbit: Jeffrey Stout, Eric Gregory, Martha Himmelfarb, Leora Batnitzky, Moulie

ACKNOWLEDGMENTS

Vidas, Cathy Kaveny, and especially Naphtali Meshel, who is not responsible for any of my mistakes. Members and attendees at the Duodecim Society, especially Nancy Duff, Peter Ochs, Vanessa Ochs, Susan Eastman, Joe Mangina, and Kendall Soulen; Robert and Blanche Jenson; Cleo Kearns; Ellen Charry again.

Colleagues in Jerusalem a second time: Brouria Bitton-Ashkelony, who got me a Lady Davis Fellowship, an office, meals, and excursions with her husband Ilon, and daily lunches at the Israel Institute of Advanced Study (even though I was a guest and a spouse and not a member); Virginia Burrus; Glenn Peers; Yitzhak and Raheli Hen; Yossi Maurey and Amir Fink; Warren Woodfin; Nina Glibetic and Gabriel Radle; Georgia Frank; Betsy Bolman; Noam Maeir, who got me lots of books; and Diana Lipton and Paula Fredriksen. I took Palestinian Arabic again from Omar Othman. I have counted up over twenty-five language teachers in my life, and he was in the top two (the other was Reginald Foster). Not that my Arabic got at all good. He told me I had to talk to strangers; but I rarely talk to strangers even in English.

In the orbit of Notre Dame's Human Distinctiveness Project, the leaders, Celia Deane-Drummond and Agustín Fuentes; the staff, especially Rebecca Artinian-Kaiser and Adam Willows; and colleagues Barbara Rossing, Nicola Hoggard Creegan, Oliver Davies, John Berkman, Todd Hanneken, Joel Hodge, Philip Rolnick, Timothy Sandoval, Arthur Walker-Jones, Rhodora Beaton, Simon Gaine, and Neil Arner.

Students and others in the Duke orbit who made the menstruation chapter less bad and are not responsible for any failures of fact or tone: Julie Morris, Deb Ebert, and, all together in an intervention, Christina Ananias, Emily Dubie, Sarah Jobe, and Aminah Bradford.

Gregory S. Williams, who read the whole manuscript, as well as Matt Elia, and the faculty who made the students available to me, especially Luke Bretherton, Jay Kameron Carter, Curtis Freeman, Laura Lieber, and Lauren Winner, the last reader of the manuscript, who made insightful additions.

At the University of Virginia, Chuck Mathewes organized the book workshop. Elizabeth Cable, Evan Sandsmark, and especially William Boyce offered formal reviews. Julie Morris, Brandy Daniels, Elizabeth Becker, Brandy Daniels, and especially Chuck, Willis Jenkins, and Paul Daffyd Jones offered constructive suggestions.

I wish to thank my dean, Timothy Johnston, for being the best dean I ever hope to have and making all these occasions possible, several times with Research Assignments providing half salary. The university also supported

xii ACKNOWLEDGMENTS

me in smaller ways, including Regular Faculty Grants, Faculty First Grants, and Kohler Grants for summer research or international travel. I thank Marc Bregman and Sarah Bregman for gifts of reading and objection, as well as other colleagues at the University of North Carolina at Greensboro during the decade I took to write the book, including Ellen Haskell, Alyssa Gabbay, Liz Bucar, Charlie Orzech, Bill Hart, Ben Ramsey, Ashlee Andrews, Greg Grieve, and Jen Feather; as well as students, especially Joseph Naron, Joe Duffield, Ian Courts, and Arthur Blankinship; and Interlibrary Loan, especially Gaylor Callahan, and Dallas Burkhardt.

In the Cambridge orbit, Sarah Coalkley, Janet Soskice, and Oliver Soskice. At Cambridge University Press, Alex Wright (also the editor, years ago, of *Sexuality and the Christian Body*). The copyeditor, Bret Workman. Anonymous readers for the press, as well as for grant agencies and journal publishers.

The scholar who had the most influence on this book was Bettina Bildhauer. When I cold-emailed her in 2011 to say she had written the best sentence I'd ever read about blood, she replied, "Good, it took me eight years to write that sentence."

From week to week I was sustained by two groups in Greensboro: the Porch Wine group of Vicki McCready, MacGregor Frank, Kay Lovelace, and Rick Bardolph; and the Italian Group: Charlie Headington, Debby Seabrooke, Maurice and Genie Schwartz, Jean Cornwell, Joanne Murphy, Tim Kircher, and Bill Ledford.

And Derek Krueger, my husband, who accompanied me in all these places and many of these thoughts.

Part I

Why We See Red

I

HOW BLOOD MARKS THE BOUNDS OF THE CHRISTIAN BODY
Overtures and Refrains

THIS BOOK HAS THREE GENESES: SIMIANS, SEX, AND SACRIFICE. All three came unbidden, presenting symptoms or unsought oracles of blood.

In the winter of 2008, trying to get a break from theology, I found myself in a boat on the Kinabatangan in Borneo, looking for orangutans. Having heard the (misleading) statistic that humans are "98% chimpanzee,"[1] I couldn't lose the idea that the biblical word for DNA might be "blood." And that brought on questions like, "What if the blood of Christ was the blood of a primate?" And "Why did God become simian?" (See Chapters 6 and 9.) I tried to treat the questions. They weren't academic, and I had other books to write. But they wouldn't go away, and my husband told me I was writing a book despite myself.

In the fall of 2008, assigned, for my sins, to write a "theology of same-sex relationships" for the Episcopal House of Bishops, I heard that "the trouble with same-sex couples is, they impugn the blood of Christ." What did that even mean? And who were these people with their strange blood-fixation? (See Chapter 5.)

In the fall of 2009, I remembered Michael Wyschogrod, whom I had first read twenty years earlier. I had been telling granting agencies I would figure out what Hebrews 9:22 meant by "without the shedding of blood, there is no remission of sin." (See Chapters 3 and 7.) I discovered that the most interesting thing about Christian commentary on that passage is how thin it is. If you look into Christian

---

[1] For a hilarious takedown of that pseudo-statistic, see Jonathan Marks, *What It Means to Be 98% Chimpanzee: Apes, People, and Their Genes*, with a new preface (Berkeley: University of California Press, 2003). Ra'anan S. Boustan and Annette Yoshiko Reed, "Introduction to Theme-Issue," *Blood and the Boundaries of Jewish and Christian Identities in Late Antiquity*, published as *Henoch* 30.2 (2008): 229–42 is elegant and compatible. Unaccountably it came to my attention only as the book was in production.

commentaries on "without the shedding of blood" you find either *domestication*, so that, in Aquinas, bloodshed needs no explanation at all, or *evasion*, as in Calvin, where "blood" means something entirely different from physical blood; it means "faith." This is a choice of frustrations: so blasé as to take sacrifice for granted, or so offended as to dismiss it outright. Briefly I hoped that Philoxenus of Mabbug interpreted the "labor of blood" as that of childbirth, but colleagues with Syriac said it wasn't so simple. (See the excursus to Chapter 4.) Origen is wonderful, but everything means something else. None of the Christian commentators I read were trying to understand what Wittgenstein called the "deep and sinister" in the appeal to blood.[2]

Then I remembered how Wyschogrod, the Jewish Barthian, does something better than all the Christian commentators I consulted. He finds blood strange. Wyschogrod neither evades blood, nor does he, by repetition, disarm it even more effectively. Here is a sample, longish but abridged:

> A dumb animal is to be slaughtered. [It emits no] sound of terror because it does not understand the instrument. It is then swiftly cut, the blood gushes forth, the bruiting begins [the sound of an artery's turbulent flow, blood rushing past an obstruction]. [T]he animal's eyes lose their living sheen. The blood is sprinkled on the altar, the animal dismembered, portions of it burned, [others] eaten by the priests who minister before God in the holiness of the Temple. This horror is brought into the house of God. [What leads from] slaughter to the holy?
>
> Sacrificial Judaism brings the truth of human existence into the Temple. It does not leave it outside. It does not reserve sacred ground only for silent worship. Instead, the bruiting, bleeding, dying animal is brought and shown to God. This is what *our* fate is. It is not so much, as [often] said, that we deserved the fate of the dying animal and that we have been permitted to escape [that] fate by transferring it. It is rather that our fate and the animal's are the same [fate] because its end awaits us, since our eyes, too, will soon gaze blindly and [fix] in deathly attention on what only the dead seem to see. In the Temple it is [we human animals] who stand before God, not as [we] would like to be, but as we truly are, [realizing] that our blood will soon enough flow as well. [We see, not the animal in place of us; we see ourselves with the animal. It is not one who dies that another may live; it is both who die together.] Enlightened religion recoils with horror from the thought of sacrifice, preferring a spotless house of worship filled with organ music and exquisitely polite behavior. The price paid for such decorum is that the worshipers must leave the most problematic part of themselves outside the

[2] Ludwig Wittgenstein, *Bemerkungen über Frazers Golden Bough/Remarks on Frazer's Golden Bough*, German and English on facing pages, ed. Rush Rees, trans. A. C. Miles (Atlantic Highlands, NJ: Humanities Press International, 1979), 8. See Chapter 7.

temple, to reclaim it when the service is over and to live with it unencumbered by sanctification. Religion ought not to demand such a dismemberment of [*the human being*].[3]

Here endeth the reading from Wyschogrod. I note that it defends Second Temple Judaism from Christian supersessionism not by mishnaic means but according to the modern pattern of aligning sacrifice with solidarity rather than sin. I return to it in Chapters 3 and 7. Here I only hope it makes blood strange.

***

IN REFERRING TO WITTGENSTEIN'S "DEEP AND SINISTER," I DO NOT mean to agree with what you might call the vulgar Girardian theory that sees violence all the way down. That would be hamartiocentric, sin-centered. Theology knows a protology before sin and an eschatology after it; the sin-story receives a frame and cannot stand in for the whole. The frame makes donation or offering broader than "sacrifice" – and it makes blood, the life-giver, wider than sacrifice too. Sacrifice does not go all the way down, but marks a subset of life-giving: life-giving under conditions of sin. Sarah Coakley's work in *Sacrifice Regained*, I think, seeks to restore sacrifice to that frame, to connect the Garden at the beginning to the Feast at the end.[4]

In any case, I work here on another front. I want to recover the strangeness of blood and then, perhaps, its even stranger logic. Part of the strangeness I want to recover is that of quantity. Why so much? Why not less? My target is not those for whom violence goes all the way down but those who would so familiarize the language of blood as to domesticate or evade it. My inquiry *relies* on the sin-free frame but now and then takes place within it, where sin gains enough reality to need remitting, and that sometimes in terms of blood.

Within the frame, we – as human or at least religious beings – can admit our solidarity both with Aztecs, who seem actually to have practiced human sacrifice (Chapter 7), as well as with any who would restore animal sacrifice in a Third Temple. I'm not in favor of either, but I want to understand what

---

[3] Michael Wyschogrod, *The Body of Faith: God in the People Israel* (San Francisco: Harper & Row, 1983), 18–19. In several editions from different publishers, the subtitle varies but the text remains the same. For ease of reading I have cut words without using ellipses.

[4] Sarah Coakley, *Sacrifice Regained: Evolution, Cooperation and God*, Gifford Lectures (Edinburgh, 2012), esp. lectures 1 and 6 at www.giffordlectures.org/lectures/sacrifice-regained-evolution-cooperation-and-god.

they tell us about what it means to be human, to admit that their deep and sinister thing is our thing, too.

***

CONSIDER THE LOGIC OF THE CLAIM "WITHOUT THE SHEDDING OF blood there is no remission of sin" (Heb. 9:22). The sentence makes blood instrumental to the remission of sin, but it's a queer sort of instrumentality. Nancy Jay suggests a thought experiment. Replace the words about blood with words about wood, and compare:

> "Without the cutting of trees, there is no building of clapboard houses."
> Surely that's sensible enough. But this:–?
> "Without the shedding of blood, there is no remission of sin."[5]

The substitution has the virtue of estranging the obvious question: How then do we use blood? To remit sin? Blood does not work like wood after all. Nor does the blood of Christ reduce to the wood of his cross (Chapters 4 and 8).

Elsewhere I warn about grandiose theory. I confess it here; later comes the part where I take it back. Emile Durkheim, Mary Douglas, Nancy Jay, and Bettina Bildhauer can help us think about the structures that blood makes in Christianity and other social groups, that cause the body individual or the body sacrificed to represent the body social.

Mary Douglas takes as axiomatic that anomalies generate pollution, taboo, and sacredness: purity and danger. But what's the *mechanism*? It's the image of the boundary. Not the boundary "itself," but its socially available *image*, its appearing in socially constructed space. The image of the boundary is the boundary salient, the boundary seen. It is first of all, for Douglas, a social boundary: a force field that society both makes and feels. But the bound that society makes, and that makes society, recruits individual bodies to represent that society in small. The business of boundedness makes both society and individual a "body," a self-enclosed unit of humanity.

As Bettina Bildhauer notes, the *Oxford English Dictionary* collects hundreds of uses of the word "body" and sums them up like this: "the material frame of man." The definition, Bildhauer comments, "singles out materiality and humanness as main features, with the word 'frame' suggesting a bound entity, carrying and unifying the human being. But this idea of a body as a material, bounded entity," she concludes, "is far from self-evident." The body takes in

---

[5] Nancy Jay, *Throughout Your Generations Forever: Sacrifice, Religion, and Paternity* (Chicago: University of Chicago Press, 1992), 1.

food, water, air, and expels waste. "Far from providing a smooth envelope, skins constantly receive and emit fluids through pores and cells, so that it is impossible to determine which atom, say, is still part of the epidermis and the intestinal lining and which is not, and which pork molecule has turned into a human molecule. Even the 'inside' of a body is full of skins, opening up many surfaces. ... We live 'as much in processes across and through skins as in processes "within" skins.' ... Despite the usefulness of the ... body as a separate, enclosed unit, ... this view is not at all obvious, and *instead needs a lot of cultural work to be upheld.*"[6]

$$***$$

FOR A GENERATION, HUMANITIES SCHOLARS HAVE IMAGINED "THE body" bounded as an envelope, not seeping with a fluid to alarm its orifices. In Bynum, Biale, Bildhauer, and Anidjar, "the body" has yielded to blood. Historians like Bynum confine blood-talk to the past; critics like Anidjar would ban it altogether. Historians or critics, those scholars hardly address the anthropological problem that blood *persists*. Strategies that only confine or sanitize are designed to fail. Blood persists because it provides a fluid to think with, a key to the scriptures, and a language in which to disagree. Internal and external critics of Christianity have protested for half a century and more that Christian blood-signaling is dangerous.[7] Yes, it is dangerous, but the protest has been anthropologically naïve. I intervene in their critique to say that Christian blood-signaling is not going away, and that the options are not exhausted by repristinating it, on the one hand, or deploring it, on the other. A third option remains: to repeat blood's language subversively, to free it from contexts of oppression or violence. This option reclaims or "mobilizes the signifier for an alternative production."[8]

$$***$$

ONLY THE BODY'S UNREMARKED BOUNDARY IS THAT OF SKIN. ITS *salient, defended, or fertile* boundary is that of blood. When something foreign penetrates the skin, or when it "leaks" (verbs I interrogate later), the envelope

---

[6] Bettina Bildhauer, *Medieval Blood* (Cardiff: University of Wales Press, 2006), 1–3, my italics, quoting Shannon Sullivan, *Living across and through Skins: Transactional Bodies, Pragmatism, and Feminism* (Bloomington: Indiana University Press, 2001), x.

[7] An example I taught for years: Joanne Carlson Brown and Rebecca Parker, "For God So Loved the World?" in *Christianity, Patriarchy, and Abuse: A Feminist Critique*, ed. Joanne Carlson Brown and Carole R. Bohn (New York: The Pilgrim Press, 1989), 1–30.

[8] Judith Butler, "Contingent Foundations," in Seyla Benhabib, et al., *Feminist Contentions: A Philosophical Exchange* (London and New York: Routledge, 1995), 35–57; here, 51–2.

turns red. Blood trickles, flows, or floods, prompting self and others to react with more or less alarm. Blood attracts attention – or society attends to blood – on the skin: the boundary of skin becomes salient with blood. The vigor with which society marks its boundaries is the vigor with which the body reacts to blood.

Moderns, medievals, and ancients all pictured the body as a sack of blood. When the sack leaked, or something punctured it, what had been inside emerged to coat the exterior. If this coating is sweat, it may draw little notice. Spittle doesn't draw much notice either, at least in a baby; more in someone older. Tears call forth concern. The leakage of sexual fluids we hide under clothes or behind doors. But blood reliably brings alarm. Unlike sweat, spit, or tears, blood is not clear. Blood's color makes it useful. Blood marks both society's investment in the individual and the individual's in society, blazes that relationship in red.

Blood is red because iron compounds transport oxygen. But society has recruited its bright, saturated color to rubricate the body and interpret life and death in terms of blood. It is not just that blood loss can lead to death. It is not just that society must care about its members. Many things share those qualities without becoming to the same extent as blood a fluid to think with. We also care about breathing and dialysis – but they do not define society as blood does. Breath is not visible. Dialysis is not natural. The importance of blood is that it combines life and death with the marks of enclosure and breach: its color and its tendency to flag the body's bounds in red when something penetrates the body, or leaves its bounds, give blood an imaging function that little else can match. "[T]he dominant medieval view of the body, as today, was that of a closed container," but "the awareness that this model could not always be upheld caused more anxiety than enthusiasm. ... Both affirmation and challenges to the dominant view of the body ... played out, crucially, through blood."[9]

***

WE SEE ANOTHER PATTERN OF AFFIRMATION AND CHALLENGE PLAY out in terms of blood when liberals contest evangelical models of atonement. Evangelicals insist that "blood" in the New Testament means "death," because "without the shedding of blood there is no remission of sin" or, in vulgar Anselmian terms, because they regard the blood of Jesus as a death that pays a

---

[9] Bildhauer, 7.

debt for sin. Liberals insist that blood means "life," citing cross-cultural studies as well as Gen. 9:4, Lev. 17:11, 14, and Dt. 12:23.[10] Indeed, Lev. 17:11 says *both* that "the life of the flesh is in the blood" *and* that "as life, it is blood that makes atonement" – complicating the claim that, in sacrifice, what makes atonement is death. Part of blood's power is to represent opposites: life *and* death, health *and* disease, kin *and* alien, treasure *and* waste. A historian lets the paradox stand: "Blood is, both physiologically and symbolically, more complex and labile because [why?] finally contradictory. Blood is life and death."[11] That is, as far as descriptive data lead – to the productive contradiction.

An anthropologist and a theologian will, however, both want to know more – more than the descriptive historian may think quite decent. *Why* does blood represent life and death? Especially when "humans much more frequently experience non-lethal blood-loss and non-bloody deaths"?[12] What is the underlying social necessity to locate the productive contradiction *here*? Why not (as an anonymous reviewer noted) in water? Or (in Vedic sacrifice) breath? Neither is red like blood. According to Bildhauer, the underlying social necessity is to uphold the body as stable. If the individual or social body is fraught with orifices, leaks, penetrations, and transfusions, they cry out to be stanched or stabilized by social *work:* society casts the complexity and instability onto "blood." The pairs of opposites always "rely on and enforce the concept of the bounded body," creating, sociologically, an "inside" and "outside" for blood to be on; "instead of seeing blood to be [intrinsically] 'more complex,'" Bildhauer contends, "the seeming complexity of blood depends on the seeming stability of the body, and vice versa. Blood was only separated into matter 'inside' and 'outside' the body because its movement was crucial" to maintaining the body as a stable sack across the boundary of which blood could move, "and the body appeared as a closed container because one location of blood is perceived to be outside and another inside."[13] Those opposites prove neither intrinsic nor innocent. Rather society invests in them all. Society creates the opposites to define, stabilize, establish something that society and individual find of high importance: their picture of themselves – their picture of themselves as bounded – as "this" and not "that," "us" and not

---

[10] Alan M. Stibbs, *The Meaning of the Word Blood in Scripture*, 3rd rev. ed. (Oxford: Tyndale Press, 1963).

[11] Caroline Walker Bynum, "The Blood of Christ in the Later Middle Ages," *Church History* 71 (2002): 685–714; here, 706–7. See extensively *Wonderful Blood: Theology and Practice in Late Medieval Northern Germany* (University of Pennsylvania Press, 2007).

[12] Bildhauer, 6.

[13] Bildhauer, 6.

"them." *Much religious creativity consists in enlarging this boundary, so that those formerly "them" are now "us," and out of death comes life, so that "death is swallowed up in victory"* (I Cor. 15:57) — *that is, finds itself enclosed within a larger body.* (See Chapter 3.)

With larger bodies we do not exactly get beyond that picture, but we can extend it productively to sublate itself. We can never leap right out of the society in which we think, but we can often use its categories in novel ways to reach beyond themselves. Judith Butler (in a passage I have quoted before, and will quote again) puts it like this:

> To deconstruct [a pair of opposites] is not to negate or refuse either term. To deconstruct these terms means, rather, to continue to use them, to repeat them, to repeat them subversively, and to displace them from contexts in which they have been deployed as instruments of oppressive power. Here it is of course necessary to state quite plainly that the options for theory are not exhausted by presuming [for example, the concept of the body], on the one hand, and negating it, on the other. It is my purpose to do precisely neither of these. . . . [My procedure] does not freeze, banish, render useless, or deplete of meaning the usage of the term; on the contrary, it provides the conditions to mobilize the signifier in the service of an alternative production.[14]

That's what Jesus does at the Last Supper. He takes the language of violent execution and turns it to a peaceful feast. "This is my body, broken for you." "This is my blood, poured out for many." He mobilizes the signifier for an alternative production. But the right mobilization and the right alternative for the signifier are hard to predict. How do we do that again?

✳✳✳

BLOOD MAY BE RED BECAUSE IRON COMPOUNDS MAKE IT SO, BUT *societies draft its material qualities, its color and stickiness, for multiple purposes of their own. I would say it in every chapter if I could. We imagine individual, social, and animal bodies as securely bounded. Inside, blood carries life. Outside, blood marks the body fertile or at risk. According to Bildhauer, society's work to maintain bodily integrity thus takes place in blood. It's the body's permeability that leaves us bloody-minded; it's in blood's terms that society makes a body. The body becomes a membrane to pass when it breathes, eats, perspires, eliminates, menstruates, ejaculates, conceives, or bleeds. Only bleeding evokes so swift and public a response: blood brings mother to child, bystander to victim,*

---

[14] Butler, "Contingent Foundations," 51–2, paragraph boundary elided.

ambulance to patient, soldier to comrade, midwife to mother, defender to border. If society is a body, society's integrity is blood's work.

***

WHEN I WRITE, NEW IDEAS RARELY SPRING FROM NOTHING. THEY bud on old growth. I want to include the budding matrix, even when several branches spread from there. I don't mind the repetitions, I like them: I call them refrains. Like refrains in hymns, I print them in italics. You can skip them once you know how they go. Or, if you like them, you can sing along.

To modify the metaphor, this chapter, like an overture, plays for the first time the principal tunes, to make them recognizable them when they come back.

***

I JUST WROTE THAT "IT'S THE BODY'S PERMEABILITY THAT LEAVES US bloody-minded." But we'll see in Chapter 4 that permeability, however often feared, isn't always bad. Jeff Stout, in a chapter called "Blood and Harmony," contrasts two organizations with different initiations into purity and permeability. One is a gang that requires new members to qualify by having killed someone different from themselves. Another trains organizers by requiring them to join two by two in mixed-race pairs. In that case, "the group was inculcating a habit of bridge-building, so that the identity-conferring boundary around the group was already rendered permeable in the very act of defining it."[15]

***

READERS OF GRANT PROPOSALS WANTED TO KNOW, ARE WE TALKING about "real" or "symbolic" blood? The short answer is, we're talking about any version of blood that carries social meaning. A distinction between "real" and "symbolic" blood only comes up once social meaning is in play: the two arise together. Consider some examples in which symbolic blood competes with physical blood for the compliment of being treated as the most "real."

In the *Dauerwunder* of late medieval Germany,[16] pilgrims regarded the substance in certain reliquaries as real, human blood miraculously kept fluid

---

[15] Jeffrey Stout, "Blood and Harmony," in *Blessed Are the Organized: Grassroots Democracy in America* (Princeton, NJ: Princeton University Press, 2010), 181–5; here, 182–3.

[16] For this paragraph: Caroline Bynum, *Wonderful Blood* (Philadelphia: University of Pennsylvania Press, 2007).

and red. Reliquary blood, liquid and bright, came to rival the wine consecrated by a priest and controlled by the hierarchy. Which was the *true* blood, the blood that bound the community together "for real"? Was it the reliquary blood, with apparently greater claims to physicality, which bound the pilgrims ecstatically with a common experience of wonder? Or was it the institutional blood, with the acknowledged accidents of wine, which bound the church into a hierarchy with priest, bishop, pope, and even dissenter or reformer? Bynum's *Wonderful Blood* details the conflict precisely where instances of reliquary blood, with greater claims to being physical, to having once flowed in human veins, gave up, albeit with excruciating slowness, the claim to be more real than sacramental blood. Eventually the hierarchy won, and the blood that maintained the deepest connections with the *social* body retained the title "true" – the blood that best connected the individual and society, the human being and God, the brothers and the Father, the body of Christ and the Body of Christ. It is of high importance that the metaphorical blood of the Eucharist became no less real in its conflict with putatively biological blood, but finally more. The exception of reliquary blood proves the rule that symbolic blood – so far from contrasting with "real" blood – instead controls what counts as real. Social power makes symbolic blood more real than physical blood, much as it makes paper money a matter of life and death. Robert Parker, writing on Greek religion, states a general principle: the "commandeering of the natural processes by society through ritual is so effective that when ritual and physical facts conflict, physical status yields to ritual."[17] In drag culture, "realness" applies to those queering gender.

If we today regard physical blood as more real, that's because of a powerful social practice called medicine. If we have learned that only a transfusion of biological blood will heal us – and certainly not red wine – medieval Christians learned the opposite: that only the drinking (or, if communion was offered in one kind, the mere sight or proximity) of consecrated wine could save them – and certainly not biological human blood.

Or consider the blood of martyrs in Ignatius of Antioch. Here too the symbol recruits the physical. Ignatius writes, "I desire the drink of God, namely his blood, which is . . . eternal life." While the "drink of God, namely his blood" refers to eucharistic wine, it also refers to Ignatius's desire, under circumstances he cannot escape, for martyrdom: "Allow me to become food for the wild beasts, through whose instrumentality it will be granted me to attain to God. I am the wheat of God, and let me be ground by the teeth of

---

[17] Robert C. T. Parker, *Miasma: Pollution and Purification in Early Greek Religion* (Oxford: Clarendon Press, 1983), 63.

the wild beasts, that I may be found the pure bread of Christ."[18] The commonplace is to trace the Eucharist to a real sacrifice (Christ's), but Ignatius boldly does the reverse: He traces a real sacrifice (his) to the Eucharist. In Ignatius, the Eucharist does not so much represent a martyr (Jesus), as a martyr (Ignatius) represents the Eucharist. The Eucharist represents, for him, so powerful a symbol that it reaches out to coopt, absorb, requisition physical realities to represent *it*. The call to *become Eucharist* so overtakes Ignatius that he warns others to resist it, for this Eucharist recruits even martyrs to represent and replicate itself. What it replicates is self-sacrifice. The paradox makes sense as eucharistic blood becomes more real than the martyr's blood.

The consecrated wine receives the high designation "the drink of God" because it alone flows with the *community's* blood, the *social* blood, which is at the same time the blood of God. Why? Because, in Durkheim's terms, that's what a totem does: identify the society with its cosmology and its god – or because, in Christian terms, that's what analogy does (*analogia sanguinis*): establish a multilevel hierarchy whereby God elevates human beings, gift upon gift, into participation in God's own life.

Social blood is more powerful, more real, more substantial than physical blood, because social blood alone conveys meaning. When the voluntary shedding of physical blood changes society, it's because social meaning changes in the process. Only when physical blood conflows with social blood does it mean; only when social blood changes does physical blood take effect. This is not to refuse the offerings of physical blood, make them vain, or deprive them of meaning, but to name their power precisely as one to change social meanings: not only to revive or resist, but also to vary, divert, re-channel, dissipate, or exhaust them. Blood's social reality becomes clear when Ignatius warns: "Be careful, therefore, to take part only in the one Eucharist; for there is only one flesh of our Lord Jesus Christ and one cup to unite us with his blood."[19] This blood carries the force of union, the social principle *par excellence*. "For drink I crave his blood, which is love that cannot perish":[20] this blood carries love, the social relation stronger than death.

---

[18] Ignatius of Antioch, *Letter to the Romans*, chapters (i.e., paragraphs) 4 and 7 in Ante-Nicene Fathers, vol. 1, trans. Alexander Roberts and James Donaldson (Buffalo, NY: Christian Literature Publishing Co., 1885), rev. and ed. for New Advent by Kevin Knight at www.newadvent.org/fathers/0107.htm.

[19] Ignatius, *Philadelphians* 4, trans. Alexander Roberts and James Donaldson, Ante-Nicene Fathers, vol. 1, ed. Alexander Roberts, James Donaldson, and A. Cleveland Coxe (Buffalo, NY: Christian Literature Publishing Co., 1885), rev. and ed. for New Advent by Kevin Knight at www.newadvent.org/fathers/0108.htm.

[20] Ignatius, *Romans* 7:3.

BLOOD THEOLOGY

The social practice called the Eucharist, communion, or the sacrament of the Lord's Supper brings the group to itself as a community, to know itself as a body, to see its blood as its own. Eucharistic disputes create and conserve ways of speaking that reveal the community's blood-sense. They work at the level of social conflict and self-definition, because both disputes about and appeals to "blood" mark the community's coming to see itself by looking at its blood.

Consider a possible exception: Catholic communion for laypeople only "in one kind," bread alone without wine. Prohibiting blood to the laity makes it no less valuable, but much more, if only the priests partake it. Fear of spilling it makes blood more precious, elevates the status of those who convey it – and shows the body porous and vulnerable all over again. And whatever you think of transubstantiation as a theory, it reveals blood's social reality as substantial, even cosmological.

***

SINCE DURKHEIM, STUDENTS OF RELIGION HAVE CALLED THE TOTEM *"The elementary form of the religious life." Since Maximus the Confessor, and reaching a high point in Thomas Aquinas, theologians have insisted on working by "analogy." In Christian theology, "analogy" has little to do with literary devices, still less with unlikely comparisons on standardized tests. In theology, "analogy" names the largest repeating structures that hold the symbol system together.[21] We need not quarrel over terms. "Analogy" is just the theological word for "totemism." Aquinas and Durkheim would agree that Christianity paints a pattern according to which the historical body of Jesus is the body of Christ; the church is the body of Christ; the bread of the Eucharist is the body of Christ; the believer makes up the body of Christ; the crucifix around her neck displays the body of Christ; and the body of Christ is the body of God. No Christianity exists without some version of this pattern, which theology calls "analogy" and Durkheim "totemism."*

Closely allied to the body of Christ is his blood, which the New Testament cites three times as often as his "cross" and five times as often as his "death."[22] This is my analogy or undersong: The blood from the cross is the blood of Christ; the wine of the Eucharist is the blood of Christ; the means of atonement is the blood of Christ; the unity of the church is the blood of Christ; the kinship of believers is the blood of Christ; the cup of salvation is the blood of Christ; icons ooze out the blood of Christ; and the blood of Christ is the blood of God.

---

[21] In Rom. 12:6, *analogia tes pisteos* names the (dis)proportionality of faith. In the twentieth century, theologians disputed among the analogy of being, the analogy of faith, the analogy of beauty, and so on.

[22] Stibbs, 1.

"The blood of Christ" works analogically in Christian theology and totemically in Christian practice. It names a large-scale structure that holds together cosmology, fictive kinship, gender roles, ritual practices, atonement for sin, solidarity in suffering, and recruits history and geography to illustrate its purposes. When conflict reveals the body as penetrable, we glimpse that the body does not define itself, but society uses its bleeding to redline its borders. Lately issues as diverse as atonement, evolution, women's leadership, and same-sex marriage seem to some Christians to threaten, and to others to revive, the symbol system that the blood of Christ structures, cleanses, and unites. In theology and anthropology, blood outside the body is matter out of place: Abel's blood cries out from the ground. But menstruation and childbirth make gendered exceptions – or engender new beginnings – where outside blood promises new life. Exegetes argue whether the blood of Christ means life or death, but blood provides the language within which they disagree.

That's how blood becomes natural for Christians to think with. How could it be otherwise? What resists analysis in terms of Christ's blood proves either irrelevant to the relations among the community, its God and its world – or a body too foreign for the system to metabolize: something that Christ's body could not digest, that Christ's blood could not cure. Such an exception could only threaten the whole system, would call up Durkheimian effervescence or outrage. Does evolution "impugn the blood of Christ"?

Natural science now seems to some Christians to threaten, to others to revive the whole analogical system by which Christianity rests on the incarnation of Christ and lives by his blood. Evolution seems to creationists to threaten the creation of humans in God's image and to relativize complementary gender roles that appeal to creation "male and female." (Chapters 6 and 9.) Sociologists of religion like Durkheim, Mary Douglas, and Nancy Jay show why the outrage of the detractors tends to the language of blood as well as why defenders seek both to avoid that language and to reclaim it.

***

AN EPISCOPAL CHURCH COMMITTEE DISPUTES SAME–SEX MARRIAGE IN terms of blood:

> "The trouble with liberals is, they can't talk about the atonement."
> "You mean, liberals talk about Abelardian atonement. You're
>   claiming liberals can't talk about *Anselmian* atonement."
> "That's right: Liberals can't talk about bloody atonement."
> "If we talk about blood a lot, you'll like it better?"
> So we did.[23]

---

[23] See Chapter 5. Conversation between myself and Grant LeMarquand, on the panel "Theology of Same-Sex Marriage," convened by the U.S. Episcopal House of Bishops, Pasadena, California, 2009. The "liberal" document talks about blood a lot – more than the conservative one. "A Theology of Marriage Including Same-Sex Couples," by Deirdre Good, Willis Jenkins, Cynthia Kittredge, and Eugene F. Rogers, Jr., *Anglican Theological*

The assumption on both sides – that Anselm talks about blood, and Abelard does not – is false. Abelard does talk about blood. He frames his argument in terms of blood. His famous atonement theory, rival to Anselm's, apparently unbloody and based on love, arises in the midst of his commentary on Romans. It forms a *quaestio* or excursus on Rom. 3:25–26, where Paul writes about "Christ Jesus, whom God put forward as an expiation by his blood." Abelard states his *quaestio*, his quest, in terms of blood: he seeks to know "what that redemption of ours through the death of Christ may be, and in what way the apostle declares that we are justified by his blood."[24] He answers that "we have been justified by the blood of Christ . . . in that [he] has taken upon himself our nature and persevered therein in teaching us by word and example even unto death . . . [so] that . . . true charity should not now shrink from enduring anything for him. . . . Wherefore, our redemption through Christ's suffering is that deeper affection in us . . . so that we do all things out of love rather than fear – love to him who has shown us such grace that no greater can be found, as he himself asserts, saying, 'Greater love than this no man hath, that a man lay down his life for his friends.'"[25] As for Abel, so for Abelard: this blood cries out.

If Anselm's own theory is bloodier than Abelard's, it is so not only in the way that Protestants remember it. While his theory does "free [the soul] from servitude" by "the blood of God" as debt-payment for insulted honor, Anselm goes on to connect the blood of the cross with that of the Eucharist: "Chew this, bite it, suck it, let your heart swallow it, when your mouth receives the body and blood of your Redeemer, for through this and not otherwise than through this will you remain in Christ and Christ in you." Today Protestant Anselmians "accept Christ" into their minds by faith: but the original Anselm accepts Christ in the Latin sense of *accipere*, "to receive in or on a part of the body," as into the belly (Cicero) or onto the lap (Vergil).[26] Anselm accepts Christ by taking him into his mouth.[27]

Review 93 (Winter 2011): 51–87. The authors are alphabetical. This article, with its companion piece by our conservative interlocutors, replies to both, and seven responses from other scholars worldwide occupies the entire issue except for book reviews.

[24] Peter Abelard, *Commentary on Romans*, in *A Scholastic Miscellany*, ed. and trans. Eugene Fairweather, Library of Christian Classics 10 (Philadelphia: Westminster Press, 1956), 280.

[25] Abelard, 283–4.

[26] *Cassell's Latin Dictionary*, ed. J. R. V. Marchant and Joseph F. Charles, rev. ed. (New York and London: Funk & Wagnall's, 1904–58), s.v. "accipio."

[27] Anselm of Canterbury, *Meditation on Human Redemption*, in *Prayers and Meditations of St Anselm*, trans. Benedicta Ward (New York: Penguin, 1973), 230–7; here, 230, lines 1–7.

It is hardly blood that distinguishes Anselm and Abelard; blood just gives them *a language in which to disagree*. Anselm holds up the blood of a debtor, Abelard the blood of a friend. For Anselm, Christ's blood reappears in the Eucharist, while for Abelard it reappears in thanksgiving. Which are the same word.

***

LOCAL THEORY. THIS IS THE PART WHERE I TAKE THE GLOBAL THEORY back. Stan Stowers is right that "sacrifice" names no single thing, but a congeries of local practices with different purposes and social locations.[28] That goes for blood discourses – local, various, socially constructed. The global theory and the local theory may seem to be at odds: but both are helpful. Some examples may fit oddly or not at all with the theory that blood constructs the body, but I don't mind. Later, Wittgenstein will tell us why we don't have to.

***

IN THE LEVITICAL MATERIAL (CHAPTER 3), BLOOD REPAIRS ruptures in social structure (sins), which also correspond to ruptures in cosmological structure, where the articulated architecture of creation breaks down and miasma or chaos sinks in. Levitical sacrifice chimes with both Genesis 1, where God creates order by separation, and the Noachide narratives, where the separations break down and the waters above the earth leak in. I ask whether the cut animal can represent the ruptured society, and the Temple can re-enclose blood poured out, to make it interior to a new and larger whole, a new social body to reunite a separated people. William Cowper's famous hymn paints the Christian picture:

> There is a fountain filled with blood drawn from Emmanuel's veins;
> And sinners plunged beneath that flood lose all their guilty stains.
> Lose all their guilty stains, lose all their guilty stains,
> And sinners plunged beneath that flood lose all their guilty stains.[29]

The trouble is that levitically there's not nearly enough blood for that. For an atonement offering, the priest only "daubs" (נָתַן) "some of the blood" on the

---

[28] Stanley Stowers, "Greeks Who Sacrifice and Those Who Do Not: Toward an Anthropology of Greek Religion," in *The Social World of the Earliest Christians: Essays in Honor of Wayne A. Meeks*, ed. L. M. White and O. L. Yarborough (Minneapolis: Fortress Press, 1995), 293–333.

[29] First published as "Praise for the Fountain Opened," in William Cowper and John Newton, *Olney Hymns* (London: various publishers, 1779).

18 BLOOD THEOLOGY

horns of the altar "with his finger" (Lev. 4:30, 4:34, 8:15, 9:9; see also 4:7, 4:18, 4:25, 16:18 and Ex. 29:12, 30:10). It works like a cleaner on a terminal or a conductant on an electrode: a little dab'll do ya. The picture in Hebrews of an altar flooded with blood is far more than a finger's worth; it is a Christian fantasy. Is there any interesting way in which Levitical sacrifice – or its representation in Hebrews – reflects the Durkheim/Douglas/Bildhauer structure?

I think there is. If meaning inheres in social practices, then material under-standing puts matter into place, and matter *out* of place gains power to destroy or restore. Genesis has *God* make meanings that way. God first creates meaning by *separation,* moving matter in and out of place: God separates the light from the darkness, the waters under the earth from the waters above the earth. Aquinas has God make separations to diversify creatures, so that what one lacks to represent God's understanding, another can supply. God makes a world where we need material difference to understand.

Blood sacrifice too works by separation: a knife parts an animal and generates blood. (Mira Balberg argues, *in order* to generate blood.[30]) Does that separation rehearse God's creation to represent understanding and restore goodness? For Mary Douglas, parting the animal shows society's division into parties, a material way to see the breach. For Nancy Jay, sacrifice "does birth better," where bloodletting exaggerates childbirth's bleeding to create a new lineage, innocent as a child.

Sacrifice, like creation, is meant as gift, this time almost unimaginably, perhaps immorally costly. When material understanding uses the costliest signaling, it takes place in blood. Blood is meaning made costly, meaning with bodies on the line. For that reason both "without shedding blood there is no forgiveness" and suicide bombings continue. Humans do use humans to think with, themselves and others – nations, sexes, animals, victims. Must we? At least we must recover and critique the ways we understand by means of blood, lest they exercise their baleful influence (in a phrase Sarah Coakley has used elsewhere) out of conscious sight.

***

THE BINDING OF ISAAC REPRESENTS A STORY WHERE BLOOD SEEPS in although the biblical narrative never mentions it. (See the next chapter.) Blood's absence tests my focus. If blood matters as much to Christian thinking as I suppose, there ought hardly to be important places where it goes missing. I claim the binding of Isaac proves the rule: There, where blood is missing from the text, Christian and (perhaps for that reason) also rabbinic

---

[30] Mira Balberg, *Blood for Thought: The Reinvention of Sacrifice in Early Rabbinic Literature* (Berkeley: University of California Press, 2017).

BLOOD MARKS THE BOUNDS OF THE BODY   19

traditions can't help themselves from reading it in. In a few rabbinic accounts it's the blood of Isaac that, at the Passover in Egypt, wards off the angel of death. In the story's Christian transformation, the beloved son of the father does die, pictured with plenty of blood.[31] *You might grant that Christian and Jewish traditions both read blood into the Isaac story, where it does not seem to belong, and argue – like Gil Anidjar – that this seepage marks a pathology rather than a feature. I think a pathology does afflict the story, but not in the blood. The pathology lies in a failure to detect the irony in God's command. Thus a sub-thesis: blood-talk is unavoidable, but irony counts.*

The sacrifice of Isaac is not the only case in which blood seeps in where it seems not to belong. Another is the crucifixion itself. Christian images cover it in blood. From Mel Brooks to Mel Gibson, the crucifixion seems to be all about blood. In the fourteenth-century painting of the Vision of St. Bernhard that graces the cover of Bildhauer's book, the crucified is swallowed up in blood. In Raphael and other painters, the crucifixion takes place to enable the collection of blood in cups (including the cover by Jacob Cornelisz). *But blood is at most incidental to crucifixion. My positivist students remind me that blood is not the cause of death. Suffocation is. You can even lash a victim to a cross so that not even hands and feet need bleed. Christ's side-wound occurs after death and would ooze coagulating gore, not frank blood. It's the picture of sacrifice – of sacrifice in blood – that colonizes the crucifixion (as the stations of the cross elaborate). Crucifixion is an unbloody death read as bloody for sacrificial interpretations. "What makes us so bloody-minded?" A social system (our own) where blood carries meaning. This system seeks to make the crucifixion, and in minority traditions also the binding of Isaac, meaningful in terms of blood, even when the story needs little or none. No blood, no meaning. The meaning of the crucifixion summons the blood. Here again, the exception proves the rule.*

***

OR CONSIDER THE FAMOUS BILLIE HOLIDAY SONG:

> Southern trees bear strange fruit
> Blood on the leaves and blood at the root
> Black bodies swinging in the southern breeze
> Strange fruit hanging from the poplar trees.

"Strange Fruit" is about lynching. Lynching is extrajudicial hanging, usually from a tree. "Strange Fruit" too "adds blood to another (usually)

---

[31] See Jon D. Levenson, *The Death and Resurrection of the Beloved Son: The Transformation of Child Sacrifice in Judaism and Christianity* (New Haven, CT: Yale University Press, 1995), 192–7.

bloodless form of death in order to identify it with the cross."[32] And yet blood-language is not strictly necessary to identify "hanging from a tree" with killing on a cross. The New Testament five times identifies hanging from a tree with hanging on a cross without ever invoking blood (Acts 5:30, 10:39, 13:29; Gal. 3:13; 1 Pet. 2:24; troping Dt. 21:23). The strange thing is that we see the blood even when it goes without saying. The blood is not overkill, it's naturalized. Mediterranean sacrifice remains incomplete without invoking blood.

***

THAT WAS ONE TEST: WHY DOES BLOOD INFILTRATE TEXTS WHERE IT GOES unmentioned? Here is a different test: There must be some cases where blood-language goes wrong. Modern creationism supplies one. (See Chapter 6.) There, blood-language makes visceral the objection to evolution. Creationists such as Ken Ham think a good God could not establish a system that runs on death not accidentally, but in principle. For them, only conscious human sin – in the Fall – could have caused the predation, extinction, and death we now observe. The limitation of that atonement theory is to cure only sin. It does not help mutability – creatures' defining ability to undergo change, whether for the good, in growth, or for ill, in falling.

The Analogy of Blood (my private title) uses Irenaeus to diagnose creationism as a softer Gnosticism, Aquinas to defend evolution as a part of providence, and sociology of religion to show why evolution's detractors tend to the language of blood – as well as why its defenders should reclaim the same language. On the way I venture a primatology of the incarnation, a sacramentology of gratitude, and recover from Maximus a cosmic theory of redemption.

In Against Heresies IV.4, Irenaeus might have been complaining about creationism when he wrote of Gnostics, "People who do not appreciate the period of growth are completely unreasonable. At the outset they refuse to be what they were made: humans who share passions with animals. They override the law of nature; they already want to be like God the Creator before they even become human. Thus they are dumber than the dumb beasts. The beasts do not blame God for not making them human! We, however, complain that instead of being made gods from the beginning, we are first human and then divine."[33]

---

[32] I quote the analysis and the lyrics from personal correspondence with Gregory S. Williams, March 1, 2019. The poem was first published as "Bitter Fruit" under the name Lewis Allan, pseudonym of Abel Meeropol, in *The New York Teacher* (1937).

[33] Irenaeus of Lyon, *Against Heresies* IV.4 in Patout Burns, ed. and trans., *Theological Anthropology* (Sources of Early Christian Thought) (Philadelphia: Fortress, 1981), 25, modified.

On Irenaeus's theory, God is perfect already; *the experiment with creatures is to see whether they can reach perfection by growing. God is stable, and creatures change. Mutability is meant for good, for growth, but turns bad, or runs down. Growth becomes suffering. What Christ comes to fix is not in the first instance sin, but flesh, what suffers and rots. On his theory, the moral running down that is sin is corollary to the physical running down that ends in death. Christ returns flesh to the way of growth.*

The biblical word joining humans to the "dumb beasts" and all flesh is "blood." Their life, like ours, "is in the blood" (Lev. 17:11, 14). The word joining humans to God is likewise blood, "the blood of Christ." Irenaeus concludes that blood is what Gnostics really want to escape (V.2), which brings the creature first growth and then salvation.

***

AS BLOOD EMERGES TO TRACE THE BODY IN RED WHEN SOMETHING penetrates it, so society sees red when new ideas threaten it. When evolution penetrates Christianity, it seems to threaten traditional cosmology, gender roles, explanations for sin. Evolution opens a social wound that bleeds with talk of blood – blood of apes and humans, blood of Christ and atonement, blood of communion and culture-war. Blood matters to Christians not only as biology. They use blood in ways too parabiological, quasibiological, pseudobiological for it to count as biology alone. Rather, blood matters to Christian theology also as a cultural symbol, a fluid to think with. Christians use blood to think with not because theologians correctly understand its biology, but because they viscerally encounter its power – its socio-conceptual power to contain opposites. Sociologically, blood means life and death, kinship and enmity, purity and contagion, vulnerability and enclosure. Whether Christians believe in evolution or not, they talk as if blood sets them at one with and apart from the "dumb beasts." In disputes with one another they invoke the blood of Christ to name what sticks them together and what cuts them apart. Those who disagree "impugn the blood of Christ" or make his body "bleed." I will repeat: This sociology of blood rubricates the community's bounds in red. *For Christianity gives blood more to mean even than the protean containment of opposites. It can surpass their binaries. In the central story of Christ's blood, Christ, on the night in which he was betrayed, did not avoid the deep and sinister means of human bloodletting, but used his blood to overcome them, as if to say, you cannot bleed me out; here, I pour my blood out for you. At what other wedding feast, suggests Jacob of Serugh, did the groom give his blood to drink in place of other wine? Theology must recover the power in the blood to turn enemies into kin and purity into vulnerability, not only for communicants but for all the creatures of the earth. If the evidence for evolution leaves creationists unmoved – if the evolutionary mysticism of Teilhard was condemned, and the evolutionary Christology of Rahner forgotten*[34] *– that is because no one connected them as the Bible did to the bloody particulars of taste and sacrifice by which humans think in their gut.*

***

WHAT DOES "THINKING" MEAN, WHEN I SAY CHRISTIANS "USE blood to think with"? In Religious Studies, "thinking" does not, primarily, refer to a private, individual mental state. You might want to study private mental states, but that's not what Religious Studies does; like sociology and anthropology, it studies groups. In Religious Studies, "thinking" encompasses public, communal practices of using language, images, and ritual. Even silent prayer or private headaches participate in the vocabulary and imagery learned and practiced among others. Christians use blood to think with when they publically "plead the blood" in prayer, praise Christ's blood in hymns, invoke the blood of atonement in theology, or accuse others of impugning that blood in disputes. Similarly, Christians use blood to think with when they drink Christ's blood in communion, venerate relics of blood in flasks, shed blood in martyrdom, or (in some traditions) prohibit menstruating women from the sacristy – as well as when their stomachs clench over those things.

***

"PLEADING THE BLOOD" IS A WAY OF IMPLORING FORGIVENESS FOR sin. It is the positive opposite of "impugning the blood," discussed in Chapter 5. When you plead the blood successfully, you are forgiven and "covered in the blood." The language of being "covered in the blood" moved, perhaps illicitly, to describe protection from misfortune as well as forgiveness for sin and rose to prominence in news reports during the COVID-19 pandemic as a protection against the virus, especially in church.[35] The application covered from COVID is odd since the blood of Jesus failed to protect Jesus himself from suffering and death; rather it resembles the suggestion of Satan that Jesus rejected, that he cast himself down from the top of the Temple (Luke 4:9). Perhaps a better application to COVID of blood's logic is that of the church responsible for an

---

[34] Karl Rahner, "Christology within an Evolutionary View of the World," trans. Karl-H. Kruger, in *Theological Investigations* 5 (New York: Crossroad, 1983 [1966]), 158–92.

[35] www.cnn.com/videos/us/2020/04/04/ohio-church-service-covid-19-pandemic-tuchman-pkg-ac360-vpx.cnn.

outbreak of over five thousand cases, some 42 percent of the total in South Korea: they donated their plasma for the recovery of others.[36]

***

I LAST CARED ABOUT TEILHARD DE CHARDIN, PALEONTOLOGIST AND PRIEST, in the dinosaur phase of childhood. There is now one place where I find Teilhard helpful: the place where he descends to blood. It comes in his Mass "On the World."[37] *Teilhard is working as a paleontologist, digging in China, crossing the Gobi by horse or camel, riding for days at a time. He is a priest; he has to say mass every day. He says mass, therefore, in his head, or under his breath, as he rides. He practices the asceticism of the paleontologist in the field; he fills his pack with picks and brushes, no altar stones, wafers, cups, or wine. How can he celebrate? His mass is "on" the world, because he takes the crust of the earth as his altar stone, its fossils as his relics. In persona Christi, Teilhard channels Paul's notion of building up Christ's body, thinks of evolution's increasing complexity, and says, "This is my body." He thinks of Christ's sacrifice, of evolution's predation, extinction, and death, and says, "This is my blood."*

This division of body and blood allows Teilhard to keep blood with expiation and frees up the body to mean solidarity and upbuilding. Can he do that? Don't body and blood do the same work in the mass? Isn't the body also broken, just as the blood is poured out? Doesn't blood build up, with healing and nourishment, just as the body does?

It depends on what your liturgy says. Greek and Protestant rites say the body is "broken"; Catholic eucharists say the body is "given." What did 1 Corinthians say? In Greek it had no verb at all. "This is my body for you" (1 Cor. 11:24). Which liturgists variously filled in. (See Chapter 6.)

Whatever the result, the "broken" translation tends to confine the body to remedy for sin. The "given" translation, however, opens the body to more than one purpose – not just remedy for sin, but also for building up the church, which suits other bits of Paul. At first I preferred "broken," but now I favor "given." It's less sin-centered and gives God more space. Even if the human being had never sinned, God could still have become incarnate to elevate humans from Eden to heaven. The body of Christ could still be the bread of heaven, even if his blood were not the cup of salvation. Teilhard suggests a felix culpa *theology of evolution: O happy fault, that merited such and so great a Redeemer. It is a theology of dramatic irony: God chose just this place – our*

---

[36] www.reuters.com/article/us-health-coronavirus-southkorea/south-korea-church-hit-by-covid-19-says-members-to-give-plasma-for-research-idUSKBN23U1QA.

[37] Pierre Teilhard de Chardin, "The Mass on the World," in *The Heart of Matter* (New York: Houghton Mifflin, 2002), 119–34.

24 BLOOD THEOLOGY

blood – to do what God always intended. Creationism, on the other hand, allows no happy fault, brooks no predation and death in the divine comedy.

Leviticus and Romans both assert that blood is "given" for the remission of sins. Their assertion turns out to be more than a tautology, because the provision of the gift explodes the occasion. In Leviticus 17:11 we read the standard "For the life (*nefesh*, person, soul) of the flesh is in the blood"; but then it continues, "and I have given it to you upon the altar to make atonement for your souls, *by reason of the life*" (RSV, *ba nefesh*). The word for "given" (נָתַתִּי) is the same as in Genesis 1:29, where God had given (נָתַתִּי) the human being every herb bearing seed to eat. The phrases are parallel – Given to eat: given to make atonement.

The parallelism in the phrasing opens the possibility of parallelism in the giving. Is atonement, according to expansive interpretations of Lev. 17:11, given already in creation itself? Especially if "atonement" means first of all making one, before it means making up for? That version of gift would tend to clinch the case that blood is good in the Garden before it repairs for sin; that blood is intended for communion before it is needed for sacrifice; that it can sanctify without any victims. Rabbis make a similar case, when they declare that God provided the ram for Isaac before the foundation of the world (Pirkei Avot 5:6).

Several New Testament passages *associate* the blood of Christ with the repair for sin and *deny* that repair exhausts its meaning, because they also assert that its provision precedes its need – precedes not only sin, but creation itself. The blood of Christ, therefore, is given first for communion, for solidarity, which becomes sacrifice only later, under conditions of sin. They have been read this way at least since Origen.[38] Romans says "they are justified by [God's] grace as a gift [δωρεάν], through the redemption which is in Christ Jesus, whom God put forward [προέθετο, also "predetermined"] as an expiation by his blood" (3:24–25). This προέθετο reappears in Ephesians, where the aorist of the verb refers not recently to the crucifixion but protologically to God's offering of blood "before the foundation of the world" (1:4, 9). Similarly, 1 Peter "destines" the "precious blood of Christ …

---

[38] Origen, *Commentary on the Epistle to the Romans*, lecture 3, section 8, The Fathers of the Church, trans. Thomas P. Scheck (Washington, DC: Catholic University of America Press, 1990), 216ff.

before the foundation of the world" (1:19–20), while Revelation calls Christ "slain" then (13:8).

We must separate, with Teilhard, in order to reunite. In both Leviticus and Romans, blood is given before it is needed. It is given, therefore, also beyond, without, or apart from need. It flows with life before it spills in death. If the remission of sin provides the ironic *occasion* for making this clear, that is just what 1 Peter spells out: the blood "indeed was destined before the foundation of the world, but was manifest at the end of times for your sake" (1:19–20). Which is to say, it's *because* the blood of God already meant kinship, communion, solidarity, love, that the shedding of blood both made sense and showed relationship. Blood was sacred before it was sacrifice.

As the incarnation makes clear, the blood of Emmanuel is the blood of God with us, the blood of one in whom all things sum up (Eph. 1:10, ASV). But Leviticus had drawn the conclusion already: all blood belongs to God. If all blood is the blood of God, the blood of my neighbor and the blood of my beast, then all blood is God with us. What if we acted that way?

***

IN THIS BOOK I DO NOT HAVE A THESIS. THERE ARE FAR TOO MANY for that. Rather I have broken out in theses. Centuries of theses. The theses may not even follow; rather they coagulate.

Or again, it is a book of bloody fragments. No book about blood could cover everything. So much is missing. There is too little about martyrdom and one remark about blood libel. I describe rather than solve the issue of eating meat, and my chapter on war ends up treating other things. I address menstruation, though it is hardly my place. I could issue more trigger warnings and quote more critics of blood-talk's dangers. There is nothing about AIDS or blood-donation or the one-drop rule or vampires or devotion to the sacred heart. Colleagues send me books about blood all the time, and everyone has a favorite anecdote. They sum up my book in a word: So you're writing a book about race. About public health. About AIDS. About haemophilia. About violence. About menstruation. About kinship. About ancestry. About atonement. About sacrifice. About communion. About the sale of plasma. All those things are reductive. Blood is not about any one of them. The point is, blood is about all of them, and more. It generates more than opposites, more than binaries, to break out into spots and drops and seepages – into patterns and into the escape from patterns. And that's also why blood makes a good metaphor for the infinite and the uncontained.

***

I CLAIM THAT BLOOD-TALK IS SOCIALLY CONSTRUCTED, AND I REPEAT that it's not going away: but perhaps, contrary to my assumption, if it's socially constructed, it *can* go away? I think about blood here as I think about gender. Any number of conservatives might have said, in any number of centuries, that "male and female are not going away." And of course in the twentieth and twenty-first centuries male and female have been changing nonstop. I don't mean that blood language is perennial and changeless. I mean that blood, like gender, is something in terms of which things change. My comparison is with Judith Butler properly understood. There is a third option beyond repristinating the terms and ignoring their power: that is to repeat the terms subversively, to queer them, to bend them like a blue note, to remove them from conditions of violence, and to mobilize them – how? – as Jesus does in the Last Supper (which is a present and a future supper).

I hope it is no flaw to raise more questions than I answer. And I hope absences of treatment and even logic will bring others to write more.

***

MANY HUMANISTS AND GRANTING AGENCIES WANT TO KNOW "what period" I'm working in. A theologian would ask a different question: what locus? This book uses history ad hoc, but it is not history. It stands, as I have said, where theology and anthropology overlap. Theology and anthropology have in common (with some other disciplines, including psychology, and parts of philosophy and literature) that they think in patterns rather than periods. Normative impulses in anthropology and theology share a tendency to reach back to claim stories of origin. They both try to outflank history by reaching back "before" it for "nature." Their reach is not overreach, if we see it as a desire to recognize the patterns that vary. Mary Douglas describes the desire for pattern as a kind of reasoning in which "the final answer refers to the way in which the planets are fixed in the sky or the way that . . . humans or animals naturally behave."[39]

I am offering, as Lauren Winner has written in a different context, "theologically motivated juxtapositions." "I am juxtaposing theological

---

[39] Mary Douglas, *How Institutions Think* (Syracuse, NY: Syracuse University Press), 46.

questions," she writes, "with social and liturgical practices with the aim of showing not causal connections, but rather affinities – affinities that illuminate both [ancient and medieval practices], and our own."[40] My interest lies in patterns that persist, neither apart from history, nor perennially, but across and through their permutations. If we stick to period, we lose the conversation between Aquinas and Bulgakov, along with its impediments. If you prefer to distinguish than to assimilate the patterns, we will be the richer for another book.

Wittgenstein has thought about this at some length, precisely in connection with such bloody topics as sacrifice:

> Historical elucidation – an elucidation in terms of historical development, is only *one* way of bringing the data together, of seeing the data together. It is just as possible to see the data in their connectedness to one another and to integrate them into a wider picture without doing so in the form of a hypothesis about their temporal development. . . . I *could* portray this idea in the form of a developmental hypothesis – or also in the pattern of a religious ceremony. . .[41]

> We can only say: where that practice and these views go together, the practice does not spring from the view, but both of them are simply there. . . . We can only *describe* and say, human life is like that. . . . One would like to say: This is what took place here; laugh, if you can. . . . The principle according to which these practices are ordered is a much more general one . . . provided in our own soul. . . . Frazer's explanations would be no explanations at all if finally they did not appeal to an inclination within ourselves. . . .

> We could almost say, the human being is a ceremonious animal. . . .

> What I want to say is: The sinister, deep thing lies not in the fact that is how the history of this practice went, for perhaps it did not go that way; nor in the fact that perhaps or probably it was like that; but in whatever prompted me to suppose it. No, this deep and sinister thing is not self-evident when we are just told the story of the performance, but it is *we* who recognize it, out of a knowledge within ourselves. . . . And if someone asked, How do you know that? I could only say, it is what my experience

---

[40] Lauren Winner, *The Dangers of Christian Practice: On Wayward Gifts, Characteristic Damage, and Sin* (New Haven: Yale University Press, 2018), 34.

[41] My translation of the following: "Die historische Erklärung, die Erklärung als eine Hypothese der Entwicklung, ist nur *eine* Art der Zusammenfassung der Daten – ihrer Synopsis. Es ist ebensowohl möglich, die Daten in ihrer Beziehung zu einander zu sehen und in ein allgemeines Bild zusammenzufassen, ohne es in Form einer Hyphothese über die zeitliche Entwicklung zu machen. . . . [D]iese Idee, *kann* ich durch eine Entwicklungshypothese darstellen oder auch . . . durch das Schema einer religiösen Zeremonie" (Wittgenstein, *Bemerkungen*, 3, 8, 16).

with human beings teaches me. . . . What I see in those stories is something they acquire, after all, from the evidence, including such evidence as does not seem immediately connected with them – from thinking about human beings and their past, about the strangeness of what I see in myself and others, the strangeness of what I have seen and heard.[42]

***

CONSIDER WHAT ROBERT BRANDOM CALLS A DE RE, IN CONTRAST with a *de dicto*, interpretation.[43] "*De dicto* interpretation aims to say what parts of a tradition have said, and is therefore constrained to prioritize those partial traditions' own ancillary commitments and cultural context." In my attempts to unearth and exhibit – in archeological fashion – robust blood-language of the past, I prioritize some of the oddities of blood's previous cultural context, for example, the medieval context of menstruation, in order to explore its significance.

"A *de re* interpretation aims to say what follows from (some of) a tradition's commitments when they are placed into the setting of the *interpreter's* ancillary commitments and cultural context." That is what I try to do when I move the unearthed blood language into a modern theological context – for example, one in which disparate treatment of women is *prima facie* unjust, and interpretations of Jesus gender his blood more female as a source of fertility and rebirth.

I also want to combine a *de re* interpretation of blood traditions (not of blood biology) with "a certain amount of internal critique, as a way of using some of the tradition's actual commitments to put critical pressure on some of its other actual commitments." For example, the traditions of thinking about blood have had actual commitments to thinking both that the blood of Jesus saves and that the blood of women defiles. I want to use the commitment to the blood of Jesus to move the language of defilement away from women's fertility and against racist thinking. In another example, I want to favor the blood of Jesus as solidarity over the blood of Jesus as satisfaction. In a third example, I want to describe two sorts of commitments to blood's logic with respect to eating meat (while leaving readers to develop the logics exposed, rather than myself choosing between them): thus I distinguish a logic in which *ascetic* commitments lead to avoidance of meat-eating, and a logic in

---

[42] Wittgenstein, 3, 8, 16.

[43] These paragraphs are in dialogue with an anonymous reader for an earlier manuscript (the one that became *Aquinas and the Supreme Court*). The material in quotation marks belongs, lightly edited, to that reader. I adapt them here to the current book. I believe the anonymous reader was Jeffrey Stout.

which *sacrificial* commitments commend laypeople to eat meat at certain times of the liturgical year (such as Easter). What does it mean if we now organize our commitments differently: no longer according to *time*, so that vegetables are prescribed during Lent and lamb at Easter, but now by *personal identity*, so that laypeople adopt vegetarianism as an identity or adhere to "Paleolithic" eating as a movement?

***

NEITHER IS MY TOPIC ETHICS. RATHER I DESCRIBE SOME SHAPES, chosen for their oddity and tellingness. Changing them, if necessary, is too unpredictable for rules or habits. Like Jesus at the Last Supper they require the intervention of religious genius or special charism: the kaleidoscopic gifts of the unexpected (like prophecy or speaking in tongues) that shake a pattern into a new shape.

***

IF, ACCORDING TO WITTGENSTEIN, MEANING INHERES IN THE USE of a word, how does it inhere in the use of a substance? "Sacrifice" and "blood" work like "meaning." They are categories to which societies recur, things to think with, when the social body sees a threat or makes thanksgiving. "Blood" like "meaning" does very large-scale cultural work. *Blood is meaning made palpable, meaning made with bodies on the line.* Blood, in a phrase, is the costliest signaling. That's why global and local theories both can help, because it's the need for costly signaling that brings up blood in such different contexts, even where it doesn't seem to belong.

Of course, "societies" do not really think; people do. The social is a cooperative enterprise, like driving on the left or speaking English. But among those decisions assemblages emerge and seem to act on their own. Our blood discourse, therefore, is a social achievement, a way in which we cooperate with one another. We can hardly avoid, but we can expand or contract it. Anselmian blood discourses contract the incarnation to those who can sin. Athanasian blood discourses expand the incarnation to those who can suffer. We cannot escape a bloody atonement. But we can expand it, lest blood come to mean too little.

***

MOSTLY I TALK IN TERMS OF SOCIAL THEORY. BUT BLOOD IS MY protagonist. Blood retains its physical qualities in our experience and in our heads. Blood is not the same as water. It's thicker and redder and leaves gore when it dries.

Blood (like bleeding) is not entirely under our control. It resists, inspires, and escapes us. Not only that: *we are conflicted about blood, and we express our conflicts in blood's terms. Blood conflicts and escapes us also because we contend among ourselves who counts as "us," and use blood-language to express and enact our cross-purposes. We use blood-language the way we use other tools like knives: to nourish, defend, and define ourselves. This makes clear that blood itself, like other tools that draw blood, turns back on the agent with an agentic capacity of its own.*[44]

While social construction illuminates the way I look at blood, a critic might observe that the social constructive and structuralist anthropological approaches – which identify humans individual and collective as the agents of blood's work – are foreign and anachronistic to many of the Christian texts, images, and attitudes I treat. In those sources, blood itself does things. Blood becomes itself the agent. A recent movement in anthropology, philosophy, and politics – "thing theory" – may prove truer to those sources. It may do more justice to another preoccupation of this book: blood's uncanny ability to persist across periods, to reappear when repressed, to seep in where it seems not to belong. Thing theory seeks to recover the agency of things, to query the anthropocentrism in which only humans act in their lordly isolation.

Jane Bennett's approach both resembles and resists the re-enchantment movement of conservative and romantic legal theories, theories that seek to evade the responsibilities with which constructivist approaches, in their constant search for hidden human agency, would burden them. Bennett encourages us to think, not only about the history of the tool's construction and the responsibility of those who made or wield it, but also about the tool itself, its side effects, its externalities: how it proves recalcitrant and ill-suited; how it resists us; how it proves clumsy – and beyond those negative or passive determinations, how the tool enables and opens things up, so easily as to unveil an agency of its own. The efficacy of objects can exceed the designs they serve (20).

"An actant," Bennett writes, "never really acts alone." It "depends on the collaboration ... or interference of many bodies and forces. A lot happens to the concept of agency once nonhuman things are figured less as social constructions and more as actors, and once humans themselves are assessed not as autonoms but as vital materialities" (21). Bodies – both ours and those of our tools, from stone hand axes to sacramental blood to concepts like race, take their power from the heterogeneous assemblages from which they also

---

[44] Jane Bennett, *Vibrant Matter: A Political Ecology of Things* (Durham, NC: Duke University Press, 2010), 35. I thank Virginia Burrus for directing me to this book.

first emerge (23–4) – in this case, a welter of humans, blood, wine, bread, cups, congregations, liturgies, priests, hierarchies, practices, warfare, menstruation, birth, violence, ramifying on and on in useful and life-giving, death-dealing and dangerous ways.

Bennett is agnostic about agency. "No one really knows what human agency is, or what humans are doing when they are said to perform as agents. In the face of every analysis, human agency remains something of a mystery. If we do not know just how it is that human agency operates, how can we be so sure that the processes through which nonhumans make their mark are qualitatively different?" (34).

Bennett admits to "anthropomorphizing" things. But she will not admit to religion. To me, thing theory seems animist at minimum. At maximum, what? Christological? Things have *rationes seminales*. They have *logoi*. I don't see how thing theory isn't religious, and thing theorists might as well say which religious ideas seem to animate their things. Otherwise theologians will make them Christological.

***

BECAUSE CHRISTIANS WORSHIP THE LOGOS INCARNATE, GOD'S OWN understanding made flesh, they have always rendered understanding material. With "My Lord and my God," Doubting Thomas used his fingers to make metaphysics palpable. Material understanding sustains the sacraments, where Christians find metaphysics and morals, grace and gratitude in bread and wine. "Taste and see that the Lord is good" (Ps. 34:8), calling the faithful to communion, proclaims the throatiest of material understandings, where God made God's understanding known in the blood of the executed Word.

This variety of understanding finds it natural to claim (with Heb. 9:22) that "without the shedding of blood there is no remission of sin." I want to recover the strangeness of the appeal to blood. It sounds quite unlike "without the cutting of trees there are no wooden houses." To answer such questions, I take the best of anthropology as irritant and stimulus.

***

HOW DO THE ANTHROPOLOGY AND THEOLOGY RELATE? A GRACE OF creation underlies anything true, including anthropology, to the extent that it's true. It's not a foundation, heavy and rigid, but a hammock, light and supple, which surrounds, suspends, and elevates.

This network of grace is knotted out in an idea of Maximus the Confessor: the idea that the Logos of God goes all the way down and rises all the way up, uplifting the hearts of things, to become their multiple principles or *logoi*. It is through those *logoi* that the Logos of God seeks "always and in all things to accomplish the mystery of his embodiment."[45] The *logoi* lie deep in the heart of things to elevate them from within and anticipate Christ's incarnation.

To put it in nuptial, not Maximian terms, God took on a body as gift, gift of God's self, in a marital mystery. "This is my body, given for you." Where sin is possible, that gift becomes an offering, a willingness; where sin is actual, the offering becomes a sacrifice. God took on a body to be with creatures, so that they could be with God; but God took the occasion to do so also as remedy for sin: God took on a body in part to do sacrifice.

Maximus makes bold to place the intelligibility of things under Christ's blood. (See Chapter 9.) This is a sacramental or even eucharistic intelligibility, one based on things' destiny in God's embodiment. If Jesus Christ becomes himself in the bread and the wine, then that is just a special case of what he seeks to do always and in all things. For Maximus, therefore, the blood of Jesus is the blood of all things: they are intelligible as they live, or build up toward God's embodiment; and in case of need, their sacrifice — perhaps! – becomes intelligible in the light of God's.

The intelligibility of the *logoi*, which is the blood of the Logos, is indeed a mystery. In the first place it means their life. But under the fallen conditions in which the Word of God suffered and died, it suggests that all things also have a share of his suffering and death. This suggestion is useful, since the suffering and death of all things is something we can observe. It expands to all things Paul's remark that "we suffer with him that we may also be glorified with him" (Rom. 8:17). By including all things in one all-embracing mysterion or eucharist, it also expands baptism to all things: it extends to all things the remark that those who are buried with the Logos are also raised with him (Rom. 8:6, Col. 2:12). Maximus's reference to Christ's blood, which is the life of all things, also makes "intelligible" their suffering and death, in the sense that it reads them into his story. It does not make their suffering negligible or intelligible, but legible: legible through his.

Christ's blood, we may infer, includes the possibility of sacrifice that every thing has to offer. Christ's blood as the blood of all things implies that all things are capable of sacrifice at need, in that all things share his life. It is Christ's blood,

---

[45] Maximus the Confessor, *Ambigua*, translated as *On Difficulties in the Church Fathers* by Nicholas Constas, English and Greek text on facing pages (Washington, DC: Dumbarton Oaks Press, 2014–15), cited by Migne number. Here 1084C-D.

on a Maximian account, that makes cooperation, procreation, evolution, and redemption all thinkable. The idea that the blood is the life, and the life belongs to God, implies that the possibility of repair remains, however much concrete sacrifices are also corrupted by sin, since there is also undoubtedly manipulated, manipulative, misguided, or just plain bad sacrifice. But it is because he regards all things as participating in a eucharistic economy of sacrifice and gratitude that Maximus puts all things under the sign of Christ's blood.

I hasten to repeat that this is no Girardian, kenotic, or sin-centered structure. Because blood first of all means life, it keeps abundance and gift at the center, and therefore the ability to deal with the rest. Girardian, kenotic, and even locally hamartiocentric structures deserve charity. But their pictures are hyperbolic. They exaggerate. Sacrifice does not mean self-immolation: it means the persistence of intention in the face of resistance. It is not the submission of the battered wife, but the free persistence of Gandhi or King – not the lack of agency, but a plenary, superlative, supererogatory agency. This plenipotentiary sacrifice emerges not from an original emptiness, but from an original abundance, the fullness of the Triune God, who is not nothing, but creates out of nothing. True sacrifice relies on God's self-offering and shares in God's fullness. This self-offering, which becomes sacrifice only when life persists against obstacles, is called God's blood. Such a part-share in the mystery of God's embodiment is not straightforward, but it roots a creature's legibility as deeply as the story allows.

Sacrifice in the Mediterranean may always be bloody, but blood is not always sacrificial. Before blood is sacrifice it is communion, the gift of life: and the blood of God is the gift of life and fellowship with God, of being born "not from the blood of human beings" but from above as a child of God (John 1:13). Thus in Leviticus blood is "the life" – and in John the divine intimacy.

✳✳✳

THIS STANDS DURKHEIM ON HIS HEAD AND VINDICATES FEUERBACH: GOD and society *are* alike in that blood begins to make visible the ways of both society and God. They reflect each other in a ruddy mirror not because God is "really" society writ large, but because (theologians should say) God funds society's capacity for sacrifice and checks its misuse. That is so, trinitarians will add, because God is a Three of whom one makes offer, one vindicates the offering, and one celebrates, guarantees, and magnifies the offering (an offer that is gift before it is sacrifice). The doctrine of the social Trinity has been put to facile uses,[46] but the classic doctrine tells us Feuerbach and Durkheim are

---

[46] See Karen Kilby, "Perichoresis and Projection: Problems with Social Doctrines of the Trinity," *New Blackfriars* 81 (2000): 432–45.

on to something: if God is fit for social projection, that's because the life of the Trinity is a community to join.

Those are some of the reasons why Mary Douglas and Thomas Aquinas, Barth and Feuerbach, Durkheim and Maximus, might meet in a single book. Not because theology and social theory, as Milbank would have it, are enemies; nor because, as Tillich might have it, they correlate on neutral ground; but rather because God created and, in giving God's own blood for human society, re-befriended them both.

***

SIMILAR CONFLUENCES OF BLOOD RECUR IN THE EARLIEST HISTORY of the little, loaded English word "bless," which derives, according to the Oxford English Dictionary, "from Old English *blóedsian,* 'to mark ... with blood ...; to consecrate.'" For better or worse, that was the word Christianizers chose, the *OED* continues, to translate "Latin *benedīcere,* and Greek εὐλογεῖν, ... 'speak well of or eulogize, praise,' ... themselves influenced by being chosen to translate Hebrew *brk,* primarily 'to bend,' hence 'to bend the knee, worship, praise, bless God, invoke blessings on, bless as a deity.'" To thicken things further, "At a very early date the popular etymological consciousness began to associate this verb with *bliss,* 'benignity, blitheness, joy, happiness,'"[47] so that the same word comes to coagulate bliss and blessing with marking by blood.

***

IN THE MOST AUSTERE OF THE FINE ARTS, YOU CAN REDUCE AN EQUATION TO simpler terms even without knowing what the variables mean. You may recognize the terms, but their import dazzles. $e^{i\pi} = -1$. Theology works similarly. Some biblical or credal statements work like operators. Theologians can apply them without (yet?) knowing what they mean; they enable theologians to generate new statements that they presume to be true, even without understanding their import. For instance, "Jesus Christ is fully human and fully God." Theologians don't know what the terms "full humanity," "full divinity," or "Jesus Christ" mean, but they use the sentence, which they hold true, to generate other sentences to be held true. Blood seems to be such an operator in Christian thought.

For Genesis (9:4–5), Leviticus (17:11, 14), Deuteronomy (12:23), Psalms (72:14), and Ezekiel (33:5), the life is in the blood.[48] In all those places, the

---

[47] *OED*, s.v. "bless." I thank Adam Tietje for alerting me to this connection.
[48] See also 1 Sam. 26:20.

Hebrew has *nephesh*, the Septuagint *psyche*, the Vulgate *anima*, and the Lutherbibel (except in Ezekiel) *Seele* – so that outside the English tradition, it is more metaphysically the *soul* that lives in the blood. For John, blood is the life of the divine intimacy: "Those who eat my flesh and drink my blood abide in me, and I in them" (John 6:56). That consensus[49] implies a further thesis. The blood of the creature, like its life, belongs to the Lord. Let us venture a generalization. In the Hebrew Bible, all blood belongs to God. For Christians, then, a corollary: all blood belongs to Christ.[50] That is just a special case of appropriating the structure of creation to the Logos, or calling the participation of all things in Christ "the *logoi* in the Logos." All blood, that is, participates in Christ's. The seas and salty water that preceded blood participate also. "One blood all nations" (Acts 17:26) is just a special case of one blood all creation.[51]

∗∗∗

IN THESE PAGES I REFER FROM TIME TO TIME TO REPAIRING THE LANGUAGES AND practices of blood. Sometimes I know what I mean, and sometimes I gesture into an unknown. But whether I understand it or not, to "repair" means to follow the pattern of Jesus. Jesus is no function of some abstract notion of repair, but repair is a notion whose contours Christians learn by discerning the recreative way of God become this creature. They can participate in God's repair of blood, because all blood belongs to God, and thus to Christ. They can participate in God's making all blood logical, that is, of the Logos. "Logical" is not simply opposed to blood, as the phrase "bloodless" or "logical" sacrifice would suggest; nor is it simply the same as blood, as if all sacrifice involved blood. Rather, "logical" is the use of blood that the Logos makes, as one who both creates and possesses blood, who gives and sheds it. That is why Irenaeus refers, in another context, to Christ's "rational blood" (*Adv. Haer.* 5.9.3).

That principle – or mystery – is less clear than we might like. For example, the logical use of blood in the crucifixion and the logical use of blood in the Eucharist are not the same, they are *ana*logical. The transition reflects a reality ungraspable in this life. The right reparative, logical, or Christoform use of blood will be mysterious, recreative, and unpredictable in advance, for all that it will look like

---

[49] William K. Gilders, *Blood Ritual in the Hebrew Bible: Meaning and Power* (Baltimore: Johns Hopkins University Press, 2004), brackets the remark "the blood is the life" in an attempt to understand Levitical ritual from its descriptions alone: but that is not the job of either rabbinics or theology.

[50] I worked out this insight in conversation with Chuck Mathewes.

[51] The word "blood" is missing from the Vulgate but present in the Greek Majority Text as well as the Syriac and the Vetus Latina (pre-Vulgate Latin text). See my review of Gil Anidjar in the Appendix.

Jesus in retrospect. The pattern of crucifixion and resurrection is not for others to follow, although God can create that pattern in them. Martyrs follow Christ, to be sure, and in exemplary fashion, but not as seeking martyrdom.

Rather, crucifixion and resurrection are for patterning the sense in senselessness, discerning a "logic" in deepest unlogic, love running over in the presence of its enemies. Where King and Gandhi fall, Christians see the pattern of Jesus. They "persevered," as Abelard wrote of Jesus, "teaching by word and example, even unto death." More mysterious still are the deaths of those who were not persevering in anything except an ordinary life. When Michael Brown, Jr., fell, and the Spirit gathered a community of witnesses called Black Lives Matter for justice and new life, dare we see a pattern of crucifixion and resurrection there?[52] (See Chapter 3.) When nameless women are snuffed out, like the concubine of Judges 19, or unnamed species go extinct, can we rightly see the pattern of Jesus – not to make their deaths any less lamentable, but to shape a lament on Good Friday?[53] Can we say that God in Christ suffers with and in them, takes their suffering up, remembers it in his hands, and memorializes it in his blood? Can we hold them in mind and repeat with Teilhard the words of Jesus, "This is my blood"? Amid so many abuses – for gaining and retaining power – is blood still apt for proper use? So used, blood would be for repair and rebirth, and for that beginning of repair in weakness which is making sense. That is why Maximus says that blood is logical.

***

"CONCIPIO, TO TAKE TOGETHER, HOLD TOGETHER . . . A. LIT. I, OF fluids, *to take in, draw in;* [of water, *concipio aquas;* of tears, *concipio lacrimas;* of air, *concipio anima*]. . . . B. . . . 4. *To comprehend, grasp.*"[54] The conception of a child or of a thought is each a special case of taking in a fluid.

How do we conceive blood, take and hold its images and usages together? Christians conceive it by taking it in. In so doing they hope to imitate Mary and conceive Jesus. But to grasp Jesus is to comprehend his blood. And to imitate Mary is to attend to women. (See Chapter 4.)

The question of this book is one of *concipimus:* how do we draw the usages of blood together, how do we draw the conceptual boundaries, the lines? And can we change them? How can we, without conceiving the Inconceivable, rechannel this dangerous fluid?

---

[52] Stephen G. Ray, Jr. "Black Lives Matter as Theology," in *Enfleshing Theology: Embodiment, Discipleship, and Politics in the Work of M. Shawn Copeland,* ed. Robert J. Rivera and Michele Saracino (Minneapolis, MN: Fortress, 2018), 83–93.

[53] I owe the last phrases to a conversation with Lauren Winner.

[54] *Cassell's Latin Dictionary,* s.v. "concipio."

Part II

Blood Seeps in Where It Hardly Seems to Belong

Blood Unnecessary and Inexhaustible

2

BLOOD AFTER ISAAC
And God Said "Na"

A PPEALING TO ABRAHAM'S SACRIFICE, JEWS, CHRISTIANS, AND Muslims all use rituals to think with blood: circumcision thinks with biological blood, the Eucharist with metaphorical blood, Eid al-Adha with blood transcended and returned.[1] But the story of Abraham's son never mentions the word "blood." Focused on Christianity, I ask why blood-talk dominates when other explanations would do, why blood seeps in where it hardly belongs. Blood provides a key for interpreting canonical texts, a spur to growth and gratitude, and a language in which to conduct disputes.

Consider the text: "Abraham built an altar there, and laid the wood in order, and bound Isaac his son, and laid him on the altar, upon the wood" (Genesis 22:10). Different versions of that story generate indigenous theories of sacrifice in Judaism, Christianity (where Isaac prefigures Jesus), and Islam (where Abraham binds Ishmael). The original story foresees a burnt offering, and an angel stops the knife. Yet rituals in all three religions commemorate the sacrifice and initiate male children with a substance named nowhere in the story: blood. In minority rabbinic accounts, it is the blood of Isaac that Israelites paint on their doors so the Angel of Death will pass over – some claiming that Isaac (like Jesus) was first killed with the knife and then resurrected,[2] or that the idea of the ram, like the Logos, preceded the creation of the world (Pirkei Avot 5:6). Commenting on the phrase "When I see the

---

[1] Peter Ochs first got me to think seriously about the Aqedah (Binding) at a Children of Abraham Institute session in Charlottesville after 9/11/2001 ("Isaac in the Eucharist," *Journal for Scriptural Reasoning* 2:3 [September 2002] at etext.lib.virginia.edu/journals/ssr/). The present chapter began when I sat in on my colleague Marc Bregman's course on the Aqedah. I thank Marc Bregman, Sarah Bregman, Steven Kepnes, and Diana Lipton for reading earlier drafts, although I have only myself to thank for neglecting their advice. See also the discussion in *Journal of Textual Reasoning* 2:1 on the Aqedah.

[2] Jon D. Levenson, *The Death and Resurrection of the Beloved Son: The Transformation of Child Sacrifice in Judaism and Christianity* (New Haven: Yale University Press, 1995), 197.

blood [of the paschal lamb] I will pass over you" (Ex. 12:13), the Mekilta de-Rabbi Ishmael glosses, "I see the blood of the binding of Isaac."[3] Which is almost to say: "I see a blood that is not there." Similarly, Pseudo-Philo has God conclude that Abraham's offering of Isaac was "acceptable before me, and *on account of his blood*, I chose them."[4] That might not be more than a drop, but Mikilta de Rabbi Shimon ben Yochai on Leviticus speaks of "Isaac son of Abraham, who gave a quarter of [a *log* of] blood upon the altar" – and rabbis further argue whether a quarter of a log is a small amount or (in Levenson's words) "all the blood a person has."[5]

Although the Qur'an criticizes sacrifice, Muslims at Mecca and at home annually kill and bleed ten million animals to commemorate Abraham's binding of his son for Eid al-Adha. Jews and Muslims initiate their sons into community with Abraham's by drawing blood in circumcision, while Christians compare baptism to washing in Christ's blood, even though they baptize in water.

Christians make Christ the Isaac figure and state as a general principle: "Without the shedding of blood, there is no remission of sin" (Hebrews 9:22) – interpreting Christ's death as bloody even though crucifixion kills by suffocation. Christian images cover it in blood. Early images portray Jesus intact and victorious on the cross; later, medieval angels collect his blood in cups. In Isaac Watts's hymn "When I Survey the Wondrous Cross," the third verse begins, "His dying crimson, like a robe, Spreads o'er his body on the tree," as if to cover and color him red. But, as I've pointed out, *blood is at most incidental to crucifixion; the picture of blood sacrifice colonizes a procedure that kills by suffocating. What makes us so bloody-minded? A social system in which blood carries meaning. This system seeks to make the crucifixion, and in minority traditions even the binding of Isaac, meaningful in terms of blood, even when the story features little or none. No blood, no meaning. The meaning of the crucifixion summons the blood. Here again the exception proves the rule.*

Blood exercises such fascination that Judaism, Christianity, and Islam race to read it in even where texts leave it to go without saying. Scholars of religion have written shelves of books on sacrifice. But why do Christians, Jews, and Muslims bring up "blood" when other explanations would suffice? Why does blood seem to explain *too much*? Why does blood seep in even where it hardly seems to belong?

---

[3] Levenson, 180–2, citing Pisha' 7.
[4] Levenson, 192, citing *Biblical Antiquities* 18:5.
[5] Levenson, 193–4, citing b. Sota 5a.

The Binding of Isaac represents a test of the blood thesis. If blood matters to Christian thinking as much as I suppose, then there ought not to be important places where it goes missing. I claim that this exception proves the rule: that here, where blood is missing from the text, Christian and rabbinic traditions both can't help themselves from reading it in. These stories get bloodier in the hands of their readers: rabbinic accounts where it is the blood of Isaac that, at the Passover in Egypt, wards off the angel of death, and the Christian transformation of the Isaac story where the beloved son of the father does die with plenty of blood. The oddity holds even if, in a kind of sibling competition, rabbis got the idea to bloody Isaac from Christian crucifixions in the first place.[6] *You might grant that Christian and Jewish traditions both read blood into this story, where it does not seem to belong, and find it a pathology rather than a feature. I think there is a pathology in the story, but not exactly in the blood. The pathology lies in the failure to detect irony. Thus a subthesis: blood-talk is unavoidable, but irony counts.* It counts because ironic blood displaces sacrifice by continuing to use its language.

I read the Genesis narrative as a trickster story in which Abraham fails to detect God's irony. I do this by attending to the untranslated word "na" with which the story begins. In most instances it seems ironic. I take it so here. "Say, Abraham, ... Have I got a proposition for you!" All of Abraham's dubious bargains begin this way – when he proposes to pass off Sarah as his sister, when he proposes to divide the land with Lot, when he negotiates with God over the cities of the plain; but when God imitates Abraham, Abraham fails to notice. Abraham is supposed to bargain or resist; unaccountably, he does neither. He just gets ready to go.

Here too a great deal depends on the ironic or transformed use of blood. Part of the Christian emphasis on blood comes, of course, from the words that Paul, the synoptics, and many communion liturgies place on the lips of Jesus himself at the Last Supper: Mt. 26:28, Mk. 14:24, Lk. 22:20, 1 Co. 11:25, or, as the Catholic rite combines them, "This is my blood of the new and eternal covenant for you and for many for the forgiveness of sins." They portray Jesus as doing a Judith Butler thing here, if I may put it that way: He takes a structure of violent oppression – death by crucifixion – and turns it

---

[6] Further sibling competition: Philo of Alexandria says (as Stroumsa recounts it), "Isaac was not, contrary to appearance, the son of Abraham, but rather of God! The maternity of Sarah is not in doubt, but Philo believes he knows that God, before giving birth to Isaac, miraculously returned Sarah to virginity. Thus we have from a contemporary of Paul's the idea that Isaac was the son of god and of a virgin!" Guy Stroumsa, *The End of Sacrifice: Religious Transformations in Late Antiquity*, trans. Susan Emanuel (Chicago: University of Chicago Press, 2009), 83, citing *De Cherubim* 42–51 and referring also to *Quod deterius potiori insidiari soleat* 124 and *De mutatione nominum* 131.

into another invitation to the eschatological wedding feast. You can't take my life from me, he says: here, I give it to you. Faced with a social structure of meaning that is not simply going away, our only choice, says Butler, is to continue to use it, to subvert it, to free it from contexts of oppression. Call this Butlerian irony. Paul and the evangelists present Jesus as something of a religious genius of that move: he remakes his violent death to renew his invitation to the feast: "This is my blood of the new covenant" – an understanding no less material, since it maintains a use of blood in the cup and among the people to convey and proliferate itself. The language that Jesus does not avoid, but affirmatively deploys to render his death meaningful, is the language of blood.

New Testament accounts of discipleship, especially Peter's, and particularly in the Gospel of Mark, emphasize that the disciples frequently or usually misunderstand, disobey, deny, betray, fall asleep, and run away. In Mark the verb "to follow" appears all but once in the imperative. The one indicative "and he followed him" applies to Bartimaeus, who started out blind and screaming. The synoptics portray God as exercising patience and forbearance to use ordinary, fallible people. Peter denies Jesus three times; Jesus once calls him "Satan" – and this is the very one whom God can use. Given his unreliability, Peter's name "the Rock" is ironic. Paul persecutes the God-fearers, and God makes him an apostle. In the Christian context, it is at least possible to entertain the possibility that Abraham, in the best of company, also fails the test – and, like the others, remains the one of God's choice. The pattern is, the human being fails miserably, and God uses him or her anyway. Many stories in the Hebrew Bible showcase tricksters who depend upon the fallibilities of those with whom they interact. Readers so formed – whether by New Testament stories or by their awareness of trickster narratives in the Hebrew Bible – may read the stories of Abraham differently.

What if Abraham misunderstands God's desires, and God goes along with him as a ghoulish exercise? Then God's command, "Take your son, your only son, Isaac, whom you love, and go to the land of Moriah," has a different tenor. The first word, standing before the imperative, goes untranslated: it is "na." The object of the verb features a long, extended pile up of appositives ("your son, your only son, Isaac, whom you love") as if the speaker is buying time while thinking out loud. It has a slow, building, deliberative quality. It says, "I know you, Abraham. You're infected by the Molochite tendency to think that child sacrifice is a good thing to do.[7] I'm

---

[7] Levenson, 50.

not sure how I'm going to persuade you that that is not what I want. Maybe I have to let you go ahead with this maniacal idea, and stop you well into the process." It says, "Okay, go ahead! I throw up my hands! Oh, no, don't let me stop you, Abraham. (Not yet, anyway.)" The command, in short, is to be read as irony. The story is not tragedy – it does, after all, have a happy ending – but it has rarely been read as dark comedy. My reading is unconventional. Is there any textual evidence for it?

It depends what you mean by "text." Certainly, my reading has the virtue of eliminating a conflict between the seeming sense of Genesis and the plain sense of Jeremiah, where God protests: "they have built the high place ... to burn their sons and their daughters in the fire; which I did not command them, nor did it come into my mind"; and again "the people have forsaken me, and ... filled this place with the blood of innocents, and have built the high places ... to burn their sons in the fire as burnt offerings ..., which I did not command or decree, nor did it come into my mind" (7:31, 19:4–5).

But is there any textual evidence *in Genesis*, which did not, after all, seek to follow Jeremiah?

I think there is just a little. It brings this chapter into that legendary category of exegesis in which everything depends upon a jot or a tittle, or in this case, a bit more – two letters. I call the chapter "And God said 'Na.'" "Na" (nun-aleph) is the particle of entreaty, usually untranslated or rendered as "please," with which God's command to Abraham begins (Gen. 22:2). Even Brown-Driver-Briggs, the standard lexicon of the Hebrew Bible, admits that it is sometimes used "ironically, as a challenge." So Is. 47:12 with "na," "Stand fast in your enchantments and your many sorceries" or Jb. 40:10 (God to Job, out of the whirlwind, with "na"), "Deck yourself with majesty and dignity; clothe yourself with glory and splendor." These, like Gen. 22:2, are both commands with the ironic or even sarcastic "na."

It is also instructive to see how Abraham himself uses the particle "na." Abraham is a trickster. From Abraham we get what I call the "na" of the dubious proposition. So Abraham uses "na" to pimp his wife and propose that Sarah lie: "Say you are my sister, that it may go well with me because of you, and that my life may be spared on your account" (Gen. 12:13). Or you get the "na" of "let's see." When "the land could not support [Abram and Lot] dwelling together," Abraham suggests dividing it, with "na": "Separate yourself from me. If you take the left ...," not with irony, but under some duress, in the sense of "Say, let's make a deal" (Gen. 13:8). Is this good for Lot? Let him beware, if Abraham proposes it. Probably the land on the left is poor.

44 BLOOD THEOLOGY

Sometimes "na" appears with a sense of warning ("beware," Judges 13:4), and, significantly, when Delilah is tricking Samson, "Tell me how you might be bound" (twice, Judges 16:6 and 16:10), and then again when Samson begs God for his strength back, Judges 16:28 – also with no innocent intent. I could go on. All these phrases start with "na."

In some cases "na" seems colorless: but in many cases it seems loaded. If it is polite, it may mask the mocking of excessive courtesy. If it starts out colorless, it marks the first stage of craving a favorable response, which may lead to bargaining and manipulation. In signal cases it becomes ironic, sarcastic, dubious, or tricky. It issues an implicit or explicit warning. "Na," in the mouth of Samson or Delilah, the prophet or the psalmist, Abraham or God, is rarely innocent.

What if God is imitating Abraham's own usages, deliberative, ironic, using his wits: "Say! I have an idea! Let's try this! Hey, Abraham, you want to sacrifice your son? The full Molochite? Okay, go ahead! See if I care! (Maybe he'll come to his senses!)" It is easy to see how this characteristic of God's might be the right way of dealing with Abraham, whom "the author of Genesis 20 portrays as an even more subtle con man than does the author of Genesis 12,"[8] in a pattern of escalating manipulation. It is easy to see how this strategy on God's part might link up with tricksters in the Hebrew Bible and moronic disciples in the New Testament. It is harder to see, of course, how it preserves the parallelism between the sacrifice of Isaac and the sacrifice of Jesus. But even that was interpreted in the early church as a trick against the devil.

Most rabbinic interpretations offer no support to mine.[9] But Midrash Tanhuma offers some:

[According to Jer. 19:5], "And they have built high places to Baal for burning their sons in the fire, burnt offerings to Baal, which I never commanded, never spoke for, and which never entered my mind" ... Moreover, it "never entered my mind" to tell Abraham to slaughter his son ... Even though I said to him (in Gen. 22:2): "Please [na] take your son," it never entered my mind that he would slaughter his son. It is therefore stated (in Ps. 89:35): "I will not defile my covenant."[10]

---

[8] Susan Niditch, *Underdogs and Tricksters: A Prelude to Biblical Folklore* (San Francisco: Harper & Row, 1987), 55.

[9] With thanks to Marc Bregman, whose attitude is interested skepticism; Sarah Bregman finds my interpretation scandalous.

[10] *Midrash Tanhuma: Genesis*, trans. and ed. John T. Townsend (Jersey City, NJ: KTAV, 1989), 124.

Mira Balberg, citing Tosefta Menachot 7.9, sums up what she calls a "particularly daring tradition" not, to be sure, about Abraham's sacrifice, but about sacrifice in general, "according to which it is not God's will that is being fulfilled through sacrifice, but rather the *offerer's* will: simply put, it is human beings who wish to make sacrifices, and God allows them to do so but certainly does not desire it."[11]

One attraction of my interpretation is that it solves the theodicy puzzle of why a good God would command child sacrifice even as a test: Abraham *fails* the test. He should have said No! After all, Abraham does sometimes say "no" to God, as in bargaining for Sodom. But this time Abraham fails to say no or even to bargain – and God can cope with that. If the command is not ironic, it's hard to tell the difference between God and the devil.

This interpretation also provides an example of what to do with difficult passages that are not going away. If we refuse to interpret Genesis 22, then we leave it to readers who suppose God really did command the killing of an innocent, even as a test – or may command it still. "Pastor, I hear a voice telling me to sacrifice my son like Abraham." Does the pastor say, "No, I don't think that's what God meant. Call this number. He's really good." Or "Better get on with it, then"?

My interpretation depends on hearing irony in a written text with no stage directions. We could hear it in a properly inflected oral performance. But for a written text there is no recourse except to other textual examples. Unless, of course, the translators helped us. They have no trouble conveying irony and sarcasm in other instances. Would it be too much to indicate the "na" in Genesis 22 with the word "Say, Abraham"? The trouble with that translation, a critic might say, is that it makes God's remark sound less like a command. But *is* it a command? God's commandments – at least the Ten – do not have "na." God is perfectly able to command something without "na." Something with "na," I argue, *is not a command*. It is at most a request: more often it is a bargaining position, a gambit.

But I need to make the case for that by piling up examples of gambits that are not commands and start with "na." It is in the nature of the case that I provide parallel evidence at some length, with or even without editorial comment, because it has to be convincing more or less on its own. I quote the Revised Standard Version (RSV) and organize it according to the speaker. Please [na] skip ahead if you don't need it. Go ahead. Feel free. Be my guest.

---

[11] Mira Balberg, *Blood for Thought: The Reinvention of Sacrifice in Early Rabbinic Literature* (Oakland: University of California Press, 2017), 84.

46   BLOOD THEOLOGY

Abraham says "Na" (usually translated "please" or "now"):

> Gen. 12:11 It came about when he came near to Egypt, that he said to Sarai his wife, "See now [na], I know that you are a beautiful woman;"
>
>   12:13 "Please [na] say that you are my sister so that it may go well with me because of you, and that I may live on account of you."
>
>   (He's pimping his wife.)
>
>   13:8 So Abram said to Lot, "Please [na] let there be no strife between you and me, nor between my herdsmen and your herdsmen, for we are brothers." [Implication: Please, let there be no strife – because there sure is tension. Please, let there be no strife: is that a threat?] 9 "Is not the whole land before you? Please [na] separate from me; if to the left, then I will go to the right; or if to the right, then I will go to the left."
>
>   18:27 And Abraham replied, "Now [na] behold, I have ventured to speak to the Lord, although I am but dust and ashes." [He says he is but dust and ashes, as he prepares to negotiate like an equal.]
>
>   18:30 Then he said, "Oh may [na] the Lord not be angry, and I shall speak; suppose thirty are found there?" And He said, "I will not do it if I find thirty righteous there." 31 And he said, "Now [na] behold, I have ventured to speak to the Lord; suppose twenty are found there?" And He said, "I will not destroy it on account of the twenty." 32 Then he said, "Oh may [na] the Lord not be angry, and I shall speak only this once; suppose ten are found there?" And He said, "I will not destroy it on account of the ten."
>
>   24:1 Now Abraham was old, advanced in age; and the LORD had blessed Abraham in every way. 2 Abraham said to his servant, the oldest of his household, who had charge of all that he owned, "Please [na] place your hand under my thigh, 3 and I will make you swear by the LORD, the God of heaven and the God of earth, that you shall not take a wife for my son from the daughters of the Canaanites, among whom I live, 4 but you will go to my country and to my relatives, and take a wife for my son Isaac." 5 The servant said to him, "Suppose the woman is not willing to follow me to this land; should I take your son back to the land from where you came?" 6 Then Abraham said to him, "Beware [na] that you do not take my son back there."

All of those cases expect negotiation. But in Genesis 22, Abraham does not negotiate. What's wrong with him?

Other cases recur as Isaac woos Rebekah – not a straightforward situation, but full of negotiation and desire. "Na" puts the powerful into a servile position.

Lot says "na":

> Gen. 19:2 [With his face to the ground] And [Lot] said, "Now behold, my lords, please [na] turn aside into your servant's house, and spend the night, and wash your feet; then you may rise early and go on your way." They said however, "No, but we shall spend the night in the square."

Blood after Isaac

47

19:7 And [Lot] said, "Please [na], my brothers, do not act wickedly. 8 Now behold, I have two daughters who have not had relations with man; please [na] let me bring them out to you, and do to them whatever you like; only do nothing to these men, inasmuch as they have come under the shelter of my roof."

Another dubious proposition; people do things they shouldn't, under duress.

Thrice-repeated "na" – Lot is really afraid:

Gen. 19:18 But Lot said to them, "Oh no, my lords! 19 Now [na] behold, your servant has found favor in your sight, and you have magnified your lovingkindness, which you have shown me by saving my life; but I cannot escape to the mountains, for the disaster will overtake me and I will die; 20 now [na] behold, this town is near enough to flee to, and it is small. Please [na], let me escape there (is it not small?) that my life may be saved."

Esau says "na":

Gen. 25:30 and Esau said to Jacob, "Please [na] let me have a swallow of that red stuff there, for I am famished." 31 But Jacob said, "First sell me your birthright." 32 Esau said, "Behold, I am about to die; so of what use then is the birthright to me?" 33 And Jacob said, "First swear to me"; so he swore to him, and he sold his birthright to Jacob. 34 Then Jacob gave Esau bread and lentil stew; and he ate and drank, and rose and went on his way.

Not a good bargain. What starts with "na" may not end well.

Isaac and Jacob say "Na":

Gen. 27:2 Isaac said, "Behold now [na], I am old and I do not know the day of my death. 3 Now then, please take your gear, your quiver and your bow, and go out to the field and hunt game for me;"
9 "Go now to the flock and bring me two choice young goats from there, that I may prepare them as a savory dish for your father, such as he loves."
19 Jacob said to his father, "I am Esau your firstborn; I have done as you told me. Get up, please, sit and eat of my game, that you may bless me."
21 Then Isaac said to Jacob, "Please [na] come close, that I may feel you, my son, whether you are really my son Esau or not." (Here the na covers suspicion.)
26 Then his father Isaac said to him, "Please [na] come close and kiss me, my son." (Na covers suspicion again.)

Rachel, Laban, and Jacob say "Na."

Gen. 30: Rachel tries to trick Leah. Rachel says "Na," but it doesn't work. Poor Rachel.

48   BLOOD THEOLOGY

Then Rachel said to Leah, "Please [na] give me some of your son's mandrakes." 15 But she said to her, "Is it a small matter for you to take my husband? And would you take my son's mandrakes also?" So Rachel said, "Therefore he may lie with you tonight in return for your son's mandrakes." 16 When Jacob came in from the field in the evening, then Leah went out to meet him and said, "You must come in to me, for I have surely hired you with my son's mandrakes." So he lay with her that night. 17 God gave heed to Leah, and she conceived and bore Jacob a fifth son.

Gen. 31: Laban's trickery is revealed with "na." Jacob is speaking to Rachel and Leah.

12 "He said, 'Lift up now [na] your eyes and see that all the male goats which are mating are striped, speckled, and mottled; for I have seen all that Laban has been doing to you.'"

Gen. 32:11: Jacob prays to God for delivery from Esau.

11 "Deliver me, I pray [na], from the hand of my brother, from the hand of Esau; for I fear him, that he will come and attack me and the mothers with the children."

Gen. 32:29: Jacob asks the angel's name (not a fair question).

Then Jacob asked him and said, "Please [na] tell me your name." But he said, "Why is it that you ask my name?" And he blessed him there.

The Joseph story is also full of tricks with "na." But we hardly need more evidence. In Genesis, only bargainers and tricksters say "na." "Na" is never colorless in Genesis. It always reveals power relations. Typically the more powerful craves something that is nevertheless in the power of the subordinate to give. In the binding of Isaac, "na" puts God in the position of the powerful at the mercy of the subordinate. Is God afraid of what Abraham will do? God experiences the helplessness of the one who loves someone flawed, and resorts to the scheming of other Genesis tricksters, scheming that can take place in deadly earnest.[12]

---

[12] "Na" in Genesis: 12:11, 12:13, 13:8–9, 13:14, 15:5, 16:2, 18:3–4, 18:21, 18:27, 18:30–32, 19:2, 19:7–8, 19:18–20, 22:2, 24:2, 24:12, 24:14, 24:17, 24:23, 24:42–43, 24:45, 25:30, 26:28, 27:2–3, 27:9, 27:19, 27:21, 27:26, 30:14, 30:27, 31:12, 32:11, 32:29, 33:10–11, 33:14–15, 34:8, 37:6, 37:14, 37:16, 37:32, 38:16, 38:25, 40:8, 40:14, 44:18, 44:33, 45:4, 47:4, 47:29, 48:9, 50:4–5, 50:17.

Blood after Isaac

Ruth says "Na."

In Ruth, the use of "na" sounds colorless:

> 2 And Ruth the Moabitess said to Naomi, "Please [na] let me go to the field and glean among the ears of grain after one in whose sight I may find favor." And she said to her, "Go, my daughter."
>
> 7 "And she said, 'Please [na] let me glean and gather after the reapers among the sheaves.' Thus she came and has remained from the morning until now; she has been sitting in the house for a little while."

But it is not colorless, just cleverer than usual. Ruth too does not ask innocently. Ruth too has a plan. Here too there is more in store for the hearer of "Na" than he foresees.

God Says "Na":

> Is. 1:18 "Come now [na], and let us reason together," says the LORD, "though your sins be as scarlet . . ."

Here the note of bargaining becomes explicit:

> Is. 36:8 "Now therefore [na], come make a bargain with my master the king of Assyria, and I will give you two thousand horses, if you are able on your part to set riders on them."
>
> 47:12 "Stand fast now [na] in your spells and in your many sorceries with which you have labored from your youth; perhaps you will be able to profit, perhaps you may cause trembling. 13 You are wearied with your many counsels; let now [na] the astrologers, those who prophesy by the stars, those who predict by the new moons, stand up and save you from what will come upon you."
>
> 51:21 Therefore, please [na] hear this, you afflicted, who are drunk, but not with wine . . .

I hate to spoil the effect, but this is sarcasm.

We should expect God's "na" to be ironic, because by saying "na" God pretends or reveals Godself to be without power, to be at the mercy of the creature God petitions; God acts the role of the supplicant. We should be wary. So Job, as we have seen.

Those left out of the conversation with "na" include those, like Sarah, who may overhear, mishear, or hear tell.[13] The story does not portray Sarah as hearing

---

[13] "Jerome Gellman notes that the role of Sarah [in Gen. 22] throws into relief the role of Abraham, representing a maternal logic [that does not bargain over sons] in direct conflict with a paternal imperative. 'Sarah is lost,' he concludes, unless the sacrificial imperative does not stand alone; unless there exists an additional, quite different central religious imperative;

the "na." Nor does it specify that she does not hear. Unlike Abraham, Sarah may be more used to hearing "na" than saying it. She may be in a better position to hear it as ambiguous and manipulative, manic and fraught with bravado, than Abraham, who hardly has the self-awareness to hear *himself* using it that way. "Say!" "Come now!" "Go ahead!" Sarah knows Abraham as prone to negotiations that start that way, a dealer also dangerously susceptible to them. These openers might well rouse exasperation in a spouse: now they would strike Sarah with terror. This is her son the bargainers are toying with. The devil, when he comes to her in Isaac's guise to tell her what is going on,[14] could hardly begin with a more chilling phrase than "I heard God speaking to Abraham, and God said 'Na . . . .'"

So too have Jews overheard Christians through the centuries: "I heard the Christians speaking to one another, and somebody said 'blood.'"

---

unless we say that Abraham personified one religious ideal and Sarah another; unless, somehow, in fairness to both Sarah and Abraham, we are to live an exquisite balance between two opposing religious commands.' This 'opposing' religious command may be reflected in that aspect of the discourse of sacrifice often left to the background in the theories we have been canvassing, the dimension that is not focused on blood, expiation, and paternity but on food, nourishment, and communal identity. Indeed, these dimensions of sacrifice may not be as easily divorced as has been implied, for the two often go together, the bloody sacrifice and immolation of parts of an animal, for instance, followed by a feast of celebration in which other parts are consumed in celebration. Here, the role of women and mothers comes to the fore in a different way and offers different possibilities for figural representation and religious practice." Cleo McNelly Kearns, "Abrahamic Sacrifice," in *The Virgin Mary, Monotheism, and Sacrifice* (New York: Cambridge University Press, 2008), 80–1 quoting Jerome Gellman, *Abraham! Abraham! Kierkegaard and the Hasidim on the Binding of Isaac* (Burlington, VT: Ashgate Press, 2003).

[14] As he does in Midrash Pirqe de-Rabbi Eliezer, 32 (72b).

3

BLOOD AFTER LEVITICUS
Separation and Sacrifice

Blood Daubed and Inexhaustible

Why do Christian and, perhaps under their influence, sometimes Jewish readers find a lot of blood where their texts show little or none?[1] Under the influence of the eucharistic "pouring out" of the synoptic Gospels, Christians interpret the New Testament book of Hebrews to need more blood than Leviticus allows. Isaac comes to bleed in a text that mentions no blood. The Gospels see blood in crucifixion, a death by suffocation. Why do people like to read blood in?

But first I depart from texts to describe animal sacrifice as it still takes place in the twenty-first century among Samaritans – and Christians.

At Taybeh in occupied Palestine, Christians slaughter around eighty sheep and goats over the course of a year on the threshold of an August and still consecrated, if ruined and roofless, Byzantine church.[2] The church is dedicated to St. George. (At Lod, another Christian village in occupied Palestine, at another church of St. George, another, smaller sacrifice cult continues annually on George's feast day.) At Taybeh, a long and sturdy steel chain, ending in two great hooks suitable for hanging a large carcass, swings in the doorway. There is an altar in the church; it is also exposed to the light and air,

---

[1] Mira Balberg, *Blood for Thought: The Reinvention of Sacrifice in Early Rabbinic Literature* (Oakland: University of California Press, 2017), especially in her central chapter "The Work of Blood" (65–107), shows how an at least somewhat similar process of inflating blood's importance takes place among the rabbis. As in Christianity, the rabbis multiply the work of metaphorical or symbolic (Balberg says "discursive") blood at a time when sacrifices no longer take place in a temple.

[2] About this practice little appears in print. See Jill Hamilton, "There Is No Role for Animal Sacrifice in Christianity" (a title that disputes its own evidence), *The Guardian*, December 15, 2011, at www.theguardian.com/commentisfree/belief/2011/dec/15/no-role-animal-sacrifice-christianity. On the cult of St. George in Cyprus, see Aaron T. Hollander, *The Multimediation of Holiness*, Ph.D. dissertation, University of Chicago, 2018.

because the roof is gone; but they do not sacrifice animals on the altar. They sacrifice in the forecourt outside and a few steps below the church, so that the sacrifice of an animal leads up to, rather than rivals the sacrifice of bread and wine. Besides, the altar inside is far too small, even for a lamb or kid.

The forecourt is made of stone, old and pitted marble. Centuries of footsteps have worn shallows and divots. Marble is porous to water, but blood absorbs poorly. An altar made to purpose would be furnished with grooves and gutters to carry off the blood: that's one of the ways you would know it's an altar. You know the forecourt is an altar in a different way: you see the blood. It pools in the swales and clogs the holes; it dries there. On a hot Saturday morning (September 19, 2015), the floor of the forecourt is stained pink and the low places show traces of gore. Exposed to the beating sun and desiccated air, everything is dead dry. At eye level the marble doorposts, as if in a Christian Exodus, show crosses and handprints in blood.

The slaughterers have brought their meat animals, not, indeed, to the altar itself, but to the threshold of the oldest and holiest place. They do not sacrifice in secret, but sign their sacrifice with handprints (I placed my hand against some to judge the size) and with the sign of the cross (any sacrifice participates in the Lamb that was slain). Local priests neither condone nor condemn, but wash their hands. The priests dislike the implications of animal sacrifice at the door of the church. But the people who continue this custom are on to something. (I am putting my own interpretation on the practice.) They seek to keep together two necessities of herding animals for food: the necessity to care for the flock, which gives the animals a share in human community, and the necessity to kill a large proportion at least of the males, so that humans can eat them for food. (Ewes, on the other hand, are good for milk and cheese, as well as more lambs.) This is not factory farming; the animals have names, faces, and distinctive marks (sometimes ruddled with red ocher): and so herders assimilate the killing of the animal to the killing of a human being, and they assimilate the killing to the willing/unwilling killing of a sacrificial victim, the one at the center of their religion, Jesus.

The air bears no tang of blood: the weather is too dry. The breeze is fragrant with oregano. I am fascinated with the blood itself: there is a lot of blood. There also is a well; no doubt they wash from it. But cleaning seems beside the point. They seem to glory in the blood. The stains and traces, handprints and crosses speak of floods.

The following spring (Wednesday, April 20, 2016), I went to Mt. Gerezim, also in the West Bank, to observe Samaritan Passover sacrifice. Samaritans are non-rabbinic, disputed Jews who stayed in Israel while non-Samaritans, *Iudaioi,* went into exile in Babylon; on the exiles' return,

Separation and Sacrifice

53

Samaritans did not join them in the Second Temple, but kept their own. Rabbinic Jews no longer sacrifice on Passover because the Temple no longer stands. While Samaritan sacrifice has been affected and interrupted by many things, Samaritans never took the destruction of the Second Temple as a reason to abandon sacrifice, and at Passover it continues to take place. Their canon includes Leviticus and lacks the exilic books that criticize sacrifice. As of January 2016, there were some 777 Samaritans, whom tourists and observers may outnumber at their Passover sacrifice.

The time of sacrifice is sunset, during a liturgy consisting largely of psalms, in a dialect called variously Samaritan or Old Hebrew. (The language of everyday intercourse is Palestinian Arabic.) The place of sacrifice is not the Samaritan temple atop Mt. Gerezim, but a wide, open platform some way down the hill, covered in matte white ceramic tiles. The platform rises slightly over the surrounding land in order to keep the surface level, and two runners or alleys (like bowling alleys or life-size gutters) interrupt it at ground level. The alleys, as wide as one or two tiles, run parallel to one another, spaced with another one or two tiles at platform level between them. But only the sides of the alleys are tiled; the bottoms of the alleys are not floored at all. They are planted with grass. Above the alleys stand steel or iron pipes painted cobalt blue.

Forty-five minutes or so before sunset, young men begin to arrive with lambs, some frisking ahead, some following behind, a few carried, in the pose familiar to Christians from innumerable paintings and statuettes of Jesus, around the necks and over the shoulders of their owners. Think again when you see those images: lambs on shoulders are destined for slaughter. Some lambs follow the grass unprompted into the grassy alleys three or four feet beneath the level of the platform; other lambs follow the young men or ride like small children on their shoulders.

The whole platform is fenced off with panels of chain-link fence in a diamond pattern to keep tourists at bay. But tourists are welcome at a distance, and busses run continuously to ferry them up and down the mountain from a parking lot at the bottom. The number of tourists may be a thousand. I don't have a press pass; I can't enter the fenced-off area; I am just another observer with a Ph.D. I am standing, most of the time, in a children's playground eight or ten feet above the platform, right above a podium where a priest leads the chanting of psalms, and twenty or thirty feet from the alleys where the sheep are munching grass. I can't see the sheep very well down there. Some of the young men are down there with them. Meanwhile, numerous sheep run by me going downhill to the right, on their way into the grassy alleys. I estimate forty to fifty sheep. The next day, newspapers

54 BLOOD THEOLOGY

report fifty. I can see what looks like a large fire being lit in a pit almost out of sight to my right. Later I learn it is a series of fires in perhaps five or six deep, cylindrical, purpose-built pits, one to a large, extended family.

Below me on the platform, everyone is wearing white. Religious officials wear surcoats of red, green, or gold brocade. Women are also on the platform, in white dresses or pantsuits, wearing their best jewelry, hair uncovered. Some of the younger men are wearing not just white, but slick white jumpsuits. They wear dark glasses against the setting sun. The jumpsuit guys look slick in more ways than one – they look overtly sexy to me – in poor taste for a religious occasion. What new style has infected the Samaritan Passover, I wonder. My impression of bad taste increases when I identify the impression of slickness as a texture of the jumpsuits: they're plasticated. Then it dawns on me that the jumpsuits are not a fashion choice. They are plasticated to wash off easily – and white to show how clean they are. Even later it dawns on me that the tiles are white for the same reason, and matte because they are nonslip.

Shortly after sunset, at some point in the singing of psalms, a cry goes up from the assembly, a sort of whoop. Slowly I realize that the jumpsuit guys are off the platform; they have slipped into the grassy alleys, and they have killed all the lambs at once. The great whoop has liturgically and effectively covered any noise the lambs might have made. Later, poring over videos online, I don't see the lambs struggle, exactly; more twitch or squirm. From my vantage point above, I see no blood at all.

After a little while, some of the jumpsuits emerge into the larger crowd of people now milling around and talking. (The chanting of psalms seems to have ended with the whoop.) The jumpsuits are entirely clean and free of blood. My colleague Gabriel Radle points out to me that the jumpsuits (I mean the guys that wear them) bear a small blaze of blood vertically on their foreheads in line with their noses – not much blood, less than Christians would use of oil at chrismation, and certainly not crossed. The jumpsuits then go directly to various people who look to be fathers, grandmothers, other relatives, speak a few words, and touch their own foreheads to the foreheads or the backs of the hands of their relatives. That's the reason I have repeated that these are "young" men: they have parents and grandparents still living. No doubt the blood transfers notionally, but to me, at a distance from the secondary recipients, transferred blood remains invisible. Later I learn from photographs online that more blood – I don't know how conveyed – is painted on the doorposts of their houses.

The atmosphere is not at all somber or grave. The atmosphere is straightforwardly festive. Platters of extremely large, round, homemade or bakery-fresh matzoh, the size of American pizzas, come in held overhead and circulate.

SEPARATION AND SACRIFICE 55

The dead lambs begin to reappear hung from the blue pipes above the grassy alleys or leaned against the blue-pipe uprights. Within a couple of hours, all the lambs are skinned, disemboweled, and hoisted on sturdy wooden spits. The spits bearing lambs are planted upright in the fire pits, five or more to a pit, depending on the size of an extended family. The pits are deep enough to hold the spitted lambs below the level of the ground; only the tips of the spits emerge above it. Below the level of the ground, and above the level of the spitted lambs, a heavy cloth tarpaulin covers each pit, each tarp weighted in turn with a mud slurry to keep things humid below. The tarps and mud smother the fire to embers. The tips of the spits stick out of the tarps and are neatly trimmed off. It is now between eight and nine in the evening, and the lambs will cook slowly for several hours until midnight. The meat must be eaten that night. As I understand it, leftovers might have been distributed, but the whole community, everyone qualified to eat it, is present, so that uneaten meat must be burned. It is hard not to read in Leviticus. As in Levitical sacrifice, and unlike the discursive sacrifice of rabbinical and Christian texts, there is more smoke than blood.

Indeed, what has been most remarkable in this whole process is the relative absence of blood. The grassy earth absorbs it from the beginning. When I get closer, at platform level, to observe the skinning and preparation of the meat, I see that the men and the carcasses are continually sluiced down with hoses, and the water runs into the alleys, thence into the ground. The meat is also treated with salt. Blood does not linger or pool. It does not seep anywhere, except into the earth. Deliberately or not, this follows the Levitical pattern that excess blood shall be removed from cultic use by being poured at the foot of the altar, that is, into the ground.

It also follows the Levitical pattern that the cultic use of blood is a matter of daubing. Indeed the blood blazed on the foreheads of the young men is hard to see at a distance, even when floodlights come on after dark; and the blood they spread to others is vanishingly small, which is to say, even through binoculars I can't see it. It dries quickly and ceases to transfer well; it turns brown and becomes yet harder to see. Little, dry, and brown, it is enough (*dayeinu*) to save the firstborn sons from the angel of death, and I read the faces of the relatives as glad, who receive the touch of the forehead of blood. Their sons and their households are safe for another year, and to celebrate the feast. A little goes a long way, and the rest is grounded.

Samaritan and Christian animal sacrifices, both in the West Bank, are close in geography, and to a tourist, no doubt, similar in substance: lambs are slaughtered in a sacred place; the meat eaten or given away; the sacrificers make signs in blood. But only tourists go to both. Practitioners are not interested in each other, to assimilate or to differentiate. Their groups are too small to be much aware of each other. No doubt both are aware of Muslim lamb festivals at Eid al-Adha. The St. George Christians have one small church in Lod, and a somewhat larger one at Taybeh, more famous for its Christian brewery. Both groups are tiny and unrepresentative minorities within their religions, just because, at large, neither Christians nor Jews sacrifice animals anymore at all.

But I am also interested in their differences, to illustrate a conceptual contrast. The Samaritan sacrifice takes place in grassy alleys below ground level and out of view; the blood sinks in; hoses run without stopping; the slaughterers wear white jumpsuits that they constantly hose and keep scrupulously clean. Of blood they need a fingertip's worth. They do not leave or keep or glory in the blood.

The Taybeh Christians sacrifice on the platform of the forecourt, over stone. It's off the altar of the church, but it's on the altar of the forecourt, which is to say, its floor of stone. They expose, they do not lower or hide their bleeding lambs; they do not pour their blood into absorbent ground, but onto stone. Pouring onto the ground removes blood from ritual use: pouring blood onto stone consecrates blood for ritual use. Their place is not too clean. The Christians at Taybeh (not at Lod) are sacrificing one at a time over the course the year. The Samaritans are sacrificing fifty at once. A singleton versus a hecatomb: why does the singleton leave more blood?

I said their place was not too clean. Maybe it is, in a Mary Douglas sense. She writes that dirt is "matter out of place," and perhaps the Christians think blood is not out of place there at all, but where it belongs. (I am reading all this in.) Their blood is a detergent. Its traces are clean essentially. It's okay to leave some there. They can keep some blood; they can make blood pudding. Christians like Samaritans eat lamb and sign with blood. Unlike Samaritans, they can leave, they can keep, they can glory in the blood.

I am not a trained ethnographer. Perhaps I have this wrong. The Samaritan site is fairly new, and constructed for the purpose; the St. George site is very old, and not supplied with hoses, although the well stands nearby. Perhaps the differences are accidental, and not cultic. Neither group, tiny minorities both, is characteristic of its religion. Are they?

The thing is, their differences line up with their texts. Leviticus calls for daubs of blood, and Hebrews calls down floods.

This Samaritan economy of blood, where a small, dry, brown amount suffices, the rest immediately removed from cultic use and returned to God through the ground, stands in contrast with the Christian economy of washing or bathing in blood, in blood without limit that keeps flowing and

SEPARATION AND SACRIFICE   57

stays red.[3] Materially, it is the move to wine that makes this possible. Theoretically, this Christian blood does not need to be *returned* to God, because it *is* the blood of God.

***

THIS CHAPTER IS A THOUGHT EXPERIMENT. ITS PURPOSE IS ONCE again to make blood strange, this time in quantity. Why multitudes of blood? My purpose is conceptual, not historical. I want to understand the paradox that Christianity finds metaphorical blood so powerful (how?) at holding a community together, more powerful, perhaps, than physical blood. I don't mean to make a supersessionist distinction from Judaism, which may show a similar development from biological to what Balberg calls discursive blood. Martha Himmelfarb notes the paucity of physical blood in circumcision and kashrut.[4] Vanessa Ochs points out that the rabbis also exaggerate, in a procedure she calls "hyperbolic reckoning."

> Eugene Borowitz maintains that hyperbole (called "guzma" in Hebrew) is "the distinctive aggadic trope." The rabbis "regularly speak of the most fundamental religious truths in terms that are variously playful, purposely shocking, wildly imaginative and . . . extravagantly exaggerated. They and their community must have shared a rich context of acceptable communication." Rabbi Ami makes a point about the ubiquity of hyperbole with this hyperbolic claim: "The Torah used hyperbole; the prophets used hyperbole; and the sages used hyperbole."[5]

Mira Balberg concludes that among the rabbis talk of blood "ritually functions as the completion of the sacrificial process in its entirety."[6]

Instead of distinguishing Christianity from Judaism, my purpose is to disrupt a Christian assumption (that blood must flood) and restore a sense of surprise. I want to trouble the notion that Christian cultic, sacrificial, or symbolic blood *must* burgeon, must gush and overwhelm, by comparing it to limited contrast cases – the *hatta't* offerings for sin – where the amount of

---

[3] Bynum plays on the enduring redness and fluidity of reliquary blood.

[4] Martha Himmelfarb, in conversation, September 2012; see her "The Ordeals of Abraham: Circumcision and the Aqedah in Origen, the Mekhilta, and Genesis Rabah," *Henoch* 28 (2008): 289–310. See also David Biale, *Blood and Belief: The Circulation of a Symbol Between Jews and Christians* (Berkeley: University of California Press, 2008).

[5] Vanessa Ochs, "Publicizing the Miracle: Optimistic Discursive Practices and the Commodities of Passover," *Contemporary Jewry*, 35 (2016): 187–202, citing Eugene Borowitz, *The Talmud's Theological Language-Game: A Philosophical Discourse Analysis* (Albany: State University of New York Press, 2006), 43.

[6] Balberg, 74.

salient blood is small, where it is "daubed" or "sprinkled." Not because I think Christians can get by with less – perhaps they can – but because I want to know why they seem to need more. Not, to repeat, to make a historical argument about when blood began to burgeon, or an interreligious argument about better or worse, but to throw a contingency into high relief, so that we can hear the conceptual question. What is the Christian theological technology by which blood burgeons? What is the anthropological structure by which it grows? I want to draw renewed attention to the excess, the nonnecessity, the gratuity of blood. I don't want to make quantities of blood perennial, but I don't want, either, to confine them to a period. Quantities of blood mark a tendency, a pattern, neither singular nor inevitable.

Another way to ask the question of structure is economic: how does "blood" flow through the system? How does the currency circulate? Quickly? Slowly? Easily? With difficulty? These are *how*-questions that we can answer more easily if we recognize alternative logical possibilities. We can become aware that blood does burgeon, by seeing that it does not have to, that it need not. I want to recover the strangeness, the excessiveness, and the gratuity of blood. The contrast case is Leviticus.

This section observes that there is initially not *enough* blood in Leviticus, which uses it only in "daubs" or "sprinkles," and uses other verbs to describe its disposal or return. (This is a mainstream interpretation, although not the only one.[7]) In Leviticus, blood is "tossed" or "dashed" against the sides of the altar or "poured out" at the altar's foot, so that the blood returns to God by being absorbed into the earth.[8] In that way by far the greatest volume of blood passes out of circulation and is put beyond cultic use. Levitical pouring out, so far from supplying vast quantities of blood, keeps the quantity small.

---

[7] For a critical survey of this consensus, see William K. Gilders, *Blood Ritual in the Hebrew Bible: Meaning and Power* (Baltimore: Johns Hopkins University Press, 2004).

[8] The burnt offering is more about smoke than blood; its mention of expiation (1.4) reflects an early stage replaced by the purification and reparation offerings discussed here (Jacob Milgrom, *Leviticus*, Continental Commentaries [Minneapolis: Augsburg Fortress, 2004], 24). The well-being offering primarily provides meat for "rejoicing" and thanksgiving (Milgrom, *Leviticus*, 28) and tosses blood against the sides of the altar to return it to God. It is the purification or purgation offering that primarily deals with expiation (*Leviticus*, 24), with the caveat that deliberate sins, at first irremediable by the sacrificial system, can be treated as "inadvertent" when confessed. Confession shows that one knows right from wrong and was not thinking of that when committing the act: thus, after confession, the sin can be treated as inadvertent and purged as such (*Leviticus*, 46).

Note that Milgrom has at least four books titled *Leviticus*. The first three contain chapter numbers in their titles, for example, *Leviticus 1–16* (Anchor Yale Bible Commentaries [New Haven: Yale University Press, 1998]). The fourth, called simply *Leviticus* without chapter numbers, abridges the first three. The abridgement is sometimes preferable as shorter and later.

SEPARATION AND SACRIFICE 59

In Leviticus 4, two applications minimize amounts of blood: blood that is "daubed" on the horns of the altar, and blood that is "sprinkled" seven times on a wall. A whole heifer, of course, produces a lot more blood than that: but the heifer is to be burned, as ash for soap. The Christian image drowns the altar in blood; Isaac Watts's "When I Survey the Wondrous Cross" "robes" Jesus in it.[9] What happens to the "rest" of the blood? It is "poured out at the foot of the altar." Don't the tossing and pouring create floods of blood already in Leviticus?

The question misunderstands the procedure. The "rest" of the blood has no cultic purpose.[10] It is simply returned to God. The ground absorbs it, as it does for an animal killed in the hunt. Pouring blood onto the ground is a religious act only in the sense that it disposes properly of excess blood; it deconsecrates, it removes from sacred use. In that sense, it is hardly even a cultic act: it neither atones for sin nor cancels impurity. Rather the reverse: pouring blood out *prevents* it from doing those things.[11] Tossing or dashing the blood onto the sides of the altar works similarly.[12] The altar, Milgrom writes, is also "an instrument for returning the life of the animal to God."[13] Levitical dashing against the altar (thence into the ground) or pouring out onto the ground directly decommissions or secularizes blood. Synoptic

---

[9] "His dying crimson like a robe, Spreads from his body o'er the tree," sometimes omitted.

[10] Except, according to Milgrom, to dissolve the logical difficulty in the H source that killing an innocent animal perpetrates its own transgression. In that case, the return of the blood (which is the life) to God is precisely what makes up for taking that life from God. Jacob Milgrom, "Prolegomenon to Leviticus 17:11," *Journal of Biblical Literature* 90 (1971): 149–56. Milgrom's interpretation seems at first to restrict to a technical matter a wording of wide application, but the solution he proposes would also seem to be of wide utility in Christianity; for example, in rendering ironic the calling down of blood upon the people in Mt. 17:25, in rebutting Abelard's charge that the killing of an innocent could only make matters worse, or in proving an exception to supersessionist readings of Hebrews 10:4.

[11] I received or conceived these ideas in a conversation with Naphtali Meshel in Princeton on January 24, 2013. If I misunderstood or exaggerated his ideas, the fault is mine.

[12] "Linguistically, the phrase ... could denote either tossing blood onto the upper surface of the altar on several places (perhaps on its perimeter) or dashing blood against several of its sides. Ancient and modern commentators are in agreement that the phrase denotes the latter." That consensus notwithstanding, Meshel thinks the phrase may have meant or included tossing blood atop the altar in a pre-Levitical past and is ritually grammatical (a meaningful operation in the system). Naphtali S. Meshel, *The 'Grammar' of Sacrifice: A Generativist Study of the Israelite Sacrificial System in the Priestly Writings with a 'Grammar' of* Σ (Oxford: Oxford University Press, 2014), 150. Could that pre-Levitical possibility leave room for the sort of Levitical science fiction that appears in the book of Hebrews, where more blood goes on top of the altar than into the ground?

[13] Milgrom, *Leviticus 1–16*, vol. 1, 251.

pouring out, on the other hand, empowers and consecrates it. These ironies mark out different ways of dealing with excess.

This interpretation implies that the *hatta't* or purification offering, with its parsimonious use of blood, is the most interesting Levitical use. The interpretation is surprising primarily if you have absorbed the Christian scheme according to which more metaphorical or symbolic blood is better (the blood of Jesus or communion), or the rabbinic scheme according to which more discursive blood is better (the blood of Mishnah Yoma). And it's surprising because while Christians focus on deliberate sins of the individual, two uses of the purification offering seem hardly to apply to sin at all: the purification offering treats *individuals* only who have committed *inadvertent* infractions or (even more mysterious to moderns, and more telling) who undergo certain breaches of the body, including leprosy and childbirth. Meanwhile the third use of the purification offering again offends a Christian sense of how forgiveness works: on Yom Kippur the *hatta't* purges even "wanton, unrepented sin."[14] But it is often overlooked: The purification offerings are more powerful than the others in that they treat the whole community rather than the individual, and because they are objective rather than subjective. They do not depend on my consciousness of sin; they do not depend on my repentance; they do not focus on my precious individuality or self-centered subjectivity: they perform an objective repair.

This is where breaches of the body come in: they are "impure because they create ambiguity about bodily boundaries."[15] More than that, breaches of the body image and represent breaches in society even apart from consciousness or will – childbirth included because of the powerful, dangerous, often excruciating widening of an opening beyond the proportions of any other mammal, from which the mother, like the society, needs to heal, and from which a living child, like a new access of justice, may emerge. Thus the purification rites do not aim to restore order to the Temple alone as a merely priestly exercise. Milgrom has been criticized for stressing the material, mechanical, and impersonal aspects of this rite, but that's to expose its objective and world-repairing function.[16] Because the purification offering

[14] Jacob Milgrom, "Israel's Sanctuary: The Priestly 'Picture of Dorian Gray,'" *Révue Biblique* 83 (1976): 390–9; here, 393.

[15] Robert C. T. Parker, *Miasma: Pollution and Purification in Early Greek Religion* (Oxford: Clarendon Press, 1983), 61.

[16] Not so much against Milgrom as because of Milgrom and in his wake, "Most scholars affirm something like the view of Daniel Stökl Ben Ezra: 'The temple ritual serves simultaneously to atone for the people and to purify the temple.'" Stephen Finlan, *Sacrifice and Atonement: Psychological Motives and Biblical Patterns* (Minneapolis, MN: Fortress Press, 2016), 11, quoting Daniel Stökl Ben Ezra, "Atonement. Judaism: Second Temple Period," in

SEPARATION AND SACRIFICE

is communitarian and objective, Milgrom says that the sinner "hopes to repair the broken relationship. He therefore seeks *more than* forgiveness."[17] The rite is powerful because it deals with the rapidly escalating *consequences* of an act or condition:[18] even what Marilyn Adams called "horrors," accidents (like parents running over their children) whose consequences, preying on our flesh-and-blood-iness, far outstrip our abilities either to intend or ward off.[19] Milgrom writes, "There is a consequence to a misdeed even performed in error. It leaves a mark that must be confronted and eventually wiped clean. The damage is done irrespective of intention."[20] Milgrom sums up this objectivity by connecting it to theodicy, to the damage that God allows. The objectivity repairs the defect in the agency of God for making a world so vulnerable to damage.[21] That is how objective, and how powerful the purification is, that the purification that works "more than forgiveness" depends not on a great but on a tiny amount, a daub, of blood.[22]

"More than forgiveness" is possible because what happens to the people, the land, and the world happens to the Temple, and what happens to the Temple happens to the world. The Temple receives and repairs the breaches in the world, so that sanctifying the Temple sanctifies the world. "What Milgrom succeeded in making clear is that sacrifice, in the Levitical texts, is not punitive or substitutionary, it is purificatory."[23] "Purification" or "purgation" are good words to describe the material procedures in the Temple: but they are poor words to capture their cosmic relational effects, unless you realize how much more widely purgation reaches than forgiveness.

In the clearest ten pages ever written on Levitical sacrifice, Milgrom lays out his material understanding of sin, altar, and blood.[24] Sin moves among the people as a "dynamic and malefic force." It floats heavily on the air,[25] like

---

    Encyclopedia of the Bible and Its Reception, vol. 3, *Athena-Birkat ha-Minim*, ed. Hans-Josef Klauk *et al.* (Berlin: de Gruyter, 2011), 43.

[17] Milgrom, *Leviticus 1–16*, 245, my italics. I owe my attention to this passage to Finlan, 11.

[18] Milgrom, "Dorian Gray," 392.

[19] Marilyn Adams, *Christ and Horrors* (Cambridge: Cambridge University Press, 2006).

[20] Milgrom, *Leviticus*, 42.

[21] Milgrom, "Dorian Gray," 398.

[22] "Daub [small quantity, direct application]. . . . Though this verb has countless denotations and shades of meaning, its technical usage for blood applications in P can be deduced from the contexts in which it appears. It is always used to designate the application of blood to a very specific spot – the horns of an altar, or the right earlobe, thumb, and big toe of a person, which can hardly be aimed at from a distance." The restrictions do not hold for non-blood contexts in P or for rabbinic literature. Meshel, 147–8.

[23] Finlan, 9.

[24] Milgrom, "Dorian Gray."

[25] Milgrom, "Dorian Gray," 393.

62   BLOOD THEOLOGY

a miasma or smog. It forms a sticky, aerial debris. "A sin committed anywhere will generate impurity that, becoming airborne, penetrates the sanctuary in proportion to its magnitude."[26] The horns of altar collect the debris by a kind of magnetic attraction.[27] "The minus charge of impurity is attracted to the plus charge of the sanctuary, and if the former builds up enough force to spark the gap, then, lightning-like, it will strike the sanctuary."[28] The miasma condenses to cling to the horns of the altar, where it disrupts the communication of the people with God; it interferes with the signal to distort or even block the love of God; it endangers the world. But blood daubed on the horns of the altar acts as a "ritual detergent"[29] to dissolve the debris of the breach, or as a conductant to discharge its power. "The altar, then, is the earthly terminus of a divine funnel for man's communion with God. It is significant that later Judaism carries the tradition that the air space above the altar is an extension of its sanctity."[30] The horns of the altar bring its receptive and conductive power to a point. Blood wiped there restores not mere hieratic purity but community among the people and with God. Blood accomplishes this objectively and holistically without resort to substitution or punishment by the power of the life itself that God has provided in it – in this case for making repair. A tiny quantity of blood works like the tiny size of the mustard seed because of the power of life within it.

The New Testament book of Hebrews follows Septuagint Levitical verbs closely – sprinkling, daubing. But synoptic accounts of the Last Supper use a verb of pouring out. Christians come to hear Hebrews in the light of the synoptics instead of in the light of Leviticus, and imagine pours of blood as cultic. The synoptic version of the Last Supper achieves supreme importance in eucharistic liturgy, where blood is poured out *(ekchunoumenon,* Mk. 4:24, Mt. 26:28, Luke 22:20) "for remission of sins" in the tradition of the Book of Common Prayer. The "pouring out" of blood becomes a cultic verb because the synoptics treat it that way.

Leviticus, our conceptual contrast case, does use the same verb *(ekcheei,* the future, in verse 4:7) in its Greek translation, the Septuagint, often consulted as the earliest external guide to the meaning of the Hebrew. But it does not use that verb in the same way. The Levitical "pouring out" does not deal with sin; daubing or sprinkling does that. Its use of "pouring out" disposes of excess blood into the ground.[31] The synoptic pouring out,

---

[26] Milgrom, *Leviticus,* 31.
[27] Milgrom, "Dorian Gray," 394–5.
[28] Milgrom, *Leviticus,* 42.
[29] Milgrom, "Dorian Gray," 391.
[30] Milgrom, *Leviticus 1–16,* 245.
[31] Naphtali Meshel defines it this way:

on the other hand, creates rather than controls sacred blood: It consecrates what Leviticus decommissions; it makes sacred what Leviticus makes secular. The uses are so different that Nestle-Aland does not cross-reference the Levitical use with the synoptic one. Leviticus and the synoptics use the same verb, but the ways they use it are not just different, they're opposed. In different senses, both uses pour out blood, and both regard that blood as belonging to God: but the Levitical rite removes from human use what the eucharistic rite reserves for human use. One minimizes and one multiplies the cultic quantity of blood.

Another way in which Christian usage mirrors and reverses Leviticus is highly suggestive. Levitical wine (offered with bread in place of an animal by the poor) must also be poured out at the foot of the altar – that is, Levitical wine, like blood, does not belong atop the altar hearth.[32]

Not for Leviticus the hecatombs of Homer or the bulls' blood of Mithraic myth, both of which contain their own exaggerations. A hecatomb, literally the sacrifice of 100 bulls, might in practice kill only a dozen. The bull of Mithras killed and dripping onto initiates standing below a grill has left no archaeological evidence and may have been invented by the Christian Prudentius. Leviticus' reception history, after multiple paradigm shifts including the First and Second Temples and their destructions, shows how drops of blood become floods in imagination: Blood (or its signaling) burgeons at need.

I digress to take up two interpretations of Leviticus, each highly interesting in its own right, and apparently as far apart as possible: Origen and Mary Douglas. We have third versus twenty-first century, religious versus secular, theological versus anthropological, christological versus historical, allegorical versus structuralist. The allegorical interpretation of Leviticus was so powerful that even now, if you pick up Origen's commentary, it is riveting. If you pick up Mary Douglas's secular anthropological interpretation of Leviticus, you find something

---

"pour": the translocation of a large quantity of blood (more than a few drops) from a high spot to a low spot using gravity. . . . In the sacrificial system of P, the object upon which blood is poured is always the base of the altar. "Pouring" applies only to the rest of the blood of a quadruped offered as a purification offering after some of its blood has been applied elsewhere. This last fact has given rise to the suggestion that pouring is not essential to the ritual, being merely a form of disposing leftover *materia sacra*.

A "Grammar" of Sacrifice (Oxford: Oxford University Press, 2014), 149. I have omitted the Hebrew, the footnotes, and the qualification that the non-sacrificial pouring out in kashrut is essential (Dt. 12:24).

[32] Milgrom, *Leviticus*, 25.

similar. She makes a case that the stacking of animal parts on the altar (think: on the grill) is supposed to represent Mt. Sinai, ringed in smoke, or the Temple, with its interior precincts. This is structuralism. Origen's allegory and Mary Douglas's structuralism have a lot in common. They both think in pictures. They require things to stand for other things; they deal in figuration. Together they exemplify what theology and anthropology share: they are ahistorical; they think in patterns; they explain, to some extent, why patterns persist.

You might think that structuralist approaches read things in. You might suspect the triad human body-social body-cosmos. You might roll your eyes at Mary Douglas's interpretation of Leviticus, where animal parts stack up to represent Mt. Sinai and the Tabernacle.[33] But allegorists also read in things like that. Leviticus matters in part because it generates interpretations, from allegorical to structuralist, that line up microcosm, mediator, and macrocosm or body, sacrifice, and universe. Origen offers a proof text so perfect and bizarre that you wonder, "who put that in there to prove Mary Douglas right?" – right that humans like to think like that. Here is Origen on Leviticus:

> Seek these offerings within yourself and you will find them within your soul. Understand that you have within yourself herds of bulls, those that were blessed in Abraham. Understand that you have herds of sheep and herds of goats, in which the patriarchs were blessed and multiplied. Understand also that within you are the birds of the sky. Marvel not that we say these are within you. Understand that you are another world in miniature and that there is within you the sun, the moon, and the stars. For if this were not so, the Lord would never have said to Abraham, "Look up to heaven and see the stars, whether their multitude can be counted. Thus will your seed be." Do not be amazed, I say, if it is said to Abraham, "Thus will your seed be as the stars are in the sky." . . . Hear further what the Savior says to the disciples: "You are the light of the world." Do you doubt that the sun and the moon are within you to whom it is said that you are "the light of the world"? . . . Since, therefore, you see that you have everything that the world has, you ought not doubt that you also have within you animals that are offered for sacrifices and from these you ought to offer sacrifices spiritually.[34]

[33] Mary Douglas, "Mountain, Tabernacle, Body in Leviticus 1–7," in *Leviticus as Literature* (Oxford: Oxford University Press, 2000) 66–86.

[34] Origen, Homily 5, para. 2, ll. 60–76, 94–7 on Leviticus, in *Homélies sur le Lévitique,* Latin and French text, ed. and trans. Marcel Robert, *Sources Chrétiennes* vol. 286 pp. 211, 214, as translated in Origen, *Homilies on Leviticus,* The Fathers of the Church, vol. 83, pp. 91–3.

It is as if Mary Douglas had hopped into a time machine to whisper in Origen's ear, "Put that in and make structuralism come true." Seriously now, what do figurative exegesis and structuralist anthropology have in common that both dwell on micro- and macrocosm, figures of body and cosmos? Do Origen and Mary Douglas both know that humans think that way?

Origen's vision imagines a lot of blood. People have herds of bulls and flocks of she-goats trooping around inside them, sacrificing which would generate ever replenishable quantities of blood. Levitical atonement offerings sacrifice cakes and small birds, occasionally a large animal. The Levitical offering, even of a large animal, needs only enough blood to daub the horns of the altar or sprinkle a wall seven times. The rest of the blood – most of it – is without cultic significance (sometimes you need the smoke or the meat) and gets tossed against the sides or poured out on the ground around the altar, to be soaked up by the earth as a way of restoring the blood, and its life, to God: not out of disrespect for the blood, but because the altar is among other things a divinely appointed instrument for grounding the power of blood, conducting it into the earth. Leviticus has no use for herds of sacrifice. Origen multiplies (imaginary) animals like an industrial slaughterhouse in Chicago.

The New Testament cites the blood of Christ, as I've mentioned more than once, three times more often than his "cross," and five times more often than his "death." The Middle Ages reserved Christ's blood in the eucharistic wine to clergy, leaving the laity with communion in bread alone: a practice that set Christ's blood more apart – as more holy, more taboo – even than his body. *Aquinas and Durkheim would both insist that blood does its conceptual work according to a specific pattern: No Christianity exists without blood-language: and no Christianity exists without some version of this bloody logic or pattern, this hematology, the analogy of blood. This kind of pattern begins to explain why Christian and, perhaps under their influence, later Jewish and Islamic readers come to find a lot of blood where their texts show little or none.*

The book of Hebrews leaps over multiple paradigm shifts in Israel's cult to Christianize Leviticus by transforming Israelite sacrifice into something that can continue after the destruction of the Second Temple. Hebrews makes the sacrificial animals stand for the sacrifice of Christ and reads atonement in a way that would become familiar as sacrifice for sin. Christian interpretations of Leviticus come to need more blood because its Christological interpretation transforms often small amounts of animal blood to wipe away particular sins and impurities in limited circumstances, into the blood of a human being slain for the sin of the world. By this logic, the sins of someone particular become Sin universal and unavoidable; blood becomes no longer a local

66   BLOOD THEOLOGY

conductant but a universal solvent. And the blood of a human being becomes
the blood of God, no longer limited in quantity to the half a *log* of blood
which, according to one rabbinic account, entirely exsanguinated Isaac
before the angel resurrected him,[35] but the blood of Jesus, not only universal
in extent but infinite in quantity, as God is omnipresent and unlimited. The
blood of *God* may indeed burgeon at need: that is its value and its property.
Blood *needs* to be unlimited, because it now atones for a community increasingly conceived as universal and for sin without particulars; and blood *can* be
unlimited, because it is the blood of the infinite God. It needs to be
unlimited; it can be unlimited; therefore it becomes unlimited. Hence the
wide popularity of hyperbolic hymns: "It reaches to the highest mountain
and it flows to the lowest valley / the blood that gives me strength from day
to day will never lose its power!"[36]

This burgeoning blood participates in the unlimited divisibility and infinite
reproduction of the sacraments: the Eucharist is available everywhere, and
every drop of wine or crumb of bread contains the whole Christ; the Eucharist
is easy to transport because the elements are available almost everywhere, and
what transforms them, provided a qualified officiant, travels through the ether
like electronic money. Similarly, profane dirt can be shoveled into the Holy
Sepulcher every day to be taken out as holy; holiness transfers commutatively
and transitively by contact and contagion. So it is also – and in advance of
eucharistic theory or of traffic in relics – almost originally for blood.

The blood of Jesus, on the other hand, has no secular function. In him, the
whole blood of an animal – a human one – has no function other than cultic.
In him, the whole blood of a human being – a human being who is also
God – never has to be returned to God, because this blood is God's own
already. All the blood is useful and available for atonement, and none of it is
left over. Indeed, since the blood is the blood of God, and God is infinite, an
infinity of blood becomes available for atonement.

Take Chrysostom:

> Do we not offer a daily sacrifice? We do, but as a memorial of His death.
> Why, then, is it a single sacrifice rather than multiple sacrifices? ... We
> always offer the same person, and not one sheep today and another one
> tomorrow, but always the same offering. ... There is a single sacrifice, and
> a single high priest who has offered the sacrifice that purifies us. *Today, we
> offer what has already been offered, an inexhaustible sacrifice.* This is done as

---

[35] Levenson, 192–7.

[36] Andraé Crouch, "The Blood Will Never Lose Its Power," Sony/ATV Music Publishing,
2005. I owe the reference to Greg Williams.

a memorial of what was done then, for he said: "Do this in memory of me." We do not offer another sacrifice, as was once done by the high priest, but we always offer the same sacrifice – or rather, we re-present it.[37]

In her fourth vision, Julian of Norwich saw the blood of Christ like this:

> I saw the body bleeding copiously in the furrows of the scourging, and it was thus. The fair skin was deeply broken into the tender flesh through the vicious blows delivered all over the lovely body. The hot blood ran out so plentifully that neither skin nor wounds could be seen, but everything seemed to be blood. ... The precious blood of our Lord Jesus Christ, as truly as it is most precious, so truly is it most plentiful. ... The precious plenty of his precious blood overflows all the earth.[38]

On the one hand, a crucifixion by itself should generate no floods of blood, because the wounds of hands, feet, thorns, and lance would generate little blood; they do not exsanguinate Christ as required by kashrut and proper disposal in the Temple. I don't mean to be positivist here, I'm just interrogating the trope.

On the other hand, Christian writers have never paid much if any attention to the paucity or absence of crucifixion blood. They assume, by a kind of sacramental causality, that crucifixion makes an unlimited quantity of blood available. And in the absence of any non-atoning use for blood, poured out to be absorbed by the ground around the altar or around the hunted kill, they imagine no blood that does not carry all the power of divine transaction.

We have different economies of excess. In Levitical sacrifice, only a small amount of blood is needed and the rest is returned to God. There is excess, in the sense of left over, but it is immediately taken out of circulation, maintaining the power of the small amount of currency in use. In Christic sacrifice, however, no currency is taken out of circulation, and we experience a hyperinflation of blood.

In economic hyperinflation, a larger amount of money chasing the same amount of goods makes the money almost worthless. But in Christianity, the opposite happened. In Christic sacrifice, an unlimited amount of blood comes to be needed as the community expands to universal extent, none of it removed from circulation. So we look to hyperinflation not in economics but in cosmology, where the universe expands exponentially out of the

---

[37] Chrysostom, *Homilies on the Epistle to the Hebrews,* 17.3 (on Heb. 9:24–26), *PG* 63.131, as cited in Guy Stroumsa, *The End of Sacrifice: Religious Transformations in Late Antiquity,* trans. Susan Emanuel (Chicago: University of Chicago Press, 2009), 74.

[38] Julian of Norwich, *Showings,* trans. Edmund Colledge (New York: Paulist Press, 1978), Long Text, chapter 12, pp. 200–1.

68 BLOOD THEOLOGY

Big Bang. Space organizes itself infinitely in non-space, a sort of creation out of nothing. The community expands because no one is discovered not to need the message of forgiveness.[39] The unlimited extent of forgiveness implies – only in sin's overcoming – a universal extent of sin, whose origin traces back so indefinitely toward the beginning as to approach the blasphemous title of "original," even though God did not create it. The blood of God is life unlimited, a light that finds shadows to illuminate as it spreads.

This is a different kind of excess, one that remains in circulation, and by a kind of hydraulic pressure *finds more things to do*.

It finds more things to do in two ways; the flood debouches in two streams, predictable and unpredictable. The predictable one is cultic: "For indeed *every* sacrifice is recapitulated in him," writes Origen.[40] Later we will ply this river when we suggest that the blood of Christ takes in not only every sacrifice for sin, but every instance of animal and human suffering. (See Chapter 6.)

But the unpredictable current spreads even more. The unlimited, unreserved, unreturned excess of the blood of God also helps explain why blood shows up in unexpected places where it hardly seems to belong, from gender roles to community boundaries to creationism to providing a language for dispute (Chapters 5–7). Multiple sociological and theological expansions mirror and suggest the burgeoning of blood: Paul's crossing of the boundaries between Jew and Gentile, creating a new whole; Nicaea's crossing of the boundary between God and creature, creating a new union; Christianity's rapid expansion, constantly exceeding its limits; and the idea that the blood of Christ was unlimited in application and infinite in value: all those transits and transgressions coalesced to produce a cosmic hyperinflation of blood. Some (like Pelagius) worried from early times about what Bonhoeffer might have called "cheap blood," but in theology, at least, the riposte was victorious that grace was free. Because this blood was not only life, but life everlasting, it pushed hydraulically into new channels and found new things to do. The power in the blood came to define or explode gender roles, to justify war or rule it out, to hold creation static or fund its evolution: blood became not just a biological or a cultic fluid, but – on family, truth, tribe, and more – the current in which argument moved and the currency in which disputes took place.

It's important to keep in mind what kind of excess this is. Not only excess paper but even excess gold can cheapen the money supply and bring inflation

---

[39] The thesis of James Alison, *The Joy of Being Wrong: Original Sin through Easter Eyes* (New York: Herder and Herder, 1998).

[40] Origen, *Leviticus*, Homily 5, p. 62.

of the bad sort. In an article by this title, *Smithsonian* reported that "Gold Rush California Was Much More Expensive Than Today's Tech-Boom California": in 1849, a dozen eggs would have cost the 2015 equivalent of $90.[41] Here too, gold created new uses for itself: ingots for eggs. We need to distinguish good new uses from bad new uses. Metaphors of buying, ransom, and debt-payment in the New Testament may lead us astray. The important thing about Christ's blood is not monetary. A better metaphor might be electricity, dangerous in quantity but almost infinitely useful when channeled. Cheap electricity did not cheapen the money supply, but found abundant and unforeseen new things to do: light, heat, transportation, cooking, industry; we are still finding new things for electricity to do.

Traditional theology does not, of course, use the metaphor of electricity. It features a different metaphor and a different definition. "Economy," in the widest sense – one that covers both the economy of finance and the *oikonomia* of God – means, according to the one important theologian with a Ph.D. in economics, Sergei Bulgakov, the human being's spiritualization of matter. "In the sweat of thy brow shalt thou eat bread" is the command; the bread of heaven the reward. A similar pattern applies to the other eucharistic element, as if to say "in the labor of the vineyard shalt thou drink wine." The blood of God is sustenance, is food and drink to us. It is, as Leviticus defines it, life itself. Better than more electricity, better even than abundant food, the blood of God is – or is meant to be – infinite life, life everlasting. If blood multiplies, burgeons, floods, it does so with the vigor of life from the source of life. If blood is "the life," as Leviticus says, that is another reason why Christians abandon the languages, images, symbols of blood only at great, perhaps unacceptable cost, and why, like life itself, the languages of blood persist and return.

Separation and Sacrifice

In what follows I take theologian's license to proceed *thesenhaft*: I entertain a host of theses; I propose them for debate. They're just theologoumena. I'm not sure I buy them all myself.

***

IN THE VEDAS, SACRIFICE CREATES THE WORLD. IN THE GOSPELS, sacrifice *redeems* it. That is, sacrifice remedies sin. But that casts sacrifice as an

---

[41] Steve Boggan, "Gold-Rush California Was Much More Expensive Than Today's," *Smithsonian* (Sept. 20, 2015), at www.smithsonianmag.com/history/gold-rush-california-was-much-more-expensive-todays-dot-com-boom-california-180956788/#J2MbopGZACucRz4H.99.

70   BLOOD THEOLOGY

afterthought, making God look careless. This is a question on which blood
throws light by indirection. For the concrete particularity of sacrifice in
blood requires division. So I pose instead a more answerable question:
would there have been division without sin?

The question is at once more concrete, because blood sacrifice requires
physical division, and more abstract, because in what follows "division"
works analogously on different levels to mean related things. The advantage
of posing the question this way is that the answer is clear: in Genesis as in
Aquinas, difference in itself is good, because God builds distinction into
Creation. Aquinas explains:

> It is said (Genesis 1:4–7) that God "distinguished the light from the darkness,"
> and "divided (*divisit*) the waters from the waters." Therefore the distinction
> and multitude of things is from God. . . . For [God] brought things into being
> in order that [God's] goodness might be communicated to creatures, and be
> represented by them; and because [God's] goodness could not be adequately
> represented by one creature alone, [God] produced many and diverse crea-
> tures, that what was wanting to one in the representation of the divine
> goodness might be supplied by another. For goodness, which exists in God
> simply and uniformly, in creatures exists manifoldly and dividedly (*divisim*),
> and hence the whole universe together participates in the divine goodness
> more perfectly, and represents it better than any single creature whatever. [*ST*
> I.47.1, translation modified to avoid masculine language for God].

Aquinas's account does not start creation from *sacrifice*, not at all. But he
does start creation from division, and sacrifice involves division, too. Can we
say that diversity represents the divine goodness, and sacrifice represents the
divine goodness under conditions needing repair? Can we even say that
diversity creates the possibility of repair?

That is: Creation's mutability gives it the possibility of growth, and, under
conditions of damage, opens it to repair. Creation's mutability provides for its
resilience.

***

SEE HOW MAGISTERIALLY AQUINAS AVOIDS A PROBLEM. HE TURNS
division into distinction. If you say that sacrifice is about separation, because
that's how it works, it sounds just as plausible. Both creation and blood
sacrifice involve separation, whether of the land from the waters, or of the
parts of an animal. But I'm not in favor of the word "separation." It makes me
nervous. It sounds too much like segregation. It seems to leave out middles.
And I'm pretty sure that purity is one of the places where blood-language

goes wrong. (See Chapter 7 on *limpieza de sangre*.) I'm suspicious of the purity that leads to schism. But Levitical purification offerings are about healing breaches, not causing them.

If we think about the *examples* in Genesis, instead of the words, we get a clearer if more complicated picture. We translate "God 'separated' the earth from the waters": but God did not keep them apart. God put them right together with their middles. Between land and water lie deltas, marshes, and estuaries, all gradations of fresh and salt, water, mud and land, myriads of middle things. In the water are shallows and sandbars and islands of all sizes. Between the waters above and the waters below are rain and clouds and lots of humidity. Between day and night are dawn and dusk. Between male and female are trans and gay and intersex. God does not "separate," in the sense of keep apart: God distinguishes, in order to put into relation. Similarly, the "separations" of sacrifice may represent a breach, but they repair a relation. They distinguish, to reunite.

***

THE HUMAN BEING PARTICIPATES IN GOD'S SELF-COMMUNICATION of goodness by becoming different. The Holy Spirit distinguishes; she will make you strange. Like priests at an altar, human beings receive themselves from God and return to God with thanks. This is an occasion for thanksgiving and self-gift, a proto-Eucharist, a distribution of gifts. Alexander Schmemann sums it up like this: "The world was created as the 'matter,' the material of one all-embracing eucharist, and [the human being as] the priest of this cosmic sacrament."[42] The priest: human beings receive the world and offer it back to God. This again is not yet sacrifice: but from the perspective of sin we can see that it *might* be. Distinction and gift both present *conditions* for sacrifice.

***

ON THIS ACCOUNT, THE DIVISION OF CHRIST'S BODY IN THE CRU-cifixion and the Eucharist just continues God's self-donation by diversifying begun at creation. It's nothing "new." It occasions thanksgiving, Eucharist, just as creation does, and it continues God's work of creation even in the face of sin. The breaking of Christ's body enables its multiplication and distribution. It enables its distribution to a diversity of people who might be made one. Under conditions of sin, God's goodness repurposes the evils of human

---

[42] Alexander Schmemann, *For the Life of the World* (New York: St. Vladimir's Seminary Press, 1998), 15.

death and Roman violence for an alternative production. The creative separation, or good sacrifice, of the multitude of things takes in and returns to purpose the separation that is suffering and evil.

***

EVEN IF HEAVEN NEEDS NO REMEDY FOR SIN, BECAUSE THERE IS NO sin in heaven, Christians need to join their sufferings to God's creative work of distinguishing to make those sufferings meaningful. Thus Julian of Norwich sees earthly sufferings and even moral failures in heaven as healed wounds and badges of honor.[43] And because they continue to need making sense of, the body of Christ (for Julian) continues to bleed.[44]

***

SACRIFICE IN THE SENSE OF SUFFERING MIGHT PARSE AS THE WORK of creative separation carried out even in the face of sin, so involving no "change" in God but the faithful communication of God's goodness. And of course when the separation takes place in a body, the body might bleed. That would be (1) the communication of goodness (of God's goodness, if it's the body of God) and (2) if suffering, then the joining of suffering to the cause of communicating goodness, and thus solidarity, overcoming of injustice, meaning, and martyrdom in the good sense of testimony to the good. In that case there's no reason why the communication of God's goodness shouldn't continue in heaven, even if it involves bleeding until the end of the world, because God's blood just is God's life, which is God's goodness.

***

THEN "THERE IS NO REMISSION OF SIN WITHOUT THE SHEDDING OF blood" could mean: There is no re-creative separation of the sin from the sinner without the communication of reparative goodness. Under the economy of God's body, the separation and multiplication that spreads goodness is the Eucharist of Christ's sacrifice.

***

WELL, THAT WAS GRANDIOSE. LET ME MAKE IT SMALLER. WHEN WE do things with blood, we engage in practices. We can keep distinct the meanings of blood, if we keep distinct the various practices we maintain with

---

[43] Julian of Norwich, *Showings*, trans. Edmund Colledge (New York: Paulist Press, 1978), Short Text, chapter 17 and Long Text, chapter 39, pp. 154–5 and 244–5.

[44] *Showings*, Long Text, chapter 12, p. 201.

respect to blood: medical practices, sacrificial practices, kinship practices, alimentary practices, purificatory practices. But such practices do overlap. And they are so many and various. Presumably they are all ones in which blood is, or at least has been, useful for something. The question is, *why is blood useful for so much?*

According to Mary Douglas, we have to make do with the tools we have and extend them by analogy. Blood is useful for so much by analogy. By analogy, we connect practices involving blood. By analogy, we connect washing the living with washing the dead. By analogy, we connect eating with kinship. Just because blood is useful in one of these contexts, we test its usefulness in another. Given our limitations, we try it, appropriate or not, and even when it looks unpromising: with social acceptance, we keep using it willy-nilly. And because we regard blood as central to the body, we regard it as central to various bodily practices, from midwifery to circumcision to mikvah to Temple to burial.

Apparently, blood is useful, among other things, for the remission of sin. So we are told.

***

MILGROM, TO REVIEW, THINKS THE SIN OF THE COMMUNITY — which, following Robert Parker's work on Greek religion, he calls "miasma" – is and sticks there like the crud that interferes with an electrical pole. Applied to the book of Hebrews, "There is no remission of sin without the shedding of blood" means: There is no cleaning off the sticky miasma that flies through the air to the altar without blood as a conductant or detergent. Why does blood work as a detergent? That depends on what the sticky stuff is.

Suppose the sticky stuff is the unformed matter from which God created the heavens and the earth by making separations.[45] It leaks out when the separations break down, when order is compromised.

Both blood and miasma – are they sticky substances? Do they both emerge from seams of separation? If so, can blood and miasma be forms of the same thing? Is miasma a bad kind of blood, matter out of place? Miasma means, the cosmos bleeds? But this is confusing, since other blood cleans miasma, whatever it is, off the horns of the altar. In this picture, miasma is not flowing blood, but drying gore. Etymologically, crud and gore both coagulate. As new nail polish softens old, blood dissolves gore.

---

[45] Israel Knohl has less speculative but suggestive remarks relating cosmologies of Genesis and Leviticus in his *Divine Symphony* (Philadelphia: Jewish Publication Society, 2003), 18–19. I owe the reference to Naphtali Meshel.

(Modern medicine would disagree that gore is bad, if gore is clotted blood, or that what blood does is clean it. Platelets perfuse the wound to lay down a healing matrix and raise up granulation tissue or proud flesh. Proud flesh grows rosy red with capillary buds.)

Other blood – the blood that is life, the blood of creative separation become the blood of sacrifice – cleans the miasma by restoring order. How does blood restore order?

That depends on understanding how "blood is the life" of a well-ordered body.

***

TO SEE WHAT BLOOD CONTRIBUTES TO THAT PICTURE, TRY a thought experiment. Consider a divided body with no attention to blood.

Genesis 15:9–18 mentions no blood. In that passage, God directs Abraham to halve several animals (a heifer, a doe goat, and a ram), and then God, in the form of a blazing pot, passes between the severed halves. This ritual establishes a covenant between God and Abraham. Robert Parker brings two comparanda: "Each spring, when the Macedonian army reassembled, it was marched between two halves of a sacrificial dog, which created what has been called an 'absorptive zone' for all its impurities." "To avert an evil omen, the Hittite army was marched through the halves of slaughtered prisoners of war."[46] This pattern uses cut animals to unite covenant partners or whole armies. It encloses those to be united between two halves of an animal. It represents those to be united within a new whole. It focuses on the bodies rather than the blood. On this picture, the horns of the altar – like those of a ram – hold power by standing apart. They can represent a breach and hold open a space for reunion. They constitute a standing absorptive zone. The horns figure the altar as an animal itself, an animal of stone – not an idol, but a figural animal to surround, hold up, and receive its life from an animal provided by God.

What Does Blood Add to This Picture?

Blood not only reactivates the altar when its horns absorb too much or crud over. More closely than divided halves, blood embraces those to be united, makes them organs in a larger whole. More intimately still, blood adds a fluid to

---

[46] Robert C. T. Parker, *Miasma: Pollution and Purification in Early Greek Religion* (Oxford: Clarendon Press, 1983), 22, text and note 20, my italics. See also Mary Douglas on animal division among the Dinka and the symbolism of the human body, *Purity and Danger* (London: Routledge, 1984), 115–16.

perfuse a body's every part; it reanimates the whole. Not only can it activate the altar's ram-like horns, but blood imitates the birthing of the heifer or the doe.

***

WE CONSTRUCT THE BODY AS A CLOSED CONTAINER, ONLY because we in society regard blood as belonging on the inside and rush to defend it when we see blood on the outside. When blood stays inside, the bounds of the social and individual body seem secure. But: Can we change the bounds of the body by redefining what counts as inside and outside? Can we redefine inside and outside by manipulating blood?

To clean away social rupture or cosmic leakage, we seem to need "outside" blood, "shed" blood. We get it by cutting animals, itself an infraction, a transgression of boundaries. We take blood from an individual to make the social body whole. *But that's only half the picture.* There is another half of the picture that we hide from ourselves. That is: the blood that cleans the altar may be used outside the animal that gave it, but then it stands *inside* a new body, a social body. The old whole, the animal, bathed in blood, now becomes an organ in the sanctuary. The sanctuary, representing society restored, re-encloses all within a larger body as blood embraces all within it. If now the sanctuary represents the social body, it wraps spilled blood into a larger whole; it double-bags the leak. A larger body now rechannels it. Blood formerly *outside* the skin becomes presently blood *inside* new veins. Blood defines a new body by creating a larger inside, a more-encompassing whole.

Cut animals represent the rupture of society caused by leaky transgressions. The broken body of the animal figures the broken body of society; it may re-present in concrete terms even violent bloodshed of one member of society against another, a palpable remedy for a palpable harm. Sacrifice does not only work to cut. Sacrifice also works to enlarge the social body. Here too an altar provides an instrument to make good on blood: here it refigures the sacrifice as an organ inside a larger body. Blood reconceived as internal enlarges the body social. It recreates peace; it restores the separated; it makes the social body whole by redrawing a boundary and staying on the new inside. It realigns cosmos and community. I'm not in favor of animal sacrifice, but I think that's how it works. (For someone who might be in favor – I can't tell – see Michael Wyschogrod's description of animal sacrifice in Chapter 1.) Is this pattern obscene or profound? Mary Douglas answers, Yes.

I'm not in favor of martyrdom, either – because I'm not in favor of persecution – but I think it works alike. Martyrs signal the rupture of society; they re-present in concrete terms the bloodshed of one part of society against

76   BLOOD THEOLOGY

another; but what makes their death martyrdom and not just murder is our
ability to read it as gathering a new society around their blood. Martyrs may
increase division, but if so that's because they fan the desire for justice, and
the desire for justice is a desire for a better society, one that has more room for
blood inside and learns to stop shedding it – or one that can turn the shed
blood into rebirth. Can martyrs also enlarge a community, rather than merely
inflame?

For better or worse, animal sacrifice attempts to pacify and institutionalize
the more charismatic and violent sacrifice of martyrs. Martyrs represent and
(once read as sacrifice) inflame or repair the social breach. Animal sacrifices
attempt to routinize and channel that energy: to represent and repair the
social breach without stooping to murder or war. Because animal sacrifices
are also usually eaten,[47] they bind even tighter the connection that at the Last
Supper seems so odd: that God in Christ should turn the worst that we can do
into another invitation to community, and even to the feast.

***

THE BLACK LIVES MATTER MOVEMENT EMERGES AROUND DEATHS
that have ceased to be mere statistics and private griefs, to become public
testimonies. It is a movement not only about Black bodies, but also about
what we might call "Black blood." Of course Black and White blood are
both red. But Black Lives Matter points out that the powers value the red
blood of a person raced as Black less than the red blood of a person raced as
White. Consider the martyrs of Ferguson and Charlotte. As in crucifixion,
blood was incidental to their deaths, deaths by shooting. In Ferguson, the
spattering of his blood mattered in forensic analyses of how Michael Brown,
Jr. was moving when a police officer shot him. Blood found its way into the
language in which the powers disputed the evidence. But more important
was the disrespect paid to his blood. The police left Brown in the hot sun of
an August day for four and a half hours while his blood turned to gore – went
from liquid and red to dry and brown. The message to his mother and others
who were standing nearby (*stabat mater*) was that his blood mattered less.[48]

---

[47] For an example from the American South, see the classic recipe for hog-killing in
"Morning-After-Hog-Butchering Breakfast," in *The Taste of Country Cooking* by
Edna Lewis, with a Foreword by Alice Waters, 30th anniversary ed. (New York: Alfred
A. Knopf, 2006), 181–8. I owe the reference to Joseph Naron.

[48] Stephen G. Ray, Jr., "Black Lives Matter as Enfleshed Theology," in *Enfleshing Theology:
Embodiment, Discipleship, and Politics in the Work of M. Shawn Copeland*, ed. Robert J. Rivera
and Michele Saracino (Minneapolis, MN: Fortress, 2018), 83–93.

Consider a second Black Lives Matter example where blood infiltrates the discourse of a shooting. The killing of Keith Lamont Scott led to the Charlotte uprising of 2016. A participant writes:

The protesters would gather every night in the same park and march through the city. At midnight the police and the National Guard would declare a curfew. Some people would go home. The rest of us would stay out and risk arrest. There was tear gas, [there were] confrontations with the cops, etc. At one point the pigs rolled over a kid with an ATV. And through it all – the [amplified bullhorns, which protestors regard as sound weapons], the tear gas, the noise, the helicopters, the sirens, the people would march. And the missionaries would come out and follow us. Anyone who participated in these protests will remember one of them. He would follow us day and night, day after day, unceasingly saying, loudly, over the crowd, again and again and again "the blood of Jesus! The blood of Jesus! The blood of Jesus!" He didn't hand out tracts. He didn't preach (in the conventional way). He didn't ask anyone if they knew Christ as their Lord and Personal Savior. He just kept chanting "the blood of Jesus! The blood of Jesus! The blood of Jesus!" for days on end in the hot sun and all night long. He got to be really annoying, which is why most of the protesters remember him. People would sometimes tell him to shut up but he would just keep chanting "the blood of Jesus!" Finally, people started, instead, chanting with him "the blood of a Black man! The blood of a Black man! The blood of a Black man!"[49]

Stephen Ray, Jr. has considered what those two things have in common, the blood of a Black man and the blood of Jesus. He compares the death of Michael Brown Jr. in Ferguson to a trickster theory of the atonement. On this theory, human flesh spurs Satan's hunger to harm, and human blood entices him to violence. Flesh and blood draw Satan like a shark, as Jonah drew the whale. Because his desire is to do evil, Satan's desire for blood only seems to value it: rather he takes advantage of it. "Satan knew full well that [Jesus] was no ordinary flesh bearer and that he was indeed the prince of the kingdom, but he thought so little of the flesh that the prince bore" that he would "consume the prince, made insignificant by the flesh he bore."[50]

Inspired by the question of Job 41:1, "Can you draw out Leviathan with a fishhook?" some trickster theories of the atonement make the flesh of Jesus veil his divinity like the bait on a fishhook (Rufinus, Nyssa). Other versions turn the cross into the hook. Augustine's version baits a mousetrap with his blood.

[49] Gregory S. Williams, personal communication, April 17, 2019.
[50] Ray, 91–2.

78 BLOOD THEOLOGY

Both the divinity and the blood imply that life itself is hiding in this flesh.
And that that life, more than the cross, is what undoes the devil.

> Far from being made weak and insignificant by the particular flesh he bore,
> Christ was enabled by it to gather a community of witnesses that would
> herald Life's victory through time and through which this power might be
> communicated to all. As with Christ, the flesh of Michael Brown Jr. made
> him imminently killable in the eyes of many and mitigated any claim of
> empathy on the hearts of too many others. In my own living it was this
> invitation to violation that was most real to me but, when I experienced the
> community called into being by the Spirit that was gathered precisely
> around Mike's Black flesh, our Black flesh, I knew that God had used his
> death to communicate something to us all. That communication? Simply
> put, in the unfolding of God's salvific plan for all of creation, Black Lives
> Matter. Michael Brown Jr. is and will be our shining Black Prince for from
> his death God has brought Life to us all and in his gaze we are enveloped in
> its power.[51]

Greg Williams pushes this further:

> When #BlackLivesMatter protests form a new social body around "the
> blood of a black man," they are taking murder and turning it into sacrifice.
> They do this by taking the mere shedding of blood and creating a sanctuary
> around it, such that what was a one-step move (take blood and put it
> outside) becomes a two step move (the blood that was outside is now on
> a new inside). This is a *felix culpa* moment. The bloody death of Mike
> Brown becomes the occasion for the repair of the social rupture that his
> death represents by putting his blood, now that it has been shed, inside
> a new social whole.
>
> People are already bleeding. Practices of protest take the blood from this
> bleeding and relocate it in productive ways, ways that do reparative work with
> the blood that has been shed. This is why protest is a better model [than
> sacrifice]. The blood is being shed anyway. Creating practices around the shed
> blood that integrate the shed blood into a new social body takes the shedding
> of blood as an occasion without making the bloodshed itself redemptive.[52]

∗∗∗

MUCH RELIGIOUS CREATIVITY CONSISTS IN ENLARGING THE
boundary of a social body, so that those formerly "them" are now "us,"
and out of death comes life, so that "death is swallowed up in victory" – that

---

[51] Ray, 91–2.
[52] Gregory S. Williams, commenting on an earlier version of the manuscript, March 25, 2019.

is, becomes enclosed in a larger body. How can inside become outside, so that blood encloses us in a larger body? Individuals become organs in a larger whole. Organs have insides of their own – the Bible mentions the interiors of hearts, kidneys, viscera. But they belong in a larger whole. They both bleed from their own interiors, and repose in the blood of the body. To bathe one's heart in blood – pictured in a medieval tapestry – means to take it out of one body and bathe it in a different blood, suggesting that it might belong to a new body or person. Just as modern accounts find in the temperature and salinity of blood an echo of an earlier ocean in which our cells still swim, so Christian accounts from multiple periods find within the social body a larger blood in which individuals find themselves enclosed as within a greater whole. Paul's metaphor of the social body speaks of "members" rather than organs, so that it too transcends metaphors of inside and outside, ingestion and enclosure, even in one verse:

> For in the one Spirit we were all baptized into one body – Jews or Greeks, slaves or free – and we were all made to drink of one Spirit. (1 Cor. 12:13)

Christians think they drink the Spirit by ingesting the consecrated wine, the spirit that is also blood and they are also enclosed in a new and living fluid, baptized into a new, unified body. Baptism takes place in water, but also in fire or blood. The newly integrated body encloses in one frame Jews or Greeks, slaves or free; hands, feet, head, eyes; prophecy, teaching, tongues, love. It overcomes divisions by drowning and regathering as one all those enclosed by the font. In the font, the baptized become a new body united by the blood of Christ. To be bathed in the blood of Christ is to become an organ in a new body: "Now you are the body of Christ and individually members of it" (1 Cor. 12:27).

But there is a specific organ of blood. I don't mean the heart; the heart is a muscle. The organ made of blood is the placenta. To be bathed in the blood of Christ is to return to the placenta and be born again.[53]

To be bathed in the blood of Christ is, of course, a metaphor of cleansing. It is also a metaphor of rebirth: babies are born with their placenta, from and with their natal blood.

Men and their texts (according to McCracken; see the next chapter) imagine that not only a newborn is bathed in "blood" (really amniotic fluid) but other organs, too: so they picture blood to work among other ways to maintain the body's unity from within. Here the metaphors of

---

[53] I owe my attention to placenta to a conversation with Aminah Bradford, Christian Ananias, Emily Dubie, and especially Sarah Jobe.

cleansing, renewal, and integration remind us that meat decays from the outside, while its interiors remain "clean," or good to eat. That's why we apply heat to the unbroken surfaces of chunks and chops and suspect ground meat, which mixes inside and outside. To be bathed in the blood of the lamb is to reacquire, by re-enclosure in cleansing blood, the innocence of an interior organ or fetal child.

Or that seems to be the medieval picture. To be more precise, the baby is bathed, not in blood, but in its amniotic fluid, the "waters" of the womb. That's another reason why the waters of baptism belong to rebirth. But medieval rebirth combines both pictures, because it takes place in the wound in the side of Christ, which gives forth both water and blood.

The blood is the life, which is intrinsically clean; the bluish-red placenta accompanies infants in the womb and follows them, as afterbirth, when they emerge from their mothers. Blood in these ways – the blood of fecundity and new life – makes new bodies and keeps them clean (cf. 1 John 3:9). The right use of blood will be to enlarge or renew bodies as clean by enclosing larger wholes.

This complex of cleansing, accompaniment, re-enclosure, and rebirth can help to explain and repair the notion that there is "no remission of sin without the shedding of blood." Sometimes, as the Black Lives Matter movement points out, the sin needing remission is real social violence. And sometimes the remedy can take the blood already shed in sin as itself the means of remission. As Gregory Williams points out, in the Black Lives Matter protests "Violence is being rescripted by social practices involving blood. But this really is about violence and, in particular, violent death." This does not mean we should take victims that peace may come. By no means. But sometimes God can make a Last Supper move, rescripting a violent death (the crucifixion of Jesus, the shooting of Michael Brown, Jr.) by social practices involving blood (protest chants, eucharistic wine). If there is a social rebirth, there is also a social reuse of blood. Is there no rebirth without an afterbirth, a shedding of placental blood?

***

IN SACRIFICE, THE ANIMAL IS DIVIDED AND BLEEDS MORE OR LESS. The parts are distributed widely among the people. That wider distribution draws together the part-takers even more closely into a social body. They ingest the body of the animal, they take it in, but find themselves overwhelmed, interior to a new body, so that the body of the sacrificial animal reasserts itself, enlarged. The smaller body of the animal, once broken open, unites the much larger body of the whole people. A new body emerges to be enlarged. Understood in terms of a divided animal, this metaphor will always be dodgy. But in terms of birth? Mothers also open. If the cervix of a human mother opened any further, it would compromise another distinctive human feature, walking on two legs.

The right way of re-enclosing individual bodies in larger wholes will not always be apparent – there will always be wrong ways to do it, and right ways can always be misused. The right ways, rightly used, will always retain elements of unpredictability and surprise. The model will be Jesus at the Last Supper, who took a structure of violent oppression, crucifixion, and turned it to a peaceful feast. His transposition was hardly predictable in advance. The image on the cover of Bettina Bildhauer's *Medieval Blood* exemplifies and exaggerates the pattern. The blood of Jesus so covers him as to reverse inside and outside. It dominates the background, so that at once it clothes, encloses, and enlarges him.[54] Picture the messianic Shiloh: "he washes his garments in wine and his robe in the blood of grapes" (Gen. 49:11).

Blood can mark these reversals because it flows and covers. The bloodied body comes to resemble its own inside; the bloodied body can resemble an organ in a larger whole. The inside of a body is always bathed in blood; the outside only at signal points, including menstruation and wounding. That's because blood marks not only external bounds but internal structure, not only wounds but veins. In society as in biology, blood carries the life of the body, both within and out of bounds. By it the community enacts unity and restores health.

***

HERE IS A QUICKER IF EVEN MORE SPECULATIVE WAY TO A SIMILAR conclusion, if you have been reading Nancy Jay. Miasma is an evil leak. In menstruation and afterbirth, blood makes an opposite and life-giving leak. Sacrifice does birth culturally, creating priestly lineages. It also releases the lifeblood that cleans up miasma. Here too the social organ named above, the-enclosure-within-the-enclosure of the Temple, resembles a womb or a placenta. Surely there is *some* significance to the sex of the red heifer. And the creative separation accompanied by fluids read as blood (what could be more obvious?) is birth.

---

[54] "Vision of St. Bernhard" (fourteenth century, Rheinland), in Museum Schnütgen, Cologne, inventory number M340.

***

HEGEMONS WANT TO FIX BLOOD IN STABLE GENEALOGIES, HIER-archs to keep it in cups under ecclesiastical control. But blood flows and escapes. Hence the attraction of flowing blood in the vial of San Gennaro, unveiled only once a year. The procession in Naples brings saintly blood to come right out of the church's "wherever," as a presidential candidate has recently put it, annual renewal in its wake. There too the blood of fertility gets out or the blood of placenta includes. The festival dramatizes blood leaving a body, to color the amniotic fluid or fill the placental organ that encloses a younger whole. How does Jesus fit these patterns? How do they bend his role and gender?

4

BLOOD AFTER THE LAST SUPPER
Jesus and the Gender of Blood

Mark 5:25–34

[25] Now there was a woman who had been suffering from a flow of blood for twelve years. [26] She had endured much under many physicians, and had spent all that she had; and she was no better, but rather grew worse. [27] She had heard about Jesus, and came up behind him in the crowd and touched his cloak, [28] for she said, "If I but touch his clothes, I will be made well." [29] Immediately the spring of her blood stopped; and she felt in her body that she was healed of her disease. [30] Immediately aware that power had gone forth from him, Jesus turned about in the crowd and said, "Who touched my clothes?" [31] And his disciples said to him, "You see the crowd pressing in on you; how can you say, 'Who touched me?'" [32] He looked all around to see who had done it. [33] But the woman, knowing what had happened to her, came in fear and trembling, fell down before him, and told him the whole truth. [34] He said to her, "Daughter, your faith has made you well; go in peace, and be healed of your disease."[1] (Mark 5:25–34 RSV modified)

I quote Mark to remind readers of the story. Yet in this chapter I interpret primarily visual and tactile evidence. Paintings and objects take us beyond texts to see how art and objects in ritual space gender blood. How does blood drawn, presented, consecrated, or drunk in church magnify blood

---

[1] SBL Greek New Testament: [25] καὶ γυνὴ οὖσα ἐν ῥύσει αἵματος δώδεκα ἔτη [26] καὶ πολλὰ παθοῦσα ὑπὸ πολλῶν ἰατρῶν καὶ δαπανήσασα τὰ παρ' αὐτῆς πάντα καὶ μηδὲν ὠφεληθεῖσα ἀλλὰ μᾶλλον εἰς τὸ χεῖρον ἐλθοῦσα, [27] ἀκούσασα περὶ τοῦ Ἰησοῦ, ἐλθοῦσα ἐν τῷ ὄχλῳ ὄπισθεν ἥψατο τοῦ ἱματίου αὐτοῦ· [28] ἔλεγεν γὰρ ὅτι Ἐὰν ἅψωμαι κἂν τῶν ἱματίων αὐτοῦ σωθήσομαι. [29] καὶ εὐθὺς ἐξηράνθη ἡ πηγὴ τοῦ αἵματος αὐτῆς, καὶ ἔγνω τῷ σώματι ὅτι ἴαται ἀπὸ τῆς μάστιγος. [30] καὶ εὐθὺς ὁ Ἰησοῦς ἐπιγνοὺς ἐν ἑαυτῷ τὴν ἐξ αὐτοῦ δύναμιν ἐξελθοῦσαν ἐπιστραφεὶς ἐν τῷ ὄχλῳ ἔλεγεν· Τίς μου ἥψατο τῶν ἱματίων; [31] καὶ ἔλεγον αὐτῷ οἱ μαθηταὶ αὐτοῦ· Βλέπεις τὸν ὄχλον συνθλίβοντά σε, καὶ λέγεις· Τίς μου ἥψατο; [32] καὶ περιεβλέπετο ἰδεῖν τὴν τοῦτο ποιήσασαν. [33] ἡ δὲ γυνὴ φοβηθεῖσα καὶ τρέμουσα, εἰδυῖα ὃ γέγονεν αὐτῇ, ἦλθεν καὶ προσέπεσεν αὐτῷ καὶ εἶπεν αὐτῷ πᾶσαν τὴν ἀλήθειαν. [34] ὁ δὲ εἶπεν αὐτῇ· Θυγάτηρ, ἡ πίστις σου σέσωκέν σε· ὕπαγε εἰς εἰρήνην, καὶ ἴσθι ὑγιὴς ἀπὸ τῆς μάστιγός σου.

represented – or only implied – in texts? I usually work on texts. But texts can be coy. To put it tautologously, pictures are more graphic. I look to discern in images and objects how blood works in Christianity both to clean and to defile – to clean and defile gender roles, and thus mostly to reinforce and sometimes to transgress them.

Consider how blood works in the Bible:

> They washed their robes and made them white in the blood of the Lamb. (Revelation 7:14)
> Without the shedding of blood, there is no remission of sins. (Hebrews 9:22)
> The city sheds blood from her midst, that her time may come, and makes idols to defile herself. (Ezekiel 22:3)

Blood is strange stuff. Sometimes it cleanses, so that red stuff makes clothes white. Even non-chlorine bleach is blue in color. So anthropologists identify blood as a "detergent." Detergent blood, like soap from ash, is made by sacrifice. But other blood defiles: the city (gendered feminine) "bleeds from her middle to defile herself." Christian rhetoric and images use blood in contrary ways, to cleanse and to defile. Those ways are also gendered. When men (Jesus, Abraham) shed blood in sacrifice, it cleanses. When women shed blood in menstruation and childbirth, it seems so powerful that men see danger. Women, in many cultures, may not sacrifice (no women priests). Men, in many cultures, must police characteristics gendered female. Blood takes on two different roles because it reinforces and complicates genders regarded as binary. If I speak of "women's blood," I don't mean to reduce women to blood, or to ignore the bleeding of transmen. Transwomen don't bleed at all. Instead, I repeat a cultural construction of gender to expose and subvert it. If we culturally construct it, why does Christ's gender even matter? The binary matters because he transgresses it; because it defines a low estate with which the stories identify him.

Mary Douglas has written, "where there is no differentiation there is no defilement." But it is also the case that, for Douglas, where there is no differentiation there is no power. Therefore, defilement can be reversed, so that "religions often sacralize the very unclean things" that they rejected. This occurs, for example, with the death of Christ. And it occurs preeminently with his blood. We must look at how the gendering of blood has made it seem unclean, and how the encounter of Jesus with the bleeding woman makes her bleeding creative.[2]

---

[2] Mary Douglas, *Purity and Danger*, 160, 159. I owe this paragraph to a question from Luke Bretherton.

This is dangerous work for a man, more so for a man with a husband. My lack of experience puts me at risk not only of blunders and bloopers, but, even worse, failures of tone and the presumption of ventriloquism. But it would be worse, I think, to write a book about blood with no chapter on menstruation and childbirth, a book in which the malestream association of blood with violence is quietly allowed to prevail.[3]

But the stories of Jesus subvert the gendering of blood in many and various ways, beginning with the virgin birth. Whether your biology is ancient or modern, the virgin birth makes strange the blood of Christ right from his conception: "Because Jesus has no earthly father, his blood is entirely the blood of his mother. It is Mary's blood that is the blood of God, Mary's blood shed on the cross, Mary's blood that works in the Eucharist. The Virgin birth queers the gender of blood by making the blood that the Son of God bleeds a woman's blood."[4]

Among many images and artifacts of blood and sacrifice, consider four standard images that gender women by means of blood. By "standard image" I mean a large collection of images that share an iconography. It's what they have in common that interests me. I focus on one commonly referred to in English as The Woman with an Issue of Blood and in Greek as the Haemorrhoissa.[5] This is the unnamed woman whom Jesus heals – or who heals herself – when she touches the hem of his cloak. In this image, overt blood never appears. For that

---

[3] Which actually happens in Gil Anidjar's *Blood: A Critique of Christianity* – where blood reduces to violence and blood gendered female is mentioned without being allowed to change the narrative.

I have six women to thank, five of them doctoral students at Duke University. One is Julie Morris, who published "Leaky Bodies" for *Christian Century* as this chapter was mostly finished, and which makes me think that, in the interchange of mutual influence between teacher and student, she must have influenced me more than I knew. The other four invited me to share the chapter with them, took it apart, and helped to put it back together again: Christina Ananias, Emily Dubie, Sarah Jobe, and Aminah Bradford. Sarah Jobe, not only a Hebrew Bible scholar but also a doula who has written a book on childbearing, *Creating with God: The Holy Confusing Blessedness of Pregnancy* (Paraclete Press, 2011), pointed out that a bloody birth is not a good thing; she and Aminah Bradford worked for hours to fix my draft. They are responsible for my attention to the placenta. The sixth is Deb Ebert, a New Zealand–certified midwife, who directed me to articles in obstretrical journals. For the errors of fact and tone that remain, I have only myself to thank.

[4] Gregory S. Williams, personal correspondence, Annunciation, 2019.
[5] For example, in the English traditions of the Gospel of Mark, the English translation of Schiller's *Iconography*, and the website of Art Resource.

reason, it seems to preserve the gendered pattern that celebrates the blood of male violence and suppresses the blood of women's fertility. But I argue it's more complicated than that, and the hidden blood undergoes a transfer that allows it to transform, transgender, and reemerge in another set of images – those of the crucifixion.[6]

Three other images offer us context. Judith and Holofernes depicts a story from the book of Judith (10:11–13:10; accepted as canonical by Catholics, Eastern Orthodox, and Anglicans), in which a woman beheads a man, Holofernes, an enemy general. The scene seems to break the rule against showing women's bloodshed, but here too it's more complicated, since the scene presents Judith "escaping" her gender to perform violence gendered male. This exception proves the rule.[7]

The scene of Bathsheba Bathing plays two roles in the plot of 2 Samuel 11:2–4. First, David sees her bathing from a tower of his palace (v. 2). Omitted from sermons and children's bibles, a second plot point spells out that Bathsheba is observing a ritual requirement to bathe (v. 4; cf. Lev. 15:19–24). A ritual bath means not only that her period has just ended; it also implies that she can't be pregnant. Thus the child she conceives must be David's – not her husband's. Here too the blood that makes the difference goes without showing.

The final image shows Jesus nursing at Mary's breast. The Greek tradition calls this image "Galaktotrophousa," the Virgin who nourishes with milk.[8] Since many traditions see milk, like semen, as whitened blood, Mary also (with other nurses and the Eucharist) nourishes with blood. This image winks in and out of use or gets plastered over as attitudes change about

---

[6] Janet Martin Soskice first drew my attention to this story and its Christological references in her fine and subtle chapter "Blood and Defilement: Christology" in *The Kindness of God: Metaphor, Gender, and Religious Language* (Oxford: Oxford University Press, 2007), 84–99. My student Julie Morris renewed my attention in a more popular account influenced by Soskice, "A Story of Two Leaky Bodies: In Mark 5, a Hemorrhaging Woman Meets a Permeable Savior," *Christian Century* (Jan. 10, 2017), www.christiancentury.org/article/story-two-leaky-bodies, from which I learned of Candida Moss, "The Man with the Flow of Power: Porous Bodies in Mark 5:25–34," *Journal of Biblical Literature* 129 (2010), 507–19. Emma Sedgwick, *From Flow to Face: The Haemorrhoissa Motif (Mark 5:24b–34 parr) between Anthropological Origin and Image Paradigm* (Leeuven: Peeters, 2015) came to my attention after this chapter was finished.

[7] Eva Straussman-Pflanzer, *Violence and Virtue: Artemisia Gentileschi's "Judith Slaying Holofernes"* (Chicago: Art Institute of Chicago, 2013) treats gender but not the sociology of blood.

[8] See Elizabeth Bolman, "The Enigmatic Coptic Galaktotrophousa and the Cult of the Virgin Mary in Egypt," in *Images of the Mother of God: Perceptions of the Theotokos in Byzantium*, ed. Maria Vassilaki (London: Ashgate Publishing, 2005), 13–22.

women's breasts. But because multiple traditions count milk as whitened blood, the exposure of a nursing breast is as close as we get in classical art to seeing blood gendered female.

Together those images raise a host of questions. What difference does it make that the Woman with an Issue of Blood never shows overt blood, while Judith and Holofernes conventionally shows floods? Do the images distinguish female-gendered blood, which men regard as secret,[9] from blood of war or sacrifice, which they regard as public? How can the woman cure herself without Jesus's conscious intention, so that he asks "who touched me"? Do both Judith and the bleeding woman, different as they are, depict women's agency and power over men? Why do images often show Judith killing Holofernes with breasts exposed? Why does the bleeding woman turn up so often on early Christian tombs? How have artists and authors used these stories to maintain or overcome gender roles? In what way do images of the bleeding woman feminize or masculinize Jesus, whose salvation they describe in terms of both sacrifice (gendered male) and rebirth (gendered female)? How have Christian artists and authors used images of women to think about Jesus – who both, like Holofernes, dies by violent execution, and, like the woman with the issue of blood, bleeds without limit?

Pictures, I learned, can also play coy. It's just that, in the church or gallery, you see so much male-gendered violence and female-gendered nakedness that the distractions of pictures can outdo the silence of texts. You study Bathsheba bathing, and there's so much to look at, you can't see what's not there. Western Christian art is frank about bloodshed by men. We're shocked at beheadings by ISIS, but Christian art displays beheadings in church. Nor does it shy from beheadings by women – if only they follow the pattern of men. Judith slaying Holofernes shows plenty of blood, one or the other half of his neck exposed obscenely for inspection like the pith of a squash. The image frees, by convention, one or both of Judith's breasts, either for her to wield the sword like an Amazon, or (which may be the same thing) to burst the bonds of gender. Images of Jael driving a tent peg into the skull of Sisera are less bloody but share the trope of exposing breasts (Antonio Molinari, Giovanni Romelli, Felice Fichelli, Gregorio Lazzarini). Judith's breasts mix a message: they sexualize her as a woman, and they bare her as a warrior. Western art shows all manner of violence; it lingers pruriently on the torture of the damned and on the piercing, flaying, and griddling of saints. But blood gendered female it does not show. The blood of women is That

---

[9] See Bildhauer, 30–8, 105; Peggy McCracken, *The Curse of Eve, the Wound of the Hero: Blood, Gender, and Medieval Literature* (Philadelphia: University of Pennsylvania Press, 2003), 84–91.

88 BLOOD THEOLOGY

Which May Not Be Seen. Sometimes the only part of a painting to suggest a woman's blood is the label underneath. At most, a painting refers to female-gendered blood by indirection. The image of Bathsheba bathing refers to blood only to wash it away. You may say, of course! But it's exactly that assumption of naturalness, of what's right and proper, that I seek to expose. I want to display, not the blood itself, but the filters of our minds, by which we have come to expect *not* to see any blood. (We men? We women taught to protect the sensibilities of men?)[10] Sometimes water stands for blood; so a woman weeps on Jesus, as he himself will come to bleed.[11] This time water hides the blood. The saints can wash themselves in the blood of Jesus, but the blood of a woman can only be washed away. Artists may cover Jesus in crimson, carmine, or vermillion, but the clear water of erasure is the only sign of Bathsheba's menstruation. Bathsheba can bathe naked, if she appears immaculate. Only immaculate women may bathe.

Jesus on the other hand can drip blood from under his loincloth and down his legs. When he drips from his loincloth the blood does not, to be sure, originate from there. It originates from the wound in his side, which figures also as a vulva. Indeed, Jesus has a womb in his wound in Latin texts, a wound sometimes called *uterus* and sometimes *vulva,* both of which Latin uses to mean "womb." Although the words for wound and womb are unrelated in either language, even Latin distinguishes *vulna* (wound) from *vulva* (womb) by a single letter. Paintings likewise play upon the opening in Jesus's side. The play is always plausibly deniable. When blood from the vulna-vulva drips below the loincloth, paintings do and do not mark Jesus with the blood of menstruation. At most they leave a trace for the viewer to interpret. But they can mark Bathsheba (whose period drives the story) only with water. The paradox is, this water is anything but transparent.

In those examples, Bathsheba, like the woman with an issue of blood, seems to reinforce a gender dichotomy, while Judith seems to cross or queer it. But perhaps both images transgress a binary, if the unlimited blood of the bleeding woman prefigures the unlimited bleeding of Jesus.

The image of Jesus and the Woman with an Issue of Blood also goes by other names. "The Hemorrhaging Woman," it's sometimes called, with studied ambiguity, after Mt. 9:20, "The Hemophiliac Woman," scholars sometimes say, misleadingly. Those names shush or misdirect. Mark's account (5:25–34) – the earliest, most rustic and plainspoken – introduces

---

[10] The purpose of a purse, a mother taught her daughter, was not to carry money, but to hide her tampons from view, so that nothing might bring to the male-gendered mind the female-gendered bleeding.

[11] Mt. 26:6–13, Mk. 14:3–9, Lk. 7:36–50, Jn. 12:1–8. I owe the connection to Sarah Jobe.

her as "a woman who had had a flow of blood for twelve years" (Mk. 5:25, *rhusei haimatos*). At her healing (v. 29), the RSV says her "hemorrhage" stopped, but the Greek deploys a different phrase, *pyge tou haimatos,* where *pyge* is a positive word usually used for a spring of water; for example, Mary became a *zoodochos pyge,* a life-giving spring, to name a church at a Byzantine source. Thus the King James refers to the woman Christologically as having a "fountain of blood." Luke (8:43–48), after Mark, also introduces the woman as having a *rhusei haimatos* but shortens the story by half and removes the word for "spring" or "fountain" to stick with the language of "issue" or "flow" (*rhusis*). Matthew (9:20–22), also after Mark, further downplays the blood: the author shortens the story by two thirds, removes all freestanding words for blood, sanitizes Mark's "flow" and "spring" with the more clinical word "hemorrhage" (which the RSV smuggles into Mark), and in one manuscript bowdlerizes even "hemorrhage" with "asthenia," or weakness.[12] That one, a royal French copy of the Greek of Matthew, manages to scrub the story of women's blood altogether.

Sermons on the story are (predictably) rare, but Chrysostom writes:

> Wherefore did she not approach Him boldly? She was ashamed on account of her affliction, accounting herself to be unclean. For if the menstruous woman was judged not to be clean, how much more would she have the same thought, who was afflicted with such a disease; since in fact that complaint was under the law accounted a great uncleanness.

The Byzantine *Catena on Mark* confines itself to the woman's faith, and – even though it's billed as Mark – follows Matthew's lead to mention blood not at all. In the West, Augustine, Luther, and Calvin reduce the concrete issue of blood to Jews and Gentiles or even to "faith."[13] In the East, Romanos and Jacob of Serugh reduce blood to sin.[14]

---

[12] The "Regius" manuscript, Paris, Bibl. Nat., Gr. 62, listed as L in Nestle–Aland.

[13] For a brief but judicious history of exegesis with important examples from Christian iconography, see Christine E. Joynes, "Still at the Margins?: Gospel Women and Their Afterlives," in *Radical Christian Voices and Practice: Essays in Honour of Christopher Rowland,* ed. Zoë Bennett and David B. Gowler (Oxford: Oxford University Press, 2012), 117–35. For texts, see Grant LeMarquand, "Appendix I: The Bleeding Woman in Pre-modern Interpretation," in *An Issue of Relevance: A Comparative Study of the Story of the Bleeding Woman (Mk 5:25–34; Mt 9:20–22; Lk 8:43–48) in North Atlantic and African Contexts* (New York: Peter Lang, 2004), 223–35.

[14] Except for metaphoric uses in Lev. 20:21 and Ez. 7:19–20, the Bible and the rabbis distinguish menstrual impurity sharply from questions of morality or sin. For a brief, reliable account, see Tirza Meacham, "Female Purity (Niddah)," in the *Encyclopedia of the Jewish Women's Archive* at jwa.org/encyclopedia/author/meacham-tirzah; the author is Professor of Talmud and Rabbinics at the University of Toronto. For an exhaustive

Except for pesky questions about marital sex and approaching the altar. Exegetical theology may disagree whether her flow of blood counts as menstruation or not, but practical theology confines the argument to menstrual terms. That's because social context uses the story to debate not Christology, but whether a bleeding woman may approach the altar or sleep with her husband (e.g., *Summa Theologiae* Supplement 64).

Prefeminist twentieth-century interpretation presents a choice of evasions that Grant LeMarquand calls "Diagnostic Exegesis" (reducing the problem to some specific disease) or the "Hermeneutics of Embarrassment" (refusing to acknowledge menstrual themes).[15] Readers from less embarrassed cultures understand what is at issue: blood that, whatever its origin, is understood to be or assimilated to menstrual blood.

Outside the Western mainstream, LeMarquand's African readers take the story as referring straightforwardly to menstruation that never stops:

> African readers cannot help but notice the blood. In evident fear, some African men with institutional church power read "power went out from him" (Mk 5:30) [to justify] separating women from holy things during menstruation. This separation is evidently meant to protect the men [such is the power of menstrual blood]. On the other hand, most African women read the story of the bleeding woman with evident empathy, noting the many dimensions of her suffering, the strength of her faith and hope, and most of all the injustice of her separation, assumed to be the reason for her stealth when she approaches Jesus. For most the implication of the woman's bleeding is clear: she would be childless (at least from the time the bleeding [began]), a great source of shame in African culture; she would be considered a danger, especially to men; she would be ostracized.[16]

What LeMarquand calls the Hermeneutics of Embarrassment in his texts, Peggy McCracken calls a "forbidden scene" in hers, and her term works even better, of course, for visual art. Texts and art identify a woman with the stereotype of women's blood – which paradoxically means she cannot conceive. Her image never shows blood and barely indicates it. Although the Woman with an Issue of Blood is often incised on amulets of a reddish-brown stone called hematite, of all the paintings and mosaics on Art Resource, not even one dresses her in red. The beautiful mosaic at

---

account, see Charlotte Elisheva Fonrobert, *Menstrual Purity: Rabbinic and Christian Reconstructions of Biblical Gender* (Stanford, CA: Stanford University Press, 2000).

[15] LeMarquand, "A Story about Blood," in *An Issue of Relevance: A Comparative Study of the Story of the Bleeding Woman* (New York: Peter Lang, 1994), 169–216; here, 173, 176.

[16] LeMarquand, p. 215. I have abridged the passage and suppressed the ellipses. I take it that when LeMarquand writes "African" he has in mind Kenyan Christians.

JESUS AND THE GENDER OF BLOOD

Monreale cloaks her in green. Nothing identifies the woman except her gesture of touching Jesus's hem. That gesture alone is her identifying mark, her attribute.[17]

(A painting of Rachel makes a single exception. Rachel cites her period to sit undisturbed atop a saddle that hides the household gods [Gen. 31:34–35],[18] and Tiepolo makes her robe a gorgeous red, perhaps because he thinks the trope a trick, and feels free to paint the joke. But the trick is deadly earnest. Because Rachel is moving with her husband, she needs the gods to protect her matriline in a patriarchal land. Nancy Jay explains: Rachel had not taken a keepsake, an heirloom, a souvenir. She was not moved by sentiment: "Rachel had stolen her family's line of descent."[19])

The emblematic gesture of the bleeding woman is not just any reaching out; all sorts of onlookers reach out. She reaches out to a particular, material thing; she reaches out to the rolled or doubled cloth that hems Jesus's garment. Because only the garment of Jesus indicates the woman's bleeding, it becomes a metonym, an index in cloth of her blood. Without denying her faith, which the artist also cannot show, we can identify a material object, a cloth, that stops her flow of blood. His hem becomes, in effect, what Bible translations elsewhere call a rag. Because it is the hem of Jesus's garment that alone identifies her, the image serves to *transfer* the index of blood from her to him. Iconographically it points, therefore, not only to her, as her gesture of identification. It points also to him, to one who will, like her, come to be identified by an issue of blood. Her past will become his future. Her emblematic touch enacts her agency and prefigures his passion. All the agency in Mark is hers; Jesus doesn't initiate anything.[20] If Jesus is passive, in Greek, he "suffers"; that is, he undergoes her touch. If the hem of his garment is the rag that tamps her flow of blood, *he* is the one who wears it. Her touch feminizes him; it figures his blood as no longer contained and male but henceforth forward and female:[21] it figures him too as one with an issue of blood. His question, "Who touched me?," detects not only a touch or a transfer but a kinship. Like hers, his issue of blood will be involuntary; like hers, his will be without limit, as it suffices to save an unlimited number and increases at the Eucharist according to need.

---

[17] I discovered too late to use Barbara Baert, "Touching the Hem: The Thread Between Garment and Blood in the Story of the Woman with the Hemorrhage (Mark 5:24b–34parr)," in *Textile: Journal of Cloth and Culture* 9 (2011): 308–59.

[18] I owe the reference to Sarah Jobe.

[19] Nancy Jay, *Throughout Your Generations Forever* (Chicago: University of Chicago Press, 1992), 41–60.

[20] A point I owe to Sarah Jobe.

[21] On "leaking," see Soskice, Morris, and Moss.

At high-church Eucharists, the hem of his garment unfurls at length or even multiplies to layer up communion linen, the clothes that both serve the chalice with its holy blood, and protect the people from the danger of the elements: a lavabo towel to dry the hands; an altar cloth to cover the table; a corporal to set a place; a veil to hang over the chalice; a pall to weight the veil; a folded napkin to clean the rim; a purificator to wipe out the chalice; a lengthy housel-cloth to overhang the altar rail, mark the sacred boundary, or bound the Sabbath space: all cloths, like the hem of Jesus, that hide and mark and ward a quantity of blood, and that at need absorb it. There is even a burse to carry the purificator – which is just Latin for the purse to hide the napkin.[22]

If the thought of all that eucharistic sanitation makes men queasy, that's just the awareness it's meant to repress. Sociological barriers, according to Durkheim, entrench, at last, in the gut. But the queasiness also holds off blood gendered female, the same gesture that, in Orthodox polity, Catholic practice, and Anglican history, forbids the altar to women. It refuses to take the blood of a woman as sacred.

Fencing off the sacred is well enough, as long as it is does justice to women and others. At Rotorua in New Zealand, St. Faith's Anglican is the oldest permanent Maori church and appears on the tourist circuit because of its gorgeous Maori carvings – and on account of the boiling mud nearby that had already sanctified the Maori site for over five hundred years. The crust of the earth is minimal at Rotorua, and the mantle, like elemental fire, seems ready to break through. The smell of sulfur and the sound of plopping mud had already heightened my nerves before I entered the church. My husband pointed out the words in raised and gilded gothic capitals along the rim of the communion table. As I approached the altar I saw the words "taboo, taboo, taboo," completely recognizable in their Maori spelling: 𝕿𝖆𝖕𝖚 𝕿𝖆𝖕𝖚 𝕿𝖆𝖕𝖚.[23] I felt the hair rise on my arms, and I didn't want to touch the altar. In Maori that is also the way to say Holy, Holy, Holy. "Tapu, tapu, tapu" is the Trisagion and the prohibition in one. In the Polynesian languages from which first Captain Cook and then anthropologists took the word "taboo," it means "sacred, prohibited, restricted, set apart, forbidden, under … protection … [in] a supernatural condition … untouchable."[24] That is

---

[22] A connection I owe to Christina Ananias.

[23] Close-ups of the altar are (perhaps appropriately) rare. But you can see the TAPU TAPU TAPU in this photo: www.rotorua-travel-secrets.com/images/maori-wall-panels.jpg

[24] maoridictionary.co.nz/search?idiom=&phrase=&proverb=&loan=&histLoanWords=& keywords=TAPU For more see Excursus 2 to this chapter.

exactly the right thing to put around an altar. It wasn't that I wasn't supposed to touch it; it was that I was having a first-order experience of taboo and I didn't *want* to touch it. To invoke Rudolf Otto's idea of the holy as the *mysterium tremendum et fascinans* is too grand. It was simpler than that. It was a shivering. So fencing off the sacred can rightly invoke religious emotions. It is not the definition of the sacred that has gone wrong. Rather, in the refusal of blood gendered female it is the definition of profane that goes wrong. The right thing to do is to include, appropriate, uphold, and honor what justly inspires awe in creation, as the Maori church takes advantage of the geothermal activity that brings the mud alive.[25] Without justice, the rite of the altar falls to the critique of Amos (5:21, 24), who hears God proclaim, "I hate, I despise your festivals, and I take no delight in your solemn assemblies. . . . But let justice roll down like waters, and righteousness like an ever-flowing stream." That is a different ever-flowing stream from that of the woman with the issue of blood. But blood-flow and justice do belong together.

In any case it's necessary to distinguish two taboos. There's a taboo in favor of the altar and a taboo against women. Those taboos are not the same, but they are tangled up. They both invest blood with power, positive or negative. Both the blood of the altar and the blood of women acquire social power from taboos – even if the second shows its power in the backhanded sense of eliciting insults from men. Thus the two taboos construct gender differentially. Despite the feminine leaking of Jesus, the blood of the altar privileges men. Despite the life-giving of menstruation and childbirth, the refusal of blood gendered female disadvantages women.

According to Nancy Jay, the two taboos support one another: a male line of cultural descent from bishop to priest depends on and stands against a female line of biological descent from mother to child. The taboos mirror and lean against each other, in order to hold each other up. The line of priestly "fathers" maintains its privilege by mimicking the line of biological mothers. In Christianity, according to Nancy Jay, the privilege of this priestly father-line is called "apostolic succession."[26]

In Nancy Jay's theory of sacrifice, descent by blood in the sense of biological connection belonged in multiple societies to women alone; men had to prove descent by cultural means. That means also involved blood, in many societies: the blood of sacrifice. It was at a common meal over a large cooked mammal that a father acknowledged his children – especially his

---

[25] As I write this the church has been closed temporarily as the boiling mud encroaches. Step away from the plopping hole! Tapu, tapu, tapu! www.nzherald.co.nz/rotorua-daily-post/news/article.cfm?c_id=1503438&objectid=11824876

[26] Jay, 112–27.

94 BLOOD THEOLOGY

sons – and created the social fact on animal flesh that modern bureaucracies create on paper (which was also on flesh when paper was sheepskin). Two incommensurable kinds of blood come together here: the maternal blood of relationship, and the paternal blood of sacrifice. It is tempting to contrast the blood of sacrifice, which Jay calls "men's childbearing" or their attempt to "do birth better,"[27] with something called "the blood of childbirth." The last phrase turns out to be a symptom of blood's logic.

On an earlier draft of this chapter, Sarah Jobe, a trained doula, wrote that "there's not that much blood at childbirth unless there is a *big* problem. [There is] lots of water/[amniotic] fluid at childbirth but not so much blood."[28]

Certain that I had gotten the contrast "blood of sacrifice"/"blood of childbirth" from Nancy Jay, I ascertained to my surprise that she never uses the second phrase. Karen Fields, in the Forward, tells a story about it:

> "I've been thinking about blood," [Jay] said, and paused. Yes, *blood.* It was odd, wasn't it, that in so many societies blood both purified and polluted. And wasn't it remarkable that the blood of childbirth and menstruation commonly polluted, while the blood of sacrifice, even of sacrificed animals, could purify? *The experience of childbirth could not have produced such an idea, [Jay] was sure,* using her own bearing of four children as a momentary example. Nor could its result, new human life [have produced the idea], for [new life] was valued everywhere. ... If neither the experience of childbirth nor its result accounted for the opposite properties of blood, what might? It was not long before Jay was talking about the opposition between childbirth and sacrifice ... as one between nature and society.[29]

Thus the "blood of childbirth" turns out to be another colonizing expression, where once again men read blood in where it hardly belongs. They imagine blood shed rather than shared.[30] They imagine (see below) a baby made of menstruum or bathed in blood, when neither is the case. (The newborn is covered in vernix, which is waxy and white.) What social forms give rise to this imagination?

Normal childbirth is neither bloodless nor hemorrhagic. There is a "bloody show," which is neither bloody (more of a blood-tinged mucus) nor much of a show, but more of a tell. "The wound in the uterine wall where the placenta shears off always bleeds," a New Zealand registered

---

[27] Jay, xxiv.
[28] Sarah Jobe, personal communication.
[29] Jay, x, paragraph boundary elided, "society and nature" reversed (my italics).
[30] An observation I owe to Greg Williams.

midwife explains. Authorities differ on what counts as normal. In Britain, 500 ml is a hemorrhage and 1000 ml is a major hemorrhage; in the US, from 2014, a hemorrhage begins at 1000 ml. By comparison, the mean blood-loss in menstruation is 30 ml, and by implication up to 80 ml is normal: a regular loss of over 80 ml may bring anemia. The same midwife comments that "although there isn't that much blood in childbirth unless there is a problem (if people are picturing floods of blood), no woman standing in the shower after giving birth with endless blood dripping down her legs would say that birth isn't bloody" at all.[31]

In normal childbirth, bleeding is incidental to birth. In crucifixion with nails, blood is incidental to death. Neither normal childbirth nor crucifixion with nails leads directly to the images of Christian atonement: blood to bathe adult bodies in, blood in floods, the blood, as Origen says, of hecatombs, or hundreds of cattle. Those ·images borrow from the infinite blood of God. Blood without exaggeration is not the same as blood without limit. That is why we might want to speak of the blood of not childbirth, but afterbirth.

The placenta, a component of the afterbirth, is, like a heart or liver, bloody by definition – not, again, in pictured floods, but neatly contained, in a flat, circular organ. The placenta is a membrane filled with blood, where mother's blood meets fetal villi to nourish and oxygenate the fetus. The mother's and the baby's blood meet but do not mix; they are united but unconfused. Nutrients and antibodies circulate.

(In the Maori language, the land makes such a tissue of circulation between the people and the sea, and is called *whenua*, which also means placenta.[32] The land, like a placenta, gives birth to the people of the land, *tangata whenua*; and they return the placenta to the earth.[33] At Rotorua, where Maori have worshipped for hundreds of years, and where the earth itself boils and

---

[31] Deb Ebert, personal communication. She supplies these references: The American College of Obstetricians and Gynecologists (ACOG) states that "experts typically report that the mean blood loss per menstrual period is 30ml per cycle and that chronic loss of more than 80ml is associated with anemia," implying that 80 ml or less is normal. ("Menstruation in girls and adolescents: using the menstrual cycle as a vital sign," Committee Opinion No. 651. ACOG, *Obstet Gynecol* 2015;126:e143–6; at www.acog.org/Clinical-Guidance-and-Publications/Committee-Opinions/Committee-on-Adolescent-Health-Care/Menstruation-in-Girls-and-Adolescents-Using-the-Menstrual-Cycle-as-a-Vital-Sign?IsMobileSet=false. WHO and Royal College of Obstetricians and Gynecologists (RCOG) classify blood loss of more than 500 ml as a postpartum hemorrhage and more than 1000 ml as a major hemorrhage. ACOG adjusted their guidelines in 2014 to classify a hemorrhage as more than 1000 ml. R. S. Kerr and A. D. Weeks, "Postpartum Haemorrhage: A Single Definition Is No Longer Enough," *BJOG* 124 (2017): 723–6.

[32] Tregear, 620, col. 2. I owe the observation to Aminah Bradford.

[33] Deb Ebert, personal communication. See also the Wikipedia article on *tangata whenua*.

plops, the placenta of the earth is thin, and something holy seems about to be born.)

In what follows, I speak of the afterbirth, which comprises the delivered placenta and fetal membranes: the place where blood was shared, in that protological state before birth. Ideally speaking, therefore, the *real* blood of childbirth – which is to say the blood of fetal *growth,* the blood that nourishes and protects the fetus through the placenta – opposes the blood of sacrifice "because it is not 'shed' at all. It is given without harm or reduction to the giver." Bracketing the distinctively human competition for resources between mother and child, that remark pictures a donation of Eden and heaven that becomes sacrifice only in between: it pictures "the protological and eschatological version of 'sacrifice' that is paradigmatically represented in Jesus."[34]

But the protological state before birth not only suggests a picture of life before sin. It also suggests a way of dealing with sin. The placenta does not only deliver nutrients. It also collects and carries off carbon dioxide and other waste from the baby's blood and transfers them for disposal to the blood of the mother.[35] Biologically, the waste and its disposal have no moral valence; eventually CO_2 and other waste become food for other creatures. And yet Christian theology has often (for good or ill) seen in waste and its disposal a metaphor for sin and its remission. Purity metaphors are often misused (see Chapter 7). Perhaps it is safer to speak with Mary Douglas of "matter out of place." It matters that the placenta not only feeds the baby but removes accumulated waste. On this picture, the placenta comes to anticipate those instruments of sacrifice – like the horns of the altar and the body of Christ – [36] that seem to attract, collect, and dispose of sin. With different figurations of quantity and place, the body of Christ, the horns of the altar, and the mother's placenta all hold blood, and they all cleanse, somehow, by means of blood. This picture suggests two ways in which the blood of Christ resembles the blood of a mother. Not only does it build up a new body. It also has the power to protect it from harm. Through the instrumentality of the placenta, the mother's blood, like that of Christ, can absorb what harms to carry it away, perhaps even, conceivably, for good uses elsewhere.

In Peggy McCracken, medieval French fathers maintained the privileges to name, claim, and dispose of their children by the fiction that the purified blood of semen formed the child.[37] Fathers and children shared blood

[34] Gregory S. Williams, personal communication, March 25, 2019.
[35] I owe this observation to a conversation with Lauren Winner. See also Jobe, *Creating with God,* 98.
[36] Cf. Jobe, 111.
[37] McCracken, 90.

because the semen conferred form, the child's very essence, making it the father's own. On that theory, the father shapes and owns the child while the mother only nourishes and incubates it. In this way, a father is related to his child by blood, and a mother is related to her child merely by food. Which is almost to say: a mother is not related to her child at all.

The blood of menstruation and afterbirth belies that simple picture – and threatens the power it upholds. Not only do men sacrifice. The bloods of menstruation and the afterbirth mark a counter-sacrifice on the part of the mother. Not to mention the pains of both, or the risk of death, by which the rabbis made Rachel a rival to Christ (Gen. 35:16–18).[38] Despite the elevation of the father's bloodline, the umbilical cord leads to the sacrificed sack of mother's blood, the afterbirth. You would think that the bleached out blood of the father in the semen could not compete with the bluish-red blood of the mother in the placenta. If you believe in the power of the blood, then the mere sight of the placenta, exposed as the afterbirth, ought to swamp the theory. "As a pregnant woman breaks open in labor," writes Sarah Jobe, "the blood and water that pour from her are perhaps as close as we will ever come to witnessing the blood and water that poured from Jesus' side on the cross."[39] In a culture where the very sight of the Eucharist sanctified, and "ocular communion" worked like darshan, seeing was believing. Like the bread of the Eucharist, the mother's blood might be food but it was not mere food. Like the wine of the Eucharist, this was sacrificial blood. If the blood of the Eucharist could make people divine, the blood of the mother could at least make them human. Couldn't it?

While the sight of the Eucharist was marked as powerful by the elevation of the elements, the ringing of bells, and the decoration of monstrances, the sight of childbirth was marked as powerful by being forbidden, by going unseen, at least by men. That was the reason, according to McCracken, that birth itself could not be shown.[40] It could not be painted, and, with exceptions that only prove the rule, men could not look upon it. Showing it would connect the birth with the afterbirth and reveal the child as living not by semen alone but also by its mother's blood. (And later by its mother's blood turned to milk.) Childbirth became the primal scene that could expose the fraud. Showing it would render undeniable that women too relate to their children by blood.

---

[38] Ellen Haskell, *Mystical Resistance: Uncovering the Zohar's Conversations with Christianity* (Oxford: Oxford University Press, 2016), 15–38.

[39] Jobe, 85.

[40] McCracken, 77–91.

98 BLOOD THEOLOGY

Or consider the birth of Jesus. Irenaeus not only accuses Gnostics of avoiding Christ's blood (*Adv. Haer.* IV.5.2); he also accuses Marcion of avoiding Christ's birth (I.27.2). Usually the most important moment of the incarnation, images of the birth of Jesus invariably show no such thing. They show the baby Jesus. They do not show his birth. They are almost Marcionite: they do not show – they refrain from showing – that Mary gives birth to God. In hiding her sacrifice, they deny her a priesthood. A few, rare images venture one step closer. They apply the strategy of Bathsheba bathing to the baby Jesus. They show him having a bath. They are showing, not the afterbirth, merely the after birth. If Moses at the Nile turned water into blood, and Jesus at Cana turns water into wine, these artists of the Nativity reverse those miracles: they thin blood into water.

Those then are some of the reasons why in the images of the Woman bleeding and of Bathsheba bathing we cannot see any blood, and why in the misnamed births of Jesus we see neither birth nor afterbirth. Those things have been hidden from us. They have been denied us. Those repressed things return, however, in the bloodying of Jesus and the baptism of believers.

Crucifixion kills by suffocation and requires no blood. Painters show Peter lashed to a cross to keep his blood from competing with Christ's. The unnecessary and excessive bleeding of Jesus feminizes and transgenders him both in physical leakiness and in generative power.[41] The power in the blood becomes paradoxically the power to overcome patriarchal distortions, because the death and resurrection of Jesus makes the blood of fertility inexhaustible and the water from his side a baptism. This figuration transfigures the story of the Woman with an Issue of Blood, a problem solved by more blood rather than less, because hidden blood becomes overt, birthwater baptizes, and placental fluids move in quantities uncountably figured to "cover" and to "bathe." The placenta is even an organ that animals and women are known to eat: their own flesh and blood without cannibalism, like the Eucharist.

(Rabbi David Kornreich raises the halachic question whether it is kosher for a woman to eat her placenta, for medicinal purposes and encapsulated into pills, and finds it "safe to conclude that שליא [the placenta] of humans is *muttar gamur* [completely permitted] according to all opinions [besides the Rambam who originally forbade the שליא of בהמה טמאה (an impure animal) which the Tur, Shulchan Aruch, Schach, Kreisi and Chavas Da'as permit].")[42]

---

[41] Graham Ward, "The Displaced Body of Jesus Christ," in *Radical Orthodoxy: A New Theology*, ed. John Milbank, Catherine Pickstock, and Graham Ward (London: Routledge, 1999), 163–81.

[42] judaism.stackexchange.com/questions/50865/is-human-placenta-kosher. I have not consulted the original article, which is in Hebrew.

Why does Christian blood seem to do "too much"? Because part of its logic is to exceed: to issue over barriers, beyond boundaries, saturating veils, exposing interiors, undamming taboos to free up the power they contain. This way the blood can be, not suppressed, sanitized, driven underground, but released to cover others to be reborn. The crucifixion needed no blood, but blood figured in its aftermath; a natural birth sheds little blood, but blood figures in its afterbirth. The crucifixion is a scene of birth, a primal scene, the scene that artistic canons forbade and Marcionite sensibilities denied.

If you crucify a woman, does she bleed? Apparently not. That's too much like menstrual blood to show. There is an example in St. Wilgefortis, sometimes called St. Julia. The painting of Hieronymus Bosch shows her in a full-length dress and proves the rule about the blood of a woman – either she doesn't bleed, or the dress is impervious. The blood of Jesus, returned to a woman, is bound anew by the rules against the blood of a woman and once again Cannot Be Shown.

That suggests, to Sarah Jobe, another picture: "The sacrifice isn't childbirth, but bleeding monthly. That sacrifice makes birth possible," as Christ's bleeding makes possible the resurrection and the birthwaters of baptism. Taken over a lifetime, childbirth is not as bloody as menstruation, because "our blood disappears into the child" of rebirth and resurrection.[43]

The symbols of water and blood interfere and belong together, life and death likewise. Part of their power lies in the fact that we can hardly keep them apart. Christians want to say, "in the blood is the life." Christians want to say, *felix culpa*, God makes the crucifixion an occasion of new life. Christians want to say, Jesus puts pain to a purpose,[44] and the Spirit brings communities out of suffering. Christians want to say, the resurrection is new birth. Under those circumstances, Christians even want to say that Jesus, at the Last Supper, turns the crucifixion into another invitation to the feast, so that suffering brings new life and prepares the resurrection.

Those reflections show why we might want to talk here not only about childbirth but also, carefully, about menstruation. Because it gets rid of an ovum, we do not want to say, menstruation is the same as birth. Because it prepares the way for a new implantation, we do not want to say, menstruation is like death. Rather, menstruation may resemble crucifixion in that it prepares – it makes ready – for new life. It reaffirms, with Leviticus, that "the blood is the life." (The Levitical taboo against menstrual blood testifies to its protean

---

[43] Sarah Jobe, personal communication.
[44] I owe the phrase, used somewhat differently, to Jobe, 84.

100   BLOOD THEOLOGY

power: men may not touch the power of life itself,[45] any more than rockets may land on the sun.) There is something about its persistence, the persistence of blood, reappearing every month: "for blood is the life thereof."

Most mammals do not menstruate. They have estrous cycles, but only Old World primates, bats, and the elephant shrew overtly bleed. Most mammals isolate their periods of fertility. Humans remain in readiness, ovulating every month – practicing, like God, the openness to new life and renewed birth. People may often freight menstruation with a binary meaning – fertility or failure, "baby/no baby" – but even in that context, its habit of bleeding is a precondition for birth, the investment and sacrifice of bloody resources that a woman's body builds up and clears out every month "just in case":[46] this menstruation is less of a lost chance, and more of a costly renewal, in view of a perhaps, seventy times seven, holding a place where life might could be, a magnificent Mightcouldlichkeit. The blood of menstruation, because of its repetition, resembles the blood of the Eucharist: and if, as Barth says, the covenant grounds the creation, we might even say that the infinite blood of the covenant supplies the repeated blood of menstruation.[47] Those are some of the senses in which "the life is in the blood." Their persistence is another paradox of blood: the crucifixion means failure turned to hope, death turned to life, pain turned to purpose. Jesus *is* the bleeding woman, with her hope revealed.

That is why she appears by convention on early Christian sarcophagi, of which the Vatican alone holds at least six. What is she doing there? The woman finds her place among a series of miracles. They express a hope for the miracle of resurrection. But the resurrection they hope for is more than a miracle. Here too her recognizable sign is the cloth (the hem of Jesus) that will absorb her blood – in order to re-release it. *Her* healing restores the possibility of new life, as does the bleeding she transfers to Jesus. Saying, "Who touched me?" he acknowledges his kinship with her, and he absorbs her blood, the better to release new life. He becomes so much like a woman with an issue of blood, that their resurrection depends on it.

But we are not finished with the taboo that both hides and teaches the power of blood, the taboo that the Western Middle Ages called the *secreta mulierum*, "the secret secretions of women." The secret not only enacts the power of blood by hedging it with conditions – see how dangerous what cannot be seen! – it also increases and inflates it. In two widely separated

---

[45] David Biale, *Blood and Belief: The Circulation of a Symbol between Christians and Jews* (Berkeley: University of California Press, 2007), 35–6.

[46] I owe the idea and the phrasing to Sarah Jobe.

[47] I owe this idea to Greg Williams.

contexts, the secrecy surrounding secretions promotes their significance to render them cosmic. Like the matter of the Eucharist, women's blood became elemental.

Bettina Bildhauer interprets the medieval book by that title, *Secreta mulierum*, or *Secrets of Women* (pseudo-Albert the Great, ca. 1300) in terms of its more revealing, fifteenth-century South German commentary.[48] The "secret of women," to this presumably male author and his implied male audience, is their "secretion," menstrual blood. Doubly full of meaning, this blood is both the secret subject matter of the book and the material secretion of a woman's body, where both meanings emerge from the same, protean, medieval German word, "*matery*".[49]

But in the Aristotelian tradition of the Commentary on the *Secreta Mulierum* the wordplay is substantive. Menstrual blood is the very matter of the human being, since "every human being ... is naturally generated from the seed of his father and the flow of his mother, which is called menstruum."[50] On this picture, menstrual blood is not only "a woman's contribution to the generation of the embryo," but it furthermore "nourishes the embryo in the womb and, after it has been further concocted into breast milk, also the baby."[51] The idea that Christ is likewise made of Mary's blood is one reason why her own parents must conceive her "immaculately": so that her blood will not taint his.[52]

In a cosmic conjecture or conceit, that is also why Maximus the Confessor associates the matter of the Logos with the blood of the Virgin. Centuries before the *Secrets of Women*, Maximus had already heard that the whole matter of the incarnation arose from the Virgin's blood: "Some among the saints say that the soul is sown by the Holy Spirit in the manner of the man's seed and that the flesh is formed from the virginal blood"[53] (a pregnant remark, to which the final chapter will return). On this conception, the blood of Mary – which is here the same as her menstrual blood – builds up the embryo and nourishes the infant. Indeed, Mary's menstrual blood, on this conception, just is the blood of Jesus.[54]

---

[48] Bildhauer, 32 n. 40.

[49] Bildhauer, 37–8.

[50] Bildhauer, 34 n. 45, her translation.

[51] Bildhauer, 33.

[52] Bildhauer, 90.

[53] Maximus the Confessor, *Questiones et dubia*, #50 (complete), trans. Despina Prassas as *St. Maximus the Confessor's Questions and Doubts* (DeKalb: Illinois University Press, 2010), p. 72. Cf. Bettina Bildhauer, *Medieval Blood,* chapter on *Materei*.

[54] For more, see Excursus 1 at the end of this chapter.

102   BLOOD THEOLOGY

But his blood is not just any blood. By communication of the attributes, the blood of the human Jesus is the blood of the divine Logos. And the Logos, with the Father and the Spirit, is the Creator God; the Logos is the one to whom theologians appropriate the structure and rationality of the world. This is not yet to say that the matter of the world is menstrual blood, but something rather stranger: the matter of the *Creator* – the humanity that is the Creator's own – consists (absent any special pleading) of menstrual blood.

This is why the Woman with an Issue of Blood really matters. Jesus is her brother, and she is his sister, not only in the generic way in which Jesus is brother to all, but also in a more familiar way in which they are alike in their leakiness; they have inherited a family's hemophilia. The whole cosmos belongs to their family, if blood, menstrual blood is the matter of creation.

Earlier I said that observing childbirth should give the lie to the Aristotelian conception that blood is "mere matter." Bildhauer, reading Judith Butler, finds grounds already in Aristotle to bridge the divide between matter and form. Bodies that matter only make sense if Butler

> uses 'matter' not as opposed to form, as one could have assumed, but in a second, different sense: as always already attracting and striving for form. This second sense of matter, *hyle*, as a material which has at the same time generative, productive powers, 'a certain capacity to originate', is also implied in Aristotelian philosophy, [Butler] explains . . . . Bodies that matter in this sense, then, are bodies that are productive and significant, that have potentiality for form inherent in their matter. So matter is here no longer opposed to form, but participating in it.[55]

The biblical version of that idea appears in the Septuagint translations of all those verses from Genesis, Leviticus, and Deuteronomy that repeat that "the life is in the blood." The Septuagint, which is often the earliest witness to what the Hebrew might mean, translates the word *nephesh* (for which English has "life"), with the Greek word *psyche*. That picture does not put the soul, or the principle of animation (the Vulgate says "anima" in the same place) in the father's semen; it places it in the blood, which belongs to the mother.

The Christological version of that idea appears as the *logoi* in the Logos, the internal significations that the Logos builds into all created things, so that things, precisely in their createdness, participate in God's design. That doctrine leads up to Maximus's most profound and famous saying: "The Word of

---

[55] Bildhauer, 86, referring to Butler, *Bodies that Matter*, 16, 32.

God (who is God) is always and in all things seeking to accomplish the mystery of his embodiment."[56] The Logos strives, therefore, to bring forth in all things the matter – the blood – the menstrual blood – from which to become incarnate; and God enables them (all things) to strive with and into the Logos. That's more than matter seeking form; more than evolution; more than a providence that leads Israel or a teleology that lures the world. That is the matter of creation seeking to become God. The paradigm for that matter is the power in the blood of a woman. That's why Maximus can also say (in another remark to which the final chapter will return) that the "logoi of intelligible beings may be understood as the blood of the Logos."[57] Maximus doesn't spell it out, but he seems to imply that it's the blood of the Virgin – her menstrual blood – that strives in all things to make the world intelligible.

In the traditions common to Maximus the Confessor and the medieval literature of secrets, blood attains cosmic significance to become the matter of the universe and even of God. That blood is not just any blood, but menstrual blood, the blood of creation. That is the deeper reason, David Biale proposes, that the rabbis prohibit husbands from having sex with their menstruating wives: because creation is too powerful, too elemental, too cosmic for them to touch.[58]

What other blood could it be? It could, of course, be the blood of sacrifice. But if menstruation and childbirth are sacrifice, and the sacrifice of the Logos brings rebirth . . . . After all, when Jesus and women, it is their own blood that they shed. Jesus and women bleed for their children. In this Jesus resembles his mother, or his mother resembles him.

"Did the woman say, /When she held him for the first time in the dark of a stable, /After the pain and the bleeding and the crying, /'This is my body, this is my blood'?"[59]

---

[56] Maximus the Confessor, *Ambigua*, translated as *On Difficulties in the Church Fathers* by Nicholas Constas, English and Greek text on facing pages (Washington, DC: Dumbarton Oaks Press, 2014–15), cited by Migne number. Here 1084C-D.

[57] Maximos the Confessor, *Ad Thalassium* 35, ed. and trans. Fr. Maximos [Nicholas] Constas in *On Difficulties in Sacred Scripture: The Responses to Thalassios*, Fathers of the Church Series 136 (Washington, DC: Catholic University of America Press, 2018), 212–14.

[58] Biale, 35–6.

[59] Frances Croake Frank, *Did the Woman Say? in Celebrating Women*, ed. Hannah Ward, Jennifer Wild, and Janet Morley (Harrisburg, PA: Morehouse Publishing, 1986). I am grateful to Nancy Duff for the reference.

Excursus 1 Is the Blood of Jesus Menstrual Blood in Thomas Aquinas and John of Damascus?

The inference that the blood of Jesus is the menstrual blood of Mary is both so cogent that Thomas Aquinas seems explicitly to admit it: "Other men's bodies are formed from the semen and the menstrual blood" (*ST* III.31.5 obj. 3) – and so shocking that he finds it necessary to distinguish it: "Of such menstrual blood infected with corruption and repudiated by nature, the conception [of Christ] is not formed; but from a certain secretion of the pure blood which *by a process of elimination* is prepared for conception" (*ST* III.31.5 *ad* 3). That sounds as if Jesus had to be protected from the very impurity he came to cure. I believe it is not meant to be. Rather, Aquinas means to distinguish the blood that remains in the body and (by the fact that it remains) is presumed pure, from the blood that leaves the body and (by the fact that it leaves) is presumed to be carrying impurities away. He does not say that there are two kinds of blood, one of which is in itself impure. His reasoning is no special pleading about the intervention of the Holy Spirit; his reasoning is Aristotelian and qualifies the conception of every human being, since "the Blessed Virgin was of the same nature as every woman" (*ad* 1).

Thomas's own remark that, so far from needing protection, "Christ came to heal what was corrupt" (*ad* 1) suggests a rather better interpretation of Mary's blood than Thomas actually offers. John of Damascus, whom Thomas quotes as his authority, had written that "the Son of God, from the Virgin's purest blood, formed himself flesh, animated with a rational soul." Aquinas takes "purest" as a restrictive adjective. But John's fuller phrasing, "her holy and most pure blood," suggests that the adjective "purest" does not filter but elevates Mary's blood. We should translate not (restrictively) "from her purest blood," but (descriptively) "from her blood most pure."[60] So far from needing filtering, the blood of Mary receives such purity from the self-forming body of Christ as to dignify her blood with an agency of its own, so that "the pure and undefiled blood of the holy and ever-virginal One made His flesh without the aid of seed" (III.13). John's mechanism of purity is just as general as the one Thomas takes from Aristotle, but here it is the work of the Logos deifying the whole human race – dignifying the Virgin as all human beings, purifying her blood as the blood of all sinners.

---

[60] John of Damascus, *The Orthodox Faith*, trans. E. W. Watson and L. Pullan *in Nicene and Post-Nicene Fathers*, Second Series, vol. 9, ed. Philip Schaff and Henry Wace (Buffalo, NY: Christian Literature Publishing Co., 1899, et al.), III.2.

JESUS AND THE GENDER OF BLOOD

Mary's blood needs no special pleading or filtering, because her purification is just the first of her son's work. His conception purifies the waters of her womb just as his baptism purifies the waters of the Jordan: not because he needs purity, but because other humans do. John includes Mary in that process because all humans need it; he does not exclude her from it out of danger to Christ. John's general principle that "creation has been sanctified by the divine blood" (III.4) applies first of all to Mary and her blood as the beginning of a sanctification that reaches back as far as sin: "He was made flesh and became [hu]man from [Mary's] pure and immaculate flesh and blood, satisfying the debt of the first mother [Eve]" (III.14). By Aristotle or Damascene, Christ's blood is not only Mary's blood, but her menstrual blood most pure.

Excursus 2 on Menstruation and the Origin of the Word "Taboo"

Speaking of things Maori – isn't there a Maori or Polynesian clue that makes the relation between "menstruation" and "taboo" much more immediate and direct? The legendary fact-checkers at *The New Yorker* have allowed their author to write "it is believed"[61] that the word "tabu" just comes from a Polynesian word for menstruation. Their careful formulation is true enough: it is so believed. The internet certainly thinks so. The internet tells you that *tapu*, the source of our "taboo," comes from *tapua,* which is widely believed (on the evidence of a Google search), to mean "menstruation." (The *b/p* variation occurs only in English and dates from Captain Cook. Polynesian languages have a single phoneme, represented in most of them by *p*.) Given the attractiveness of such a claim, it is frustrating that "*tapua*" appears in no Polynesian dictionaries.

All the formulations with "*tapua*" with an *a* as the first vowel – which turns out not to be the actual word – seem to descend from Judy Grahn.[62] Grahn cites Robert Briffault's classic *The Mothers*, a sort of proto-feminist *Golden Bough*. Briffault writes, "The Polynesian word 'tabu,' or 'tapu,' appears to be closely allied to the word 'tupua' [first vowel a *u*], which in Polynesian languages signifies 'menstruation.'"[63] Grahn has changed the first vowel of *tupua* from *u* to *a* (which are distinct, indeed far apart, in Polynesian languages), no doubt without conscious intent. The change does tend to improve the fit between the original *tupua* and the targeted *tapu* to promote it from a theory to a meme.

Briffault cites Tregear's venerable *Maori-Polynesian Comparative Dictionary* of 1891.[64] Under "tapu" (472 col. 2), a warrior touching a menstruating woman comes as the sixth and last example, but Tregear gives no indication of an etymological relationship, nor even any indication that the last example gives rise to the concept. It would almost be surprising, of course, if menstruation did not appear as an *example* of taboo.

Briffault's *tupua* with a *u* for the first vowel does appear in Polynesian dictionaries. Under *tupua* (with a *u* as the first vowel), as actually referenced

---

[61] Jerome Groopman, "Pumped: The Story of Blood" (review of *Nine Pints*), *The New Yorker*, vol. 94, no. 44 (Jan. 14, 2019), 58–64; here, p. 60, col. 1.

[62] Judy Grahn, *Blood, Bread, and Roses: How Menstruation Created the World* (Boston: Beacon Press, 1994), 4.

[63] Robert Briffault, *The Mothers: A Study of the Origins of Sentiments and Institutions*, 3 vols. (New York: Macmillan, 1927); here, vol. 2, 412. A one-volume, abridged version is more common but lacks the relevant discussion.

[64] Edward Tregear, *Maori-Polynesian Comparative Dictionary* (Wellington, NZ: Lyon and Blair), 1891. Searchable facsimile: archive.org/details/maoripolynesiano1treggoog/

by Briffault, we find again no reference to menstruation. But every page displays its first and last words in the header, and on that page *tupua* rides the header. So you could be forgiven for thinking that you were in that entry when you *did* glimpse a word related to menstruation. Higher up in the same column as *tupua*, but under the verb *tupu/tubu,* "to increase, to grow," we find the compound *tubukohi* (with a *b*) for menarche (p. 557, col. 1, s.v. *tupu; ko* and *hine* are both terms for "girl," s.v. *kohine,* p. 156, col. 1); it seems to mean something like "a girl grown up," in my conjecture: not much like taboo. The only verb defined as "menstruate" – and presumably there are also other verbs – is *maringi*, "to spill" (p. 217, col. 1). At the end of the volume lies a simplified English-to-Maori dictionary; under the English word "menses" (p. 679, one column), it gives two choices, *tahe* and *pakehe*. At the end of the trail, there appears to be no evidence that Polynesian languages derived the word *tapu* or taboo from a word for menstruation.

I wish it were true. The fact that we would like so much for it to be true, that we note with such satisfaction the idea that it should be true, and that we take it so readily to be true – those are facts about ourselves. I'm not suggesting that anyone is consciously trying to massage the evidence. But our wish fulfillment, with its chain of subconsciously motivated misprisions, is telling. Briffault takes a compound from *tubu* "to grow" and transfers it to *tupua*. Grahn takes the *a* from *tapu* and improves *tupua* to *tapua*. No one checks back to see what the menstruation words might be. Such beliefs and conjectures say something about us. We would certainly like to think that menstruation is *the* taboo, the Original Taboo, the Ur-taboo – because perhaps it is among the strongest taboos for us.[65]

---

[65] The standard etymology, "set apart, forbidden," is, after all, just a definition. Either that is as much as we know, or the word is composed of the element *ta*, in its meaning of "to mark" (p. 437, col. 1, definitions 14–16), as perhaps in "tattoo" (s.v. *tau,* p. 487 col. 1); and the intensifier *pu* (p. 864, col. 1, "exceedingly"). Again the etymology is suggestive even if it is not secure: taboos and blood both mark intensively.

Excursus 3 The *Pneuma* Is in the Blood

Late Antique Greek *pneuma* was a fluid *stuff*, not transcendent God; as such it animated and circulated in blood and semen, which had much to do with Paul's metaphors of the Holy Spirit creating "children" of God (literally sons, or children who inherit). The idea persisted well into the Middle Ages, including Aquinas.[66] Semen is also another form of blood – the kind that makes children blood relatives to their fathers.[67]

In the bits of Aristotle that separate matter and form, a child resembles mother and father for different reasons. The mother supplies the matter, but the father supplies the movement and origin. The father, therefore, contributes to the fetus its "shape and character."[68] Philo reports that "similarities of body and soul ... are preserved in seminal principles (*en tois spermatikois logois*)."[69] But – and here is where adoption and natural birth come together – a Greek or Roman father has to formally accept even his biological child, admitting it into the family by ritual.[70] This ritual is sacrifice, the ceremonious slaughter and eating together of a large animal. The father offers a sacrifice, legitimates the child, and gives the child a name. Baptism, the ritual drowning that makes a child of God, and Eucharist, the ritual breaking that names Christians after Christ, both retain elements of a father's accepting children by sacrifice. In inheritance disputes, family members had to testify that a father had admitted his heirs to family feasts. So Apollodorus testifies: "[My adoptive father] conducted me to the altars and to the members of the extended family and the clan. With them the same law applies both when someone introduces a natural son or an adopted son: he must swear with his hand on the sacrificial animal [about] the child whom he introduces, whether his own or an adopted son."[71]

Through the ritual of shared sacrifice, even adopted children "shared blood" with their adoptive fathers and brothers:[72] "Greek texts intuit an

---

[66] See the discussion at the end of the next chapter.

[67] For more about this, see Rogers, "How the Semen of the Spirit Genders the Gentiles," in *Aquinas and the Supreme Court: Race, Gender, and the Failure of Natural Law in Thomas's Biblical Commentaries* (Oxford: Blackwell, 2013), 289–97.

[68] Caroline Johnson Hodge, *If Sons, Then Heirs: A Study of Kinship and Ethnicity in the Letters of Paul* (Oxford: Oxford University Press, 2007), 94–5.

[69] Quoted in Hodge, 27.

[70] Hodge, 27.

[71] Quoted in Hodge, 29.

[72] Hodge, 27; Jay, 107–8.

analogy between sacrifice and men's control of childbirth because sacrifice actually effected paternal control of children."[73] "Through sacrifice, children [receive] a place in the father's lineage; through ritual, men beget their heirs."[74] Nancy Jay puts it even more starkly: male sacrifice seeks to give birth culturally, by *cultus* or, literally, cutting; men seek, in short, to "do birth better."[75]

It is thus that the *pneuma* of the father naturalizes associations with sacrifice and feasting, fire and wine: because of deeply rooted cultural (or cultic) *practices*. Those associations do not float free of embodied activities like killing and eating; they arise from them.

Paul insists that Gentiles receive sonship of God by adoption (*huiothesia*, placing sons). Greco-Roman eulogies and encomia say that adopted children resemble their adoptive *patres*: but how? Indeed, children resemble even *invented* ancestors, and they resemble adoptive ones even when everybody knows they're adopted. Thus Julius Caesar claims descent from the goddess Venus, and Cicero continues to record genealogies he recognizes as decked out with "feigned triumphs" and "too many consulships."[76] If Cicero winks at inventions even as he perpetuates them, how much more easily can the rhetoric of family resemblance accommodate the adopted who may learn their posture and character from adoptive *patres*, absorbing it, as we say in English, from the air? That's not so far from saying, from the *pneuma*, which also means air. "The historian Diodorus of Sicily describes the heritage of Publius Scipio, who was not only born to a famous father, but also 'given in adoption to Scipio.' Diodorus goes on to cite both the birth *and* the adoptive family to prove the worth [of Publius]: 'Sprung from such stock, and succeeding to a family and clan of such importance, he showed himself worthy of *the fame of his ancestors*.'"[77] Which set of ancestors? Both. Is there a *pneuma* theory for adoption? Can it animate the air or circulate in the household? Certainly: but my application to adoption is an inference; so far I have no sources to tell me so directly.

Reading Durkheim would also make you think so. According to Durkheim, societies establish facts when they entrench them in individual

---

[73] Stanley Stowers, "Greeks Who Sacrifice and Those Who Do Not: Toward an Anthropology of Greek Religion," in *The Social World of the Earliest Christians: Essays in Honor of Wayne A. Meeks*, ed. L. M. White and O. L. Yarborough (Minneapolis, MN: Fortress Press, 1995), 293–333; here, 301.

[74] Hodge, 27.

[75] Jay, 17.

[76] Hodge, 19, 32.

[77] Hodge, 30, citing Diodorus, *Bibliotheca historica XXXI.26.4*, ed. and trans. Francis R. Walton (Cambridge: Harvard University Press, 1957).

minds, and societies entrench facts in individual minds when they meet together in "reunions" and generate "moral effervescence,"[78] social "juice" or electricity, such as at sacrifices, family feasts, Tigers' games, or the donning of the gowns. In Christianity, the social juice is the Holy Spirit – unless of course it's blood – and one of the effervescent reunions is the baptism with its extended families and fictive kin or godparents. I would like to say: Paul's adoption metaphors depend on a Greco-Roman adoption discourse according to which adopted sons resemble adoptive fathers by *pneuma*, which circulated both in the semen or blood (for biological children) and in the air or in the household (for adopted children). *Pneuma* would have circulated also in the blood and meat and community of sacrifice, as it does in the Eucharist, to leaven the bread and enflame the wine. Certainly, *Christianity* has a *pneuma* theory for adoption. It's called baptism. In it we find both sacrifice – by drowning – and birth done better, in the womb of the font. The Spirit, a fluid, extends by *krasis*, or mixing, into the water. So it extends all the more readily into that sacrifice in which the Son makes brothers by sharing his blood, into that mixed substance that modern Greek calls *krasi*, the wine: which celebrates the wedding feast that a father throws for his son, where the son says to his spouse, "this is my body, given for you."

The Spirit, I propose, is, even in antiquity, not *merely* a physical thing, but a *para*physical thing: one that works with and alongside but exceeds the physical. (I reclaim the notorious phrase of Romans 1 that refers to excessive Gentile love of men for men or women for women, because Paul repeats it in Romans 11 to describe the excessive love of Gentiles by God.[79]) Later theologians would think about the Spirit in terms of immanence and transcendence, but the ancients had no moderns to go by. Paul, as it happens, uses notably parabiological or paraphysical metaphors to include Gentiles. If Jews are God's children by nature, Gentiles become God's children by adoption; they are "fellow" heirs; the Spirit must *teach* them to call God "Father," which Jews already know; in Romans 11 Gentiles form branches *grafted* explicitly *para phusin*, in excess of nature, into the unaccustomed clefts of the Jewish olive tree. Normal would be to graft sweet or oil-rich olives onto

[78] Emile Durkheim, *The Elementary Forms of the Religious Life* (New York: Free Press, 1965), 240–2.

[79] See Eugene F. Rogers, Jr., "The Spirit Rests on the Son Paraphysically," in *The Lord and Giver of Life: Perspectives on Constructive Pneumatology*, ed. David H. Jensen (Philadelphia: Westminster/John Knox, 2008), 87–95, 174–6; "Paul on Exceeding Nature: Queer Gentiles and the Giddy Gardener," in F. S. Roden, ed., *Jewish/Christian/Queer: Crossroads and Identities* (Aldershot, Hants.: Ashgate, 2009), 19–33; and "How the Semen of the Spirit Genders the Gentiles," cited above.

the more vigorous rootstock of a wild tree; but God does the opposite, grafting *wild*, good-for-nothing olives onto a perfectly good domestic stock. This God is no longer the sober agriculturalist of Eden but a loopy plant-fancier: this God is a giddy gardener.[80] All these metaphors are paraphysical: they extend even to the breaking point the metaphors of kinship. Paul's "Spirit of adoption" also works paraphysically, expanding nature according to Greco-Roman adoption theory, where the father's *pneuma* is not just "spirit," but seminal fluid. Somehow, it causes both biological and adoptive children to resemble him.[81]

Shall we apply this analysis also to the wine, which is the blood of the community: *pneuma* animates blood, and therefore wine? On this view, the spirit in the wine is not only alcohol: it goes deeper: it belongs also to the blood. Christians certainly *pray* that the Spirit will be in the blood: "Send forth Thy Holy Spirit upon these Thy creatures of bread and wine that they may be fitted to become the Body and Blood of Thy Son."[82]

---

[80] These sentences first appeared to different purpose in "Giddy Gardener," 25–6.

[81] This idea first occurred to me in conversation with Stanley Stowers; it seems to be implied, but never quite stated, in Stan Stowers, "Matter and Spirit, or What Is Pauline Participation in Christ," *The Holy Spirit: Classic & Contemporary Readings*, ed. Eugene F. Rogers, Jr. (Oxford: Wiley-Blackwell, 2009), 92–105.

[82] Variations are common; this version appears in *Eucharistic Devotions* (London: Joseph Masters, 1870), 34. Greg Williams suggested that I quote it here.

Excursus 4 on Philoxenus of Mabbug

Why does the history of exegesis connect the blood of sacrifice so rarely to blood gendered female? (For the answer, see Nancy Jay.) In the history of exegesis of Hebrews 9:22, "without the shedding of blood there is no remission of sin," most commentators take blood so for granted that they have little to say – it's a premise for them, nothing they have to justify. The one exception I know of seems so far-fetched that one has to reach for subconscious motivation, Freudian repression, or a hermeneutics of suspicion to explain the connection between the labor of asceticism and the labor of childbirth that seems, after Nancy Jay, to leap to the eye. The Syriac bishop, theologian, and translator Philoxenus of Mabbug (d. 523) is plenty suggestive in his "Letter to Abba Symeon of Caesarea"[83] – even if he doesn't seem to know what or how much he's suggesting. I put some leading questions in square brackets.

> The practice of the commandments is not accomplished simply and by chance, for it is written that "without the shedding of blood there is no forgiveness of sins." [How does that follow exactly?] Our nature first received renewal [What does "renewal" mean? Can it mean rebirth?] through the incarnation of Christ, and it participated in his passion and death. Then, after the renewal of the shedding of blood [What does "renewal of the shedding of blood" mean? Presumably it means "after the renewal wrought by Christ's shedding of blood. "But am I wrong to think of women's monthly renewal of the shedding of blood?] our nature was renewed and sanctified and became able to receive his new and perfect commandments. . . . [N]ow there is a secret labor [Can this include labor in the sense of bringing to birth, or must it be only work and nothing else?] that accompanies the new spiritual commandments. When the soul keeps these through the circumspection of the fear of God, they renew it, sanctify it and secretly heal all its members. . . . The operation of the commandments is perceived only by the healer and the healed, after the likeness of the woman who had an issue of blood.

My leading questions suggest, in short, that there is no forgiveness of sins without rebirth and the labor thereof, so that the blood without which there

---

[83] Philoxenus of Mabbug, "Letter to Abba Symeon of Caesarea," in Erik Heen and Phillip D. W. Krey, *Hebrews*, Ancient Christian Commentary series, New Testament vol. 10 (Downers Grove, IL: IVP Academic, 2005), under Hebrews 9:22. Although modern scholars attribute the text to Philoxenus, it comes down to us among the writings of Isaac of Ninevah, and hence the Ancient Christian Commentary takes it from *Ascetical Homilies of St. Isaac the Syrian*, trans. Holy Transfiguration Monastery [Dana Miller] (Boston: Holy Transfiguration Monastery, 1984), 427–48; here, 436.

JESUS AND THE GENDER OF BLOOD 113

is no remission is the blood of fertility. This genders feminine both the believer and the blood. Furthermore, it does so secretly, hiddenly, or circumspectly, because the blood of childbirth recalls the woman with an issue of blood, where the blood of healing keeps itself secret. The blood of life, that is, remains as secret as the blood of menstruation to men, or the rebirth of the heart, wherein Christ is born within the believer.

Perhaps this interpretation is what Harold Bloom calls a strong misreading. The Syriac text hardly supports it. The word for labor or working is *'amla,* which is not used for the labor of childbirth. One correspondent writes that, since the blood of renewal is that of the cross, Philoxenus's "blood is definitely *not* gendered female, [not] blood associated with menstruation or childbirth [but] clearly is gendered male, sacrificial blood (thinking back to Nancy Jay, so to speak)."

Well, yes, the blood of Hebrews 9:22 must always be the labor of the cross, but that could include the labor of childbirth. And yes, Evagrian asceticism is a work this text genders male, but must the text mean that alone? After Bynum made it commonplace that in the West the monk – especially the Cistercian – labors to give birth with the labor of Mary, in the East, later than Philoxenus, Symeon the New Theologian considers spiritual pregnancy. Philoxenus does not know those texts. Consider another text that aligns men's and women's labor, one that Philoxenus does know:

In Genesis 3, God curses both the woman (v. 16) and the man (v. 17) with labor/pain/suffering (עִצָּבוֹן). That word distinguishes in order to unite; man and woman alike are punished with עֶצֶב, labor, whether on the land or in childbirth. In the Syriac Bible, the Peshitta, the word in both verses is also the same; it is *ci'ba',* which means pain, as in childbirth or illness. In both Hebrew and Syriac, Genesis unites the gendered labor of men and women under a single word that includes childbirth. In Philoxenus, therefore, we find a tension between prominent Evagrian words that exclude the labor of women and the tacit Genesis intertext that includes it.

Is it possible that an underlying or even unconscious picture connects the blood of atonement to the labor of childbirth – but has been rendered appropriate to a male, ascetic recipient and somewhat wider audience by using words from the Evagrian tradition of male ascetics – in order to avoid words for labor gendered feminine?

My correspondent's reference to Nancy Jay is pregnant. Jay argues not only that sacrifice produces a blood and a line gendered male, while childbirth, which men interpret as bloody, produces a "blood" and a line gendered female. Jay argues also that those separated things belong together, because sacrificing traditions attempt to create a male patriline that "does birth better," that is, culturally rather than biologically. The blood of sacrifice, gendered male, *is also* a "blood" of childbirth. Or more accurately, the blood of sacrifice is one that men associate culturally with childbirth, even though biologically childbirth ought not to produce too much bleeding. Or even: For Nancy Jay and her readers, the blood of sacrifice, gendered male, *just is* the imagined "blood" of childbirth, transmuted into the culture of a patriline, a culturally constructed lineage of fathers and sons. The imaging of childbirth that gives sacrifice rise must therefore be present even when hidden. Thanks to Jay, I'm wondering whether these sacrificial versions of labor are gendered male in such a way that they hide, deny, repress, or repel connections otherwise apparent between ascetic labor and labor of childbirth. If childbirth becomes a metaphor that the ascetic must avoid, then that has its own interest. In "Marian Dogmas and Taboos," Cleo Kearns has done something much more sophisticated with instances where Catholic devotion to Mary grants her priestly attributes (as when she offers Christ in the Temple at his circumcision) and then runs screaming in the other direction with Jay-inflected denials.[84] Jay, like Genesis, genders in order to unite. Jesus, like the ascetic, sacrifices in order to renew; his blood, like the labor of childbirth, brings new life, as innocent as a baby. Childbirth, especially if it turns out like Rachel's, is also sacrifice.

Stillbirth, miscarriage, and menstruation as well. In the twelfth century, Rabbi Joseph Bekhor Shor argued that women need not be circumcised, because they menstruate. Circumcision is sacrifice: therefore menstruation is also.[85] Nancy Jay would see that logic as backwards and reverse it. Menstruation is naturally sacrifice. Circumcision is menstruation done culturally, by cutting.

---

[84] Cleo McNelly Kearns, *The Virgin Mary, Monotheism, and Sacrifice* (Cambridge: Cambridge University Press, 2008), 258–92.

[85] Shaye Cohen, *Why Aren't Jewish Women Circumcised: Gender and Covenant in Judaism* (Berkeley: University of California Press, 2005), xv, 192–8, 205–6. I owe my attention to these passages to Ellen Haskell.

PART III

Blood Makes a Language in Which to Conduct Disputes

Family, Truth, and Tribe

BECAUSE THE BLOOD OF CHRIST ACTS AS TOTEM OR TOUCHstone, Christians also conduct their disputes in the languages of blood.

The disputes in Part III invoke the language of blood, whether they touch blood's reality or not. This Part is not social ethics, but cultural anthropology where theology overlaps. It shows how blood-talk circulates underground, and bubbles to the surface, when civic reasoning grows anemic.

The disputes Christians conduct in terms of blood include the largest issues. Rival theories of atonement depend on whether Christ's blood means his life or his death. Creationists reject evolution because animal death before human sin would seem to limit the scope of Christ's blood. Lefevrite Catholics say women's hands on a chalice defile the blood of Christ,[1] while liberal opponents appeal to Mary's sacrifice in childbirth. Ex-gay ministries claim same-sex

---

[1] Nancy Jay, *Throughout Your Generations Forever: Sacrifice, Religion, and Paternity* (Chicago: University of Chicago Press, 1992), 120–7.

couples "impugn the blood of Christ"; defenders say they revive it. The examples press social issues that lean on blood's logic: Do same-sex couples count as family? Is evolution true? Which if any wars are just? The last three examples disclose current blood discourses of family, truth, and tribe.

Blood does not explain everything. But it explains aspects at the margins that otherwise escape us. The point is not life *or* death, death bloody *or* unbloody. The point is that blood discourse governs all those cases as the language in which Christians argue them. The topic is not blood biological or symbolic, but any kind of blood invested with meaning, any type of blood that funds dispute.

5

BRIDEGROOMS OF BLOOD
Same-Sex Desire and the Blood of Christ

I

From 2007 to 2009 I sat on an expert panel to advise the House of Bishops of the U.S. Episcopal Church on "a theology of same-sex relationships" – that was the charge.[2] Of everything the panelists said – Ph.D.s teaching at respected institutions – the most arresting to an anthropologist of religion might be "The trouble with same-sex relationships is, they impugn the blood of Christ."[3] They do *what*? "Impugn the blood of Christ." After I got over being offended, I found myself fascinated. What could the statement possibly mean? What would an anthropologist say? The original remark attempted a hazing; the final result bestowed a gift, the gift of blood made strange. The familiar, domesticated language of "the blood of Christ" became again, as it was in the beginning, the occasion of offense. What tribe was this, with their strange ways and their even stranger bloody-mindedness?

This chapter turns on two sentences. The first you have just read: same-sex couples "impugn the blood of Christ." I use Religious Studies categories to understand that sentence, which I call the antithesis; I conclude

---

[2] Our reports occupy the entire issue of the *Anglican Theological Review* 93.1 (Winter 2011), consisting of a "liberal" paper, a "traditionalist" paper, a response to each "side" by the other, and further responses by multiple authors around the Anglican Communion. My work appears in "A Theology of Marriage Including Same-Sex Couples," by Deirdre Good, Willis Jenkins, Cynthia Kittredge, and Eugene Rogers, *Anglican Theological Review* 93 (2011): 51–87 (authors alphabetical; Rogers 75%), and "Liberal Response," by Deirdre Good, Willis Jenkins, Cynthia Kittredge, and Eugene Rogers, *Anglican Theological Review* 93 (2011): 101–10 (authors alphabetical; Rogers 40%). Online at Same-Sex Relationships in the Life of the Church offered by the Theology Committee of the House of Bishops. A short account of the panel's work appears in Eugene F. Rogers, Jr., "Same-Sex Complementarity," *Christian Century* 128.10 (May 17, 2011): 26–9, 31.

[3] The remark does not appear in the publications above. It took place orally at one of the panel meetings in Pasadena, I believe in 2009.

that blood-of-Christ language, like same-sex couples, is not going away, but can only be reclaimed. Then I use theological categories to elaborate a second sentence, which I call the thesis: The thief on the cross is the bride of Christ. Thus two opposing sentences: Same-sex couples impugn Christ's blood; and The thief on the cross is his bride. Repurposing a phrase from Exodus 4:25, I observe (with others) that Christ is a bridegroom of blood.

II

I argued in the previous chapter that blood acquires gendered roles because we use it to reinforce two genders regarded as binary – and that Jesus's use of blood (because Jesus is God) exceeds, explodes, and necessarily queers gendered categories.[4] Gendered blood is no ancient prejudice only, but marks Christianity today. Nancy Jay observes that Catholics and Eastern Orthodox, who regard the Eucharist as chiefly reenacting Christ's sacrifice, call their leaders "priests" (meaning *sacrificers*) and restrict that role to men, while Protestants, who regard the Eucharist as chiefly reenacting Christ's supper, call their leaders "ministers" (serving a meal) and more easily open that role to women. Anglicans, in between, are split.[5]

"Ex-gay" ministries also use blood-of-Christ language to police gender roles. Blood is supposed to wash gay people with the atonement, even as self-accepting gay people say they don't need cleansing. The blood of Christ is supposed to unite Christians in the cup of the Eucharist, even as debates over sexuality divide the churches. The blood of Christ is supposed to protect the apostolic succession, even as bishops protect priests for sexual crimes. To conservative Christians, those *failures* of the blood of Christ bring nothing less than a cosmological disturbance.

"Impugning the blood" is the negative, in some versions of Christianity, of "pleading the blood," which arises from the book of Revelation: "And they overcame him by the blood of the Lamb" (12:11).

> We can and should remind Satan of the power of Jesus's blood. There is nothing wrong with saying "I plead the blood of Jesus" when under spiritual attack. . . . [T]here is nothing magical in the statement; the power is in the authority conferred to us through the shedding of Christ's blood. When we plead the blood, we are acknowledging that we are not worthy to be a part of God's kingdom, but His blood has made us worthy. And as priests of this new blood covenant in Christ, we have been given authority to deal with the enemy.[6]

---

[4] I owe the second half of this sentence to comments by Gregory Williams in similar words.

[5] Nancy Jay, *Throughout Your Generations Forever: Sacrifice, Religion, and Paternity* (Chicago: University of Chicago Press, 1992), xxiv, 113–14, 115, 126–7.

[6] Ray Beeson, *Signed in His Blood: God's Ultimate Weapon for Spiritual Warfare* (Lake Mary, FL: Charism House Book Group, 2014), 166.

"He placed his hands upon his own body and for twenty minutes pleaded the Blood of Jesus, saying, 'I plead the Blood of Jesus,' over and over again. The result of this attack on Satan's effort to destroy him was that he was completely healed [of ptomaine poisoning]. Others find that the simple repetition of the one word 'Blood' is sufficient. There are no rules; it is the simple offering of the Blood of Jesus in faith, as priests of the New Testament, which brings results. God will hear the Blood-cry and will respect that which it has purchased for us."[7]

To some anti-gay Christians, same-sex couples seem to impugn, mock, or slander the blood of Christ, by implying that there is something the blood of Christ cannot heal or change. Some conservative Christians with doctorates and social work degrees have argued that accepting same-sex attraction is, as their article titles it, "A Slippery Slope that Limits the Atonement," explaining that "The Gospel of Jesus Christ is a gospel of change, and we (including those who struggle with homosexual attraction) cannot sink lower than the arms of the Atonement can reach."[8]

Apparently, same-sex couples command greater superpowers than mere slander; anti-gay Christians credit them with overcoming the atonement altogether. Families, clergy people, and ex-gay ministries plead the blood of Christ and invoke it to cover the sin.[9] *And it doesn't work.* The blood of Christ can cover murder, and it can't change gay people? That's the cosmological disturbance. Something seems to be stronger than the blood of Christ. *And it's same-sex couples?*

Of course, there is another answer. Same-sex couples don't threaten belief in the atonement, if homosexuality is not in itself a sin – or not any more infected with sin than heterosexuality is. In that case, the blood is pleading not guilty.

III

Durkheim, Mary Douglas, Nancy Jay, and Bettina Bildhauer illuminate blood-structures in Christianity and other social groups that cause the body individual or the body sacrificed to represent the body social.

---

[7] Ray Beeson, *Signed in His Blood* (Lake Mary, FL: Charism House Book Group, 2014), 166–7, quoting H. A. Maxwell Whyte, *The Power of Blood* (n.p., n.d.), 74.

[8] A. Dean Byrd, Ph.D., MBA, MPH; Shirley E. Cox, DSW, LCSW; and Jeffrey W. Robinson, Ph.D., "A Slippery Slope that Limits the Atonement," *FAIR (Foundation for Apologetic Information and Research)*, 2009, www.fairmormon.org/archive/fairmormon-journal/fj200507-html. The first author led the National Association for Research & Therapy of Homosexuality in attempting to change sexual orientations.

[9] On the blood of Christ invoked to prevent or remove evils of other kinds, see also Samuel Olaweraju, "The Efficacy of Prayer in the Blood of Christ in Contemporary African Christianity," *Africa Journal of Evangelical Theology* 22 (2003): 31–49.

120   BLOOD THEOLOGY

Blood may be red because iron compounds make it so, but societies draft its color and stickiness for multiple purposes of their own. We imagine individual, social, and animal bodies as securely bounded. "Inside," blood carries life. "Outside," blood marks the body at risk. According to Bildhauer, society's work to maintain bodily integrity thus takes place in blood. It's the body's permeability that leaves us bloody-minded; it's in terms of blood that society makes a body. The body becomes a membrane to pass when it breathes, eats, perspires, eliminates, ejaculates, menstruates, conceives, or bleeds. Only bleeding evokes so swift and public a response: blood brings mother to child, bystander to victim, ambulance to patient, soldier to comrade, midwife to mother, defender to border. When society is a body, society's integrity is blood's work.

Since Durkheim, students of religion have called the totem "the elementary form of religious life." Since Maximus Confessor, and reaching a high point in Thomas Aquinas, theologians have insisted on working by "analogy." In Christian theology, "analogy" is no literary comparison, but names competing accounts of the largest repeating structures that hold the symbol system together. But theologians and anthropologists need not quarrel over terms. "Analogy" is just the theological word for "totemism." Or, "totemism" is just the secular word with which sociology acknowledges analogy. Aquinas and Durkheim would agree that Christianity paints a pattern according to which the body of Jesus is the body of Christ; the church is the body of Christ; the bread of the Eucharist is the body of Christ; the believer belongs to the body of Christ; the crucifix around her neck displays the body of Christ; and the body of Christ is the body of God. No Christianity exists without some version of this pattern, which theology calls "analogy" and Durkheim "totemism."

Closely allied with the body of Christ is his blood, which the New Testament cites three times as often as his "cross" and five times as often as his "death." The blood from the cross is the blood of Christ; the wine of the Eucharist is the blood of Christ; the means of atonement is the blood of Christ; the unity of the church is the blood of Christ; the kinship of believers is the blood of Christ; the cup of salvation is the blood of Christ; icons ooze the blood of Christ; and the blood of Christ is the blood of God.

"The blood of Christ" works by analogy in Christian theology and as totem in Christian practice. It names a large-scale structure that holds together cosmology, fictive kinship, gender roles, ritual practices, atonement for sin, solidarity in suffering, and recruits history, geography, and martyrdoms to its purposes. Unlike cleansing/defiling and inside/outside, the analogical or totemic structure escapes the binary, although it can uphold or undermine binaries at need. When conflict reveals the body as penetrable, we glimpse that the body does not define itself, but society uses its bleeding to redline its borders. Lately issues as diverse as atonement, evolution, women's leadership, and same-sex marriage disturb and revive the symbol system that the blood of Christ structures, cleanses, and unites. In theology and anthropology, blood outside the body

BRIDEGROOMS OF BLOOD 121

is matter out of place: Abel's blood cries out from the ground. But menstruation and childbirth present an alternative picture, where outside blood promises new life. Exegetes argue whether the blood of Christ means life or death, but blood provides the language within which they disagree.

Given that status, blood becomes "natural" for Christians to think with. How indeed could it be otherwise? Something that resisted analysis in terms of Christ's blood would be either irrelevant to the whole complex of relations among the community, its God, and its world, or something too foreign for the body of Christ to digest, something the blood of Christ could not clean or cure. Such an exception could only threaten the whole system, would call up what Durkheim called moral effervescence, and what its defenders call outrage.

Sex and gender issues now seem to some Christians to *threaten*, to others to *restore* the whole analogical system by which Christianity rests on the incarnation of Christ and lives by his blood. Same-sex marriage is now the most controverted of those claims. *Sociologists of religion like Durkheim and Mary Douglas help show why conservatives invoke the language of blood and liberals seek first to avoid and then at length to reclaim it. Avoidance only forces blood language underground, to exercise its baleful influence out of conscious sight.* Mary Douglas tells us why. And Jesus shows us what to do about it.

IV

In *How Institutions Think*, Mary Douglas writes about Durkheim. "Durkheim thought the reaction of outrage when entrenched judgments are challenged is a gut response directly due to commitment to a social group."[10] Directly? Isn't that a bit strong? Durkheim and Douglas think not. When a dissident challenges entrenched judgments without communally recognized reasons, the reaction is visceral: "that's not what we do" or "that's not playing by the rules." You can't neglect community norms without making the hearer's blood pump faster and her blood pressure go up. The group calls the dissident to account: Give *our* reasons. If the challenger gives reasons that seem instead to undermine the community and its practices of thinking, the insult rises to a different level. If I, as the listener now join the challenger in adopting reasons that lead out of the community's thinking, then what the challenger is leading outside the community is not an argument but *me*. I cannot adopt the new view without isolating myself from my allies and support. I become a heretic or traitor. I change sides, where the "sides" define the community's boundary. From in, I go out. The social body bleeds. The challenger,

[10] Mary Douglas, *How Institutions Think* (Syracuse, NY: Syracuse University Press), 10.

therefore, is not persuading me to change my *mind*, so much as tempting me to change my loyalty – to betray and isolate myself. The boundary-crossing reason threatens me with self-betrayal, abandonment, perhaps worse. If that threat seems future, I feel fear. If the threat seems present, I feel anger. I dare not let challenging reasons put me outside the gate.

Social solidarity explains appeals even to nature and nature's law. Douglas points out that individuals, "as they pick and choose among the analogies from nature those they will give credence to, are also picking and choosing their allies and opponents and the pattern of their future relations."[11] The dissident reason does not so much break the rules of the cosmology, as it breaks the bonds of the society, the society that coheres because it constructs its cosmology together. A convention acquires social reality, Douglas says, when "the final answer refers to the way in which the planets are fixed in the sky or the way that . . . humans or animals naturally behave."[12] That's why the blood of Christ comes up. It's cosmological.

"According to [Durkheim's] theory, the elementary social bond is only formed when individuals entrench in their minds a model of the social order." They furnish their minds as, Douglas says, as "society writ small."[13] Such minds *know* that to cross the frontiers of thought is to leave the group. That is why an attack on cosmology attacks the group and "rouses emotions to its defense."[14] The group shares a worldview to sustain its solidarity. The group that classifies together, stays together. That bond made visible and defensible is what Durkheim calls "the sacred," where commitment becomes explicit and solidarity gets practice. In the decades around the turn of the twenty-first century, in multiple denominations and around the world, that bond and boundary has run right through same-sex relationships and trans people.

Years ago, a UVA undergrad in my course "God, the Body, and Sexual Orientation" said she'd spent hours arguing with a hallmate about same-sex relationships. She was winning the argument, she said, when her hallmate just walked away. "Why did she [the hallmate] walk away?" the student asked. "Because," I said, "you weren't really asking her to change her mind; you were asking her to leave her community. If she changes her mind about this, she crosses a line; she's out." *That's* how not only same-sex relationships, but even *views* about them, attract the power nowadays to impugn the blood of Christ. It happens four ways:

[11] Douglas, 63.
[12] Douglas, 46.
[13] Douglas, 45.
[14] Douglas, 113.

One, the blood of Christ in the atonement is supposed to cure sin. Homosexuality did traditionally count as sin.[15] But gay people – and the pastoral experience of conservative counselors themselves – both suggest that the atonement does not, in fact, cure homosexuality. So same-sex relationships impugn, or fight against, this blood of Christ with an effectiveness that alarms their critics. In anti-gay versions of the atonement, same-sex relationships defeat the blood of Christ. That makes a cosmological disturbance.

Two, the blood of Christ in communion is supposed to keep the community together. A member of our panel came from a diocese that had recently split. He said he couldn't go to communion with us, and he teared up. His ecclesiology not only allowed, but required him to keep up the communion fellowship; nevertheless, he said, he couldn't do it. The blood of Christ in communion wasn't working either.

Three, the blood of Christ marks not only the external boundaries of a community, when it bleeds; blood marks also the internal lines, the veins. Blood means bonds *and* bounds. And the most prominent internal line – in all the heteronormative denominations, from Catholic to Baptist, runs between male and female, often because male and female marks the internal line between clergy, gendered male, and laity, gendered female. Thus finally:

Four, in versions of Christianity that see the Eucharist as more a sacrifice than a meal, same-sex relationships seem to undermine the homosocial fathering of the hierarchy, "ordination," the way in which sacrifice defines a community of fathers and sons by "doing birth better." That, minus the application to same-sex relationships, is Nancy Jay in her Religious Studies classic, *Throughout Your Generations Forever*. The Roman paterfamilias recognized his biological and adopted sons at family sacrifices so that if they were admitted to the sacrifice, they counted as sons; the Roman church continues the episcopal fathering of priests at the sacrifice of the mass, making same-sex relationships especially fraught.[16]

To my question, *How* do same-sex relationships impugn the blood of Christ, the answer is fourfold: they disrupt the curing of the atonement and cause a cosmological disturbance; they disrupt the unifying of communion and tempt schism; they disrupt traditional gender roles and bring social change; and they disrupt the fathering of the hierarchy that itself takes

---

[15] Or same-sex sexual activity. "Homosexuality" emerged in medical discourse and entered Christian theological discourses only in 1928, when it gave rise to both "therapeutic" and rights discourses, according to Heather White, *Reforming Sodom: Protestants and the Rise of Gay Rights* (Chapel Hill, NC: University of North Carolina Press, 2015).

[16] Nancy Jay, *Throughout Your Generations Forever: Sacrifice, Religion, and Paternity* (Chicago: University of Chicago Press, 1992), 45–60, 112–27.

124   BLOOD THEOLOGY

place in sacrifice and bring us full circle back to the sacrifice of the atonement. Christianity articulates the effects of all four disruptions – atonement, communion, gender roles, and patriline – in terms of blood.

Having understood Christian blood discourse as an anthropologist, my task now as a theologian is to repair it. If anthropology explains that same-sex couples can count as a cosmological disturbance, theology replies that the real cosmological disturbance (as Sarah Coakley points out in another context) is the incarnation.[17] It is Jesus the Logos, after all, who is the boundary-crossing reason *par excellence*. It's hardly surprising, therefore, if Christology should queer gender roles.

                                    V

Conservatives make sexuality a mark of human lack of control, and thus homosexuality a special sign of the fall. Taking homosexuality as the hallmark of the fall was not always the case, but responded to the claim not to need curing by the blood of Christ – a claim that becomes more threatening, the more its critics suspect that it's true. Goodness then seems to depend upon mortifying a sinful body on the pattern of bloody atonement. The pattern invites women and sexual minorities to "take up their cross and follow Jesus." Ask whether someone making that demand is willing to join you on the cross, as Jesus joined the thief. Ask who holds the hammer and the nails.

I propose to keep blood and desire together in a marital theory of the atonement safe for same-sex couples: The thief on the cross is the bride of Christ. I elaborate its elements in order.

1. *The good thief.* The thesis opposes theft with gift. The original sin took by force or too soon what God would give as gift. In that it resembles rape. But God always intended the human being for fellowship with God. When the snake said, "you shall be like God,"[18] that was true. Only, divinity was not to be gained by grasping. In the Philippians hymn (Phil. 2:6–11) Jesus precisely reverses the fall by "counting equality with God not a thing to be grasped."

If the original sin stretched up to seize divinity, then the fall did not occur, as so often, because the body, being lower, let us down – but because the mind, overreaching, tipped us over. Adam did not stoop and fall down, but craned too high and fell over. After the fall, the body told the truth and gave

---

[17] Sarah Coakley, *Flesh and Blood: The Eucharist, Desire and Fragmentation*, The Hensley Henson Lectures, 2004–5, Oxford University. Lecture 1, 18–22 of typescript.

[18] Gen. 3:5, Ps. 82:6.

the mind the lie: you are no god, but creature still. The fall did not result in the body corrupting the mind. The fall resulted in the mind scorning the body for proving it wrong.[19] In "counting equality not a thing to be grasped," Jesus reverses the grasping; it is precisely to the thief, the grasper, that Jesus has come.

The thief on the cross. Why does Jesus not climb *down* from the cross? Why does he stay *up*? On the vulgar Anselmian theory, he stays up to pay a debt for sin. On my theory – which accords well with other bits of Anselm, as I'll show – Jesus stays on the cross in solidarity with the thief. In becoming incarnate, Jesus reverses the scorn of the body by re-befriending it, and just so keeps faith with the thief. "This day you will be with me in paradise." *With me.* Jesus cannot consummate the thief's desire by abandoning him. He can only consummate the thief's desire – which is his own – by staying with him.[20] This is the pattern: Jesus will give by grace, what Adam would take by force.

The thief on the cross is the bride. All Christians, of whatever gender, count as brides of Christ. And all Christians, of whatever gender, stand with the penitent thief. They enact and repeat this at Orthodox communion, when they pray,

> accept me today as a communicant of Your Mystical Supper, for
> I will not speak of this Mystery to Your enemies,
> nor like Judas will I give You a kiss,
> but like the penitent thief I confess to You:
> O Lord, remember me when You come into Your kingdom.[21]

In the West, a similar insight frees Anselm to use erotic imagery in his *Meditation on Human Redemption.* At communion Anselm addresses himself: *"Taste the goodness of your Redeemer. Be on fire with the love of your Saviour. Chew the honeycomb of his words, suck their flavour which is sweeter than sap, swallow their wholesome sweetness. Chew by thinking, suck by understanding, swallow by loving and rejoicing. [Anselm's not finished yet.] Be glad to chew, be thankful to suck, rejoice to swallow. ... See, Christian soul, here is ... the cause of your redemption. ... Chew this, bite it, suck it, let your heart swallow it, when your mouth receives the body and blood of your Redeemer. Make it in this life your daily bread, for through this and*

---

[19] Sebastian Moore, "The Crisis of an Ethic Without Desire," in *Jesus the Liberator of Desire* (San Francisco: Crossroad, 1989), 89–107, reprinted in *Theology and Sexuality: Classic and Contemporary Readings,* ed. Eugene F. Rogers, Jr. (Oxford: Blackwell Publishers), 157–69.

[20] Donald MacKinnon, "Evangelical Imagination," in *Religious Imagination,* ed. James McKay (Edinburgh: University of Edinburgh Press, 1986), 179.

[21] Mark Glen Bilby, *As the Bandit Will I Confess You: Luke 23.39–43 in Early Christian Interpretation,* Cahiers de Biblia Patristica 13 (Turnhout: Brepols, 2014).

126   BLOOD THEOLOGY

not otherwise than through this will you remain in Christ and Christ in you ... [To accept Christ, for Anselm, means to accept him into your mouth.] Cleave to him, my soul, and never leave off. Good Lord, do not reject me; I faint with hunger for your love; refresh me with it. .... Take me and possess me wholly, who with the Father and the Holy Spirit are alone blessed to ages of ages. "[22] Anselm can use such language, by the way, not only when convention genders his soul feminine, but even in male–male relations, calling his teacher *amplectissime*, a vocative superlative campier than a showtune: "most embraceable you."

Anselm's atonement takes place by a marital exchange of bodily fluids. Debt payment belongs in a married household. Where else but in marriage do adults freely pay one another's debts? The Bridegroom did not bleed but for the love of the bride, so that even in Anselm, God meets God's demand with God's body's gift and pays a debt with a bodily donation. Anselm calls himself by baptism "betrothed to Christ" and therefore "a dowager with the Holy Spirit,"[23] in the technical sense of a widow receiving for life a share of her husband's estate. You'd think Anselm's abbey was Downton.

No one has put it more familiarly than the hymn:

> The Church's one foundation/Is Jesus Christ her Lord; ...
> From heaven he came and sought her/To be his holy bride;
> With his own blood he bought her,/And for her life he died.

And no one has put it more vividly than Jacob of Serugh:

> The King's Son made a marriage feast in blood at Golgotha;
> There the daughter of the day was betrothed to him, to be his,
> And the royal ring was beaten out in the nails of his hands;
>
> With his holy blood was this betrothal made ...
> he led her into the Garden – the bridal chamber he had prepared for her.
> At what wedding feast apart from this did they break
> the body of the groom for the guests in place of other food?[24]

Under patriarchy, the woman suffers for the man. Jesus, the bridegroom subverts and atones for that pattern. Here one gendered male suffers for one gendered female. That brings us back again to sacrifice, its abuses and reversals. I quote Judith Butler once again:

---

[22] *Meditation on Human Redemption*, ll. 7–12, 163–9, 265–71.

[23] Anselm of Canterbury, *Oratio II (formerly Oratio III)* in *Opera Omnia*, ed. F. S. Schmitt (Edinburgh: Thomas Nelson, 1951), vol. 3, p. 80, ll. 7f.

[24] Jacob of Serugh, *Homily on the Veil of Moses*, 11.141–51, trans. in Sebastian Brock, *Studies in Syriac Spirituality*, Syrian Churches Series 13 (Poonah, India: Anita Printers, 1988), 95.

To deconstruct [a binary] is not to negate or refuse either term. To deconstruct [the] terms means, rather, to continue to use them, to repeat them, to repeat them subversively, and to displace them from contexts in which they have been deployed as instruments of oppressive power. ... [My] options ... are not exhausted by presuming [the terms of a binary], on the one hand, and negating it, on the other. [I propose] to do precisely neither of these. ... [My procedure] does not freeze, banish, render useless, or deplete of meaning the usage of the term[s]; on the contrary, it [can] mobilize the signifier[s for] an alternative production.[25]

Christianity's paradigm for that procedure is Jesus's announcement, "This is my body, given for you."[26] Catholic eucharistic theology makes it a marital remark.[27] With it, Jesus subverts and redeploys a structure of violent oppression – crucifixion – and turns it to a peaceful feast. He reverses the movement of the fall, which counted divinity a thing to be grasped. Jesus re-befriends the body and creates the bread of heaven, by counting divinity nothing to be grasped. At the Last Supper, he performs a deathbed wedding, as if he said: "You can't violate my body; here, I give it to you."[28] He becomes a bridegroom of blood: you can't exsanguinate me; drink this, all of you. Gethsemene's bitterest cup becomes the toast at a wedding feast.

Marriage therefore interprets the atonement. In both cases, a body is given to another with all its precious fluids. In both cases, the gift begins in desire and ends in charity. Jesus did not die for his spouse because his desire was faint, but because his passion was great.[29] Jesus takes on the body to befriend it, to rescue it from scorn; he gives it in commitment to another. The atonement, like marriage, does not bypass the body, but elevates it as gift.

The remaining issue in the marriage debates was complementarity: whether two women or two men may represent Christ and the church. Elsewhere I argue they must.[30] Otherwise the incarnation leaves out women and the church leaves

---

[25] Judith Butler, "Contingent Foundations," in Seyla Benhabib, et al., *Feminist Contentions: A Philosophical Exchange* (London and New York: Routledge, 1995), 35–57; here, 51–2, paragraph boundary elided.

[26] This paragraph is quoted with small changes from Eugene F. Rogers, Jr., "Marriage as an Ascetic Practice," *INTAMS Review, The Journal of the International Academy of Marital Spirituality* 11 (2005): 28–36.

[27] John Paul II's eucharistic theology, Bernard Cooke's sacramentology. For a similar usage, see David Matzko McCarthy, "The Relationship of Bodies: The Nuptial Hermeneutics of Same-Sex Unions," *Theology and Sexuality* 8 (1998): 96–112.

[28] For a longer version of this interpretation, see Eugene F. Rogers, Jr., *Sexuality and the Christian Body: Their Way into the Triune God* (Oxford: Blackwell Publishers, 1999), 249–68 and Rogers, "Nature with Water and the Spirit: A Response to Rowan Williams," *Scottish Journal of Theology* 56 (2003): 89–100; here, 92–6.

[29] Moore, "Desire," in Rogers, 158.

[30] Rogers, "Same-Sex Complementarity."

out men. Typology does not close off representation, but opens it up. Otherwise typology becomes sub-Christian, inadequate to the incarnation and confining an infinite God. Here, however, I leave that argument to close with same-sex examples from Thomas Aquinas and Symeon the New Theologian.

Aquinas's anti-gay use of "contrary to nature" is well known.[31] But he also seems to know something about the Greek, which is *para phusin*. *Para* is in origin a spatial preposition, meaning alongside or beyond, as in parallel or Paraclete, which is not the same as *anti* or *contra*. We preserve it in paralegal and paramedic, who work alongside and not against. Aquinas notices that Paul *repeats* the phrase *para phusin* in Romans 11:24. There it describes God's love for Gentiles – the same ones whom Paul had characterized with same-sex desire in Romans 1:26–27. Aquinas sees that Paul's reuse of paraphysical language in Romans 11 must destabilize rigid accounts of God and nature. Aquinas explains that God's acting "*contra naturam,*" as the Vulgate translates Romans 11, *just is* "natural," in the analogical sense of "natural-to-God": "That which *God* does, is not against nature [*non est contra naturam*], but is simply natural [*sed simpliciter est naturale*]. Since every creature is naturally subject to God, whatever God does in the creature is simply natural, even if it is not natural according to the proper and particular nature of the thing in which God does it, for example, when God enlightens the blind and raises the dead."[32] As a piece of conceptual analysis, this clarification may look pedestrian. But as a piece of exegesis, it is remarkable. Aquinas's understanding of Paul prompts him to contradict the Latin Bible. The Vulgate says *contra naturam*: Aquinas says, "*Non.*" Aquinas replaces a simple negation, *contra,* with an emphatic positive, *simpliciter.* Aquinas is following the Greek (and not the Vulgate) with precision. For Aquinas, exceeding or moving beyond nature belongs to God's identity as boundary-crossing spreader of goodness. God acts paraphysically in the incarnation itself.

Paul's "Spirit of adoption" also works paraphysically, expanding nature according to Greco-Roman adoption theory, where the father's *pneuma* is not just "spirit," but seminal fluid, which causes both biological and adoptive children to resemble him.[33] Interpreting Romans 8:17 on becoming children of God, Aquinas makes bold where moderns may blush:

---

[31] The following three paragraphs derive from Eugene F. Rogers, Jr., "Romans and the Gender of Gentiles," *Soundings: An Interdisciplinary Journal* 94 (2011): 359–74 and developed in Rogers, "How the Semen of the Spirit Genders Gentiles," in *Aquinas and the Supreme Court* (Oxford: Wiley-Blackwell, 2013), 289–97.

[32] *In Rom.* 11:24 in P. Rapheal Cai, O.P., ed., *Super epistolas S. Pauli lectura,* 8th rev. ed., 2 vols. (Truin: Marietti, 1953), §910b. Cf. *Summa Theologiae* I.105.6 *ad* 1.

[33] Stan Stowers, "Matter and Spirit, or What Is Pauline Participation in Christ," ed. Eugene F. Rogers, Jr., *The Holy Spirit: Classic & Contemporary Readings* (Oxford: Wiley-Blackwell, 2009), 92–105. For more, see Chapter 4.

This is clear from a comparison to physical children, who are begotten by physical semen proceeding from the father. For the spiritual semen proceeding from the Father is the Holy Spirit. And therefore by this semen some human beings are [re]generated as children of God. —1 John 3:9: "Everyone who is born of God does no sin, since the semen of God remains in him [*semen Dei manet in eo*]."[34]

If "*semen*" in Latin means both semen and seed, Aquinas places it without apology in its sexual context. Again, Aquinas usually genders the human soul feminine, to God's male – and then removes God from a particular gender as beyond categories and source of all. But here, quoting 1 John, Aquinas uses masculine pronouns without comment for both sides of a sexual encounter by which God regenerates, refathers, or even breeds and seeds Gentiles. Surely Aquinas didn't have a sense of humor, did he? In any case his account retains the spirit of Paul's desire to shock – and it puts a different spin on how to be born again in the Middle Ages. Of course, semen is also another form of blood – the kind that makes children blood relatives to their fathers.

For a second example, I quote Symeon, the New Theologian. In his *Tenth Ethical Discourse*, a rebel has fought against the Emperor of the Christians for many years. Like the Prodigal, however, the rebel returns. "When he approached the Emperor and embraced his feet [shades of Ruth 3:4, 7–8?], he wept and asked forgiveness. Seized by unexpected joy, the good emperor immediately accepted him. ... Raising him up, the emperor 'fell upon his neck and kissed him' [Lk. 15:20] all over, and on his eyes, which had been weeping. Then ... he ordered ... a crown and robe and sandals ... [as] he was wearing [and] himself clothed his former ... rival. ... [Shades of the Prodigal, Lk. 15:20, 22 and of Jonathan, 1 Sam. 18:4.] And not only this, but night and day he was rejoicing in him and being glad, and embracing [him] and kissing his

---

[34] *Et hoc est manifestum ex similitudine filiorum carnalium, qui per semen carnale a patre procedentes generantur. Semen autem spirituale a Patre procedens, est Spiritus Sanctus. Et ideo per hoc semen aliqui homines in filios Dei generantur.* – *I Io. III, 9: "Omnis qui natus est ex Deo peccatum non facit, quoniam semen Dei manet in eo"* (*In Rom.* 8:17, §636). The Greek of the passage from 1 John is *sperma*. The observation that "semen" also means "seed" and recalls (say) the parable of the sower only reinforces the connection evident elsewhere in Romans between sexual and agricultural images. For more on medieval sexual metaphors, see Linda Coon, "What Is the Word If Not Semen?" in Leslie Brubaker and Julia Smith, *Gender and the Transformation of the Roman World* (Cambridge: Cambridge University Press, 2003), 278–300; Caroline Walker Bynum, *Jesus as Mother* (Berkeley: University of California Press, 1984), 110–69; and Eugene F. Rogers, Jr., *After the Spirit* (Grand Rapids, MI: Eerdmans Publishing, 2005), 120.

mouth with his own .... So much did he love him exceedingly [shades of David, 1 Sam. 20:41] that he was not separated from him even in sleep, laying down with him and embracing him on his bed and covering him all over with his cloak [as Boaz did for Ruth, Ruth 3:9–15], and placing his own face upon all his members."[35]

---

[35] Symeon. the New Theologian, *Ethical Discourses* 10, lines 235–73, in *On the Mystical Life: The Ethical Discoures*, trans. Alexander Golitzen, 3 vols. (St. Vladimir's Seminar Press 1995), vol. 1, 150–1, as modified in Derek Krueger, "Homoerotic Spectacle and the Monastic Body in Symeon the New Theologian," in *Towards a Theology of Eros*, ed. Virginia Burrus and Catherine Keller (New York: Fordham University Press, 2006), 99–118; here, 100–1. Krueger worries that I am hearing things in the resonances I suggest in brackets, because Symeon echoes the action rather than the words of the LXX.

6

RED IN TOOTH AND CLAW
Creationism, Evolution, and the Blood of Christ

DOES EVOLUTION TOO "IMPUGN THE BLOOD OF CHRIST"? *Natural science now seems to some Christians to threaten, to others to revive the whole analogical system by which Christianity rests on the incarnation of Christ and lives by his blood. Evolution seems to creationists to threaten the creation of humans in God's image and to relativize the complementary gender roles that appeal to creation "male and female."*

This chapter uses Irenaeus to diagnose creationism as a softer Gnosticism, Aquinas to defend evolution as a part of providence, and sociology of religion to show why evolution's detractors tend to the language of blood – as well as why its defenders should reclaim the same language.

Like all the chapters in this section, this one performs a test. Modern creationism supplies a second case in which blood-language goes wrong. In modern creationism, blood-language determines whether evolution can be true, because it is blood-language that makes the objection to evolution visceral. In *One Blood,* leading creationist Ken Ham finds evolution too bloody for a good God.[1] A good God could hardly use predation, extinction, and death as a means. A good God could not establish a system that runs on death not accidentally, but in principle. Blood also sets humans at one with or apart from the "dumb beasts." But Ham relies on too narrow an atonement, where the blood of Christ makes up only for sin. According to creationists, only conscious human sin – in the fall – could have caused the bloody predation, extinction, and death we now observe. The limitation of their atonement theory is to cure sin alone. It does not help mutability – creatures' defining ability to undergo change, whether for the good in growth, or for ill in falling. From Irenaeus, Athanasius, and Maximus in antiquity to Marilyn

---

[1] Ken Ham, Carl Weiland, and Don Batten, *One Blood: The Biblical Answer to Racism* (Green Forest, AZ: Master Books), 1999.

131

132   BLOOD THEOLOGY

Adams, Teilhard de Chardin, Hans von Balthasar, and Sarah Coakley in the present, proposals not short on blood place suffering within solidarity and make room for evolution. Secular citizens too can hope wider atonements prevail.

The staying power of creationist objections to evolution cries out for explanation. It depends on the use of blood language. The appeal to scripture is a smokescreen. Both William Jennings Bryan, and, a century later, Ken Ham connect evolution with the blood of predation and the blood of apes, and both also connect evolution with the blood of atonement. They object that evolution is red in tooth and claw. They object that it connects humans and animals. They object that it separates violence (assimilated to sin) from human responsibility. All three objections come in terms of blood: the blood of the hunt, the blood of kinship, and the blood of atonement.

As we have seen, blood becomes important to societies that image the social body on the individual human (or sacrificial animal) body, because blood reveals the body as porous and vulnerable and, for that reason, as needing cultural work to remain whole and bounded. Blood is the place where society conducts that work. In the evolution-creationist debates too, blood language is ineliminable from Christian discourse and indeed from discourses that model the social on the individual body. The only solution, I suggest, is not to avoid the language of blood, but to continue to use it in ways that broaden its focus from human sin to human and nonhuman suffering.

I also argue that creationist appeals to scripture secretly come second to blood. Evolution violates creationists' understanding of Christ and his blood quite apart from the appeal to scripture. It's the structural importance of the blood discourse in Christian contexts apart from evolution – atonement, communion, images of Christ on the cross, images from Leviticus to Revelation about blood as a cleanser – that explains why creationists' blood-critiques of evolution don't yield, but persist.

Evolutionist and creationist Christianity disagree in terms not of metaphysics but of blood. Creationists mount a blood-critique of evolution. It makes their objections more salient that tooth and claw are red, that evolution's violence is bloody. Incarnational Christianity is also bloody. The analogy of blood animates both. It displays the full totemic power of the sociology of blood. We dare not drive it underground, only to hide it from sight.

Thus science and theology – together or apart – work at the level of society and culture. *For Christianity gives blood more to mean than even the protean containment of opposites. In the central story of Christian blood, Christ, on the night in which he was betrayed, did not avoid the deep and sinister means of human bloodletting, but used his blood to overcome them, as if to say, you cannot exsanguinate me; here, I pour my blood out for you. At what other wedding feast, suggested Jacob of Serugh in the* previous chapter, *did the groom give his blood to drink in place of other wine?* Now, what else this means divides one Christian from another. Does it mean payment, solidarity, recapitulation? But in those disputes the appeal to blood is frank. *Theology must recover the power in the blood to turn enemies into kin and purity into vulnerability, not only for communicants but for all the creatures of the earth.*

Atonements Narrow and Broad

Irenaeus on Creation, Blood, and the Good of Time. In *Against Heresies*, as I wrote in the first chapter, *Irenaeus might have been complaining about creationism when he wrote of Gnostics, "People who do not appreciate the period of growth are completely unreasonable. At the outset they refuse to be what they were made: humans who share passions with animals. They override the law of nature; they already want to be like God the Creator before even they become human. Thus they are dumber than the dumb beasts. The beasts do not blame God for not making them human! We, however, complain that instead of being made gods from the beginning, we are first human and then divine."*[2]

In Irenaeus, it marks God to be stable, and creatures to change. *God is perfect already: the experiment with creatures is whether they can reach perfection by growing. Mutability is meant for good, for growth, but turns bad, or runs down. Growth becomes suffering. What Christ comes to fix is not in the first instance sin, but flesh, what suffers and rots. On this theory, the moral running down, which is sin, is corollary to the physical running down, which ends in death. Christ returns flesh to the way of growth.*

In Irenaeus, Gnostics scorn growth, and thus the world, as not good enough for us – with ingratitude they regard themselves as too good for growth, and thus for the world. In that diagnosis of Gnosticism, as in modern creationism, Irenaeus points to a flight from matter not in general, but from its duration and development, its history and time. Gnostics and creationists share a world of punctiliar perfection. Of course, Irenaeus did not have creationism in mind. But his reasoning applies. Like Gnostics, creationists mistrust the temporal aspect of matter, specifically that material creatures take time to grow and develop. Creationists want a young earth and preformed

---

[2] Irenaeus of Lyon, *Against Heresies* IV.4 in Patout Burns, ed. and trans., *Theological Anthropology* (Sources of Early Christian Thought) (Philadelphia: Fortress, 1981), 25, modified.

species. Like Gnostics, they dislike that human beings are animals. And like Gnostics, they want humans to be made spiritual, distinct from animals, godlike "from the beginning": and, more than that, they want other animals to be from the beginning as they are now, and complain that instead of being made dogs from the beginning, dogs are first wolves and then dogs.

Irenaeus's recovery of time goes deeper than the humans and the dumb beasts. His whole soteriology avoids punctiliar perfection, because creaturely perfection is a coming to be. The difference between Creator and creature distinguishes two perfections: perfection-from-the beginning differs from perfection-through-becoming. God enjoys perfection from the beginning, but humans reach perfection: they are to grow. The whole idea of species preformed from the beginning in their perfection runs against Irenaeus's distinction between the Creator (who enjoys perfection) and the humans (who receive it over time).

The incarnation, too, needs time. The work of salvation is to recapitulate – to re-title, re-narrate, re-head, re-enact – the life of the creature, to do it over right. The repair takes time, first in the lifetime of Jesus, in which he encounters human frailties and failures in order and creates them again from within; and then in the history of the church, which slowly spreads the contagion of holiness from person to person and age to age. This means that the forensic, Anselmian debt-payment model, beloved of creationists as well as others, would look inadequate from Irenaeus's point of view, because it reduces to a point: the point of Christ's passion and death rather than his whole life; it fixes on a point in his story rather than unfolding throughout it. Creationists resemble Gnostics, because both have a problem with time.

Their attempt to take creatures out of time means that creationist atonement can make up only for sin, focused at the point of the fall (although its consequences continue), and tends to see sin as a plurality of right-or-wrong point-transgressions, punctiliar sin*s*, rather than as the time-extended habits by which humans grow in virtue or vice (*felix dilatio*, O happy delay!).[3] Finally, this picture tends to collapse *suffering*, the very undergoing of which involves time, and which returns analysis to the frailty of human and other animal life, where vulnerability *continues*, so that extending the creature extends its risk.

If what Christ shares with us is passion, suffering, undergoing, then for Irenaeus what redeems it is the right use of time, for growth rather than decay, the right use of time-bound vulnerability and risk. Those are qualities

---

[3] For more on *felix dilatio*, see Eugene F. Rogers, Jr., *After the Spirit* (Grand Rapids: Eerdmans and London: SCM, 2005), 11, 64, 104–11, 124, 129, *et al.*

that animals share with us more clearly than they sin. Whether or not animals sin, they grow, they suffer, they undergo vulnerability and risk. On this picture, as in Julian of Norwich, sin is a variety of suffering – moral suffering – which wounds our very agency.[4] Christ restores agency by healing the moral harm, doing over, making amends, making good on the evils of the past – but in doing that he has also, not incidentally, overcome the wrong uses of vulnerability and risk, time and decay, frailty, failure, and death, all of which we clearly share with other creatures. Nor do those things exhaust recapitulation, as sin governs debt; rather, recapitulation covers all the things that can go wrong or need repair in the course of a life. That is in part because recapitulation takes time, and in part because it's narrative, since time leaves room and narrative infinitely expands all the things that repair could cover.

Irenaeus next complains that Gnostics want to escape not only time but also blood, which both marks the creature and brings salvation (Against Heresies 5.2). The biblical word joining humans to the "dumb beasts" is blood. Their life, like ours, "is in the blood" (Lev. 17:14). The word joining humans to God is likewise "the blood of Christ" – appearing (as I've noted before) three times as often as Christ's "cross" and five times as often as his "death." Irenaeus writes that Christ "graciously poured out Himself," in a phrase that tacitly identifies "Himself" with his blood (5.2.2), which Irenaeus calls "the bond of union between soul and body" – so that later Irenaeus can use the Christological expression "rational blood" (5.9.3) – which in Greek is "logical blood" – since it is the Logos that unites God with God's body. In denying the goodness of creation and its development, the Gnostics also deny "blood," the sign of the created humanity of God.

Irenaeus makes blood central to his recapitulation theory, because Christ's death (which Irenaeus interprets as bloody) recapitulates and repairs the death of Abel, whose blood had cried out from the ground. Recapitulation takes up and renarrates "historical" or "earlier" deaths, that is, ones earlier in the biblical stories. Christ recapitulates and repairs the death of Abel – and all other "effusion of blood from the beginning" – by himself bleeding, this time in a redemptive way. For Irenaeus, Christ's blood does not make up for sin by presenting a payment to a hostile Father. Rather Christ first shows solidarity with victims by bleeding as they bled, then turns their blood to a new purpose by giving it redemptively.

Furthermore, recapitulation reaches backward more effectively than debt-payment: Debt-payment is extrinsic: recapitulation remakes an interior. Like others, this is a queer use of blood, not negating or repristinating its cultural

---

[4] Julian of Norwich, *Showings* (the Long Text), chapter 39.

uses, but repeating to subvert and repurpose them, liberating them from "contexts of oppressive power" (fraternal murder, state execution), turning them to a peaceful feast. But it is precisely this repurposing that Gnostics shut down when they deny flesh and blood. They take half of Butler's false alternative, the alternative of purity and refusal, and miss, according to Irenaeus, the whole point. There can be no recapitulation without blood, and therefore no salvation, because without blood there is no human being to be saved. There is no solidarity and no living life properly without blood. Here, blood means life undertaken in solidarity, not violence undergone in payment.

It is no accident that Irenaeus pauses not on sex or hunger, but moves directly to murder, a sin of blood, and fratricide, a sin in society. Blood figures time (as in the biblical begats), and blood figures time not only in terms of life and growth, but in those sins also that take time away. The blood Cain spills takes time from Abel. The blood of fratricide infects society from brother to brother. The example raises without resolving the issue of carnivory and animal sacrifice, since God objects to the killing of Abel but accepts Abel's sacrifice of a sheep. Indeed, God mysteriously objects to Cain's sacrifice of the fruit of the ground, and then to his sacrifice of Abel, the strange fruit in which the ground brings forth blood. Cain can't win. It is our vulnerabilities and sufferings (in which we are like sheep, we can be killed) that Irenaeus focuses on, because – when Christ sheds his blood aright – it is those vulnerabilities and sufferings that receive repair:

> And if the blood of the righteous were not to be inquired after, the Lord would certainly not have had blood. But inasmuch as blood cries out from the beginning, God said to Cain, when he had slain his brother, *The voice of your brother's blood cries to Me* (Gen. 4:10). And as their blood will be inquired after, He said to those with Noah, *For your blood of your souls will I require, [even] from the hand of all beasts* [Gen. 9:5]; and again, *Whosoever will shed man's blood, it shall be shed for his blood* [Gen. 9:6]. In like manner, too, did the Lord say to those who should afterwards shed His blood, *All righteous blood shall be required which is shed upon the earth, from the blood of righteous Abel to the blood of Zacharias the son of Barachias, whom you slew between the temple and the altar. Verily I say unto you, All these things shall come upon this generation* [Mt. 23:35–36]. He thus points out the recapitulation that should take place in his own person of the effusion of blood from the beginning, of all the righteous men and of the prophets, and that by means of Himself there should be a requisition of their blood.[5]

---

[5] Irenaeus, *Against Heresies* V.14, trans. Alexander Roberts and William Rambaut in *Ante-Nicene Fathers*, vol. 1 (Buffalo, NY: Christian Literature Publishing Co., 1885).

Teilhard on Body and Blood, Evolution and Sacrifice. If the evidence for evolution leaves creationists unmoved – if the evolutionary mysticism of Teilhard was condemned, and the evolutionary Christology of Rahner forgotten – that is because no one connected them as the Bible did to the bloody particulars of taste and sacrifice by which humans think in their gut. But in one pregnant phrase Teilhard descends to blood, and changes everything. It comes in his "Mass on the World."[6] Teilhard is working as a paleontologist, digging in China, crossing the Gobi on horse or camel, riding for days at a time. As a priest, he has to say mass every day. He fulfills that duty, therefore, in his head, or under his breath, as he rides. He practices a paleontologist's asceticism rather than a priest's; he has filled his pack with picks and brushes, not portable altar stones. How is he to celebrate? He is supposed to consecrate the bread, not on any table, but upon a stone, to make it an altar. His mass is – note the preposition – "on" the world, because he takes the earth itself, its very stones, as his altar. Consecrating in persona Christi, Teilhard channels Paul's notion of building up Christ's body, thinks of evolution's increasing complexity, and says, "This is my body." He thinks of Christ's sacrifice and of evolution's predation, extinction, and death, and says, "This is my blood." He separates body and bread to give them different work.

Brilliant: but how is this even a possible move? Don't "body" and "blood" belong together, because both come in a sacrificial context? Isn't the body "broken" (1 Cor. 11:24) just in order to bleed? Or not? The Gospels do not agree: they say "given," not "broken" – and sometimes 1 Corinthians does, too. Thereby hangs a tale.

At first it looks as if "broken" fits better with my thesis. Broken bodies shed blood. But "broken" makes it difficult to defend Teilhard's insight that blood and body might do different work: blood for sacrifice and body to build up. "Broken" proves more common in Greek and Protestant liturgies. Catholic liturgies have "given." The different readings trace back to different translations of 1 Corinthians 11:24. The *textus receptus* has *klomenon*, broken. But the oldest texts lack any verb at all to read, "this is my body for you, *to soma to huper humon.*" By the principle that scribes tidy texts up, New Testament scholars infer that a more difficult reading came first, the *lectio difficilior*. Thus the Nestle-Aland critical edition supposes that someone added *klomenon* later to make the sentence prettier, and favors readings without it as earlier. So in Nestle-Aland, the body is neither "broken" nor explicitly "given," but simply "for you." Because the Vulgate also follows that pattern *(hoc est corpus meum pro vobis)*, Catholic eucharists line up with the earlier

---

[6] Pierre Teilhard de Chardin, "The Mass on the World," in *The Heart of Matter* (New York: Houghton Mifflin, 2002), 119–34.

texts. The KJV has "broken," influencing creationists, among others. In English-language texts, Calvinist liturgies have "broken" and Anglican liturgies vary, but now follow the RSV with "given." If we seem far from creationism at the moment, note that their theology of atonement depends on brokenness.

Whatever the result, the "broken" translation tends to confine the body to remedy for sin. The "given" translation, however, holds open "the body for you" for more than one purpose – not just remedy for sin, but also for building up the church, which suits other bits of Paul. This allows Teilhard to keep blood with expiation but frees the body for solidarity and upbuilding. Early in this research, I would have preferred "broken" as more honest about the sacrificial aspects – but *now I prefer "given." It's less hamartiocentric and gives God more space. Even if the human being had never sinned, God could still have given himself to elevate human beings from Eden to heaven. The body of Christ could still be the bread of heaven, and Christ's blood the cup of elevation. Teilhard suggests a felix culpa theology of evolution: O happy fault, that merited such and so great a Redeemer. Creationism allows no happy fault, brooks no predation and death in the divine comedy.*

Although most accounts of the Eucharist do not distinguish the bread's work as Christ's body from the wine's work as Christ's blood, a few do. The Liturgy of St. Basil for the washing of the hands distinguishes "Your most precious Body, and Your life-giving Blood," implying that the first avails for "the forgiveness of all my sins," while the second associates the blood with "life everlasting." For this reason too Maximus associates blood with the God to whom it belongs and the divinity humans gain from the Logos: "perhaps the 'flesh' of the Logos is the perfect return and restoration of nature . . . and the 'blood' is the future divinization."[7] Thomas Aquinas makes a similar distinction (*ST* III.74.2), quoting Ambrosiaster on 1 Cor. 11:20: "this sacrament 'avails for the defense of soul and body'; and therefore 'Christ's body is offered' under the species of bread 'for the health of the body, and the blood' under the species of wine 'for the health of the soul,' according to Leviticus 17:14: 'The life of the animal [Vulgate: 'of all flesh'] is in the blood.'" In Anglican traditions, the pre-communion Prayer of Humble Access ends, "Grant us therefore, gracious Lord, so to eat the flesh of thy dear Son Jesus Christ, and to drink his blood, *that our sinful bodies may be made clean by his*

---

[7] Maximos the Confessor, *Ad Thalassium* 35, ed. and trans. Fr. Maximos [Nicholas] Constas in *On Difficulties in Sacred Scripture: The Responses to Thalassios*, Fathers of the Church Series 136 (Washington, DC: Catholic University of America Press, 2018), 212–14.

body, and our souls washed through his most precious blood, and that we may evermore dwell in him, and he in us."[8]

Teilhard has exploited this openness to differential meaning beautifully – and changed it. All four earlier examples follow Leviticus to associate blood with "life," "soul," or "divinization." Teilhard however allows the "blood" language to carry New Testament themes of sacrifice and the body language to take on Pauline themes of building up the body, a *sensus plenior*. This may not work as *historical* exegesis, but it does work by the Augustinian–Thomistic theological principle, that any meaning of the text that is true, *and* that the words will bear, *is* a meaning of the text, and that it is a fault "so to confine the text to one meaning, as to expose the faith to ridicule."[9] That is in effect what creationists are doing when they confine the atonement to the breaking of the body for sin, and leave the Eucharist no way to absorb the predation, extinction, and death that the incarnation also takes on.

Teilhard's Christology of evolution begins to work only as, like God in Christ, humans too are vulnerable to predation, blood, and death, and we are able to resign ourselves, to offer ourselves up.[10] And that is moral in turn only if God, too, in becoming animal, becomes vulnerable to predation, blood, and death. And *this* is what takes place in a cosmic redemption and a cosmic Eucharist: Christ as head of all creation takes responsibility for the violence of evolution, although you can see that the creationist answer enjoys the advantage of simplicity.

God has a sense of irony and takes the worst that human beings can do as the occasion for the building up. God is made sacrifice, that we might be made God. Dare we say: God's sacrifice enables the predation and extinction by which at least one hominin species arose to worship God? This works only

---

[8] This is from the long-lasting version of the 1662 *Book of Common Prayer.* The prayer was removed from the US book in 1979 but approved for Roman Catholic churches of the Anglican rite in 2013.

[9] *quia ab infidelibus veritas fidei irridetur, cum ab aliquo simplici et fideli tamquam ad fidem pertinens proponitur aliquid quod certissimis documentis falsum esse ostenditur . . . ne aliquis ita Scripturam ad unum sensum cogere velit, quod alios sensus qui in se veritatem continent, et possunt, salva circumstantia litterae, Scripturae aptari, penitus excludantur,* Thomas Aquinas, *De potentia* 4.1.r, citing Augustine, *De Genesi ad litteram* 1; see other forms of *cogere* in the replies to 4.2.14, 15, and 16. *Quaestiones disputatae de potentia Dei*, trans. English Dominican Friars (Westminster, MD: The Newman Press, 1952); online edition ed. Joseph Kenney at isidore.co/aquinas/QDdePotentia.htm. For discussion see Bruce Marshall, "Absorbing the World," in *Theology and Dialogue: Essays in Conversation with George Lindbeck*, ed. Bruce Marshall (Notre Dame, IN: University of Notre Dame Press, 1990), 90–7.

[10] This is where Teilhard takes it, in the reading of Robert Hughes III, who makes a spirituality out of it. See Hughes, *Beloved Dust* (New York: Continuum, 2008).

if God elects, not us or other animals for sacrifice, but God's own self for sacrifice and us for divinity. Athanasius must work cosmically or not at all.

Meat and Vegetable Offerings. That is also why for most of Western history meat eating – human predation and herding – has worked liturgically. "The architecture and economy associated with animal sacrifice dominated ancient civic and domestic life, from the city square ringed with monumental temples to the city meat market and the private home."[11] For most of Christian history, too, meat-eating has had more to mean than it does; theologically, meat-eating was first paschal and then dominical, belonging first to Easter, derivatively to Sunday, and finally to any meal that recalled the sacrifice of God. So it was that Mary Douglas, crypto-theologian, defended eating fish on Fridays: meatless Fridays marked the last time that meat meant anything sacrificial in Western Christendom.[12] These days, vegetarianism is full of meaning; meat has less to mean. In due course our meat animals, too, have had less and less to mean, so that we treat them more and more as commodities standing in their own filth than as sacrifices like ourselves deserving of respect. Barth, the rabbis, and four out of five anthropologists agree that meat-eating has usually transcended itself to mean more; now it means less than vegetables. Between this world and the next, Christians practice a Eucharist which both is and is not meat and blood.

The Eucharist, however, is not entirely of the present, but makes the bread of heaven. That's why it's not only cannibalistic but also vegetarian. The pattern of crucifixion is backward-looking, for making sense of tragedy. This reverses the pattern according to which the Eucharist is a memorial: The Eucharist looks forward to a time without sacrifice, but not a time without sacrifice in its past. The Eucharist does not bypass or erase sacrifice, because self-sacrifice is *a* logical response to sin, suffering, and loss, and because unwilled sacrifice is a wound or womb deserving of permanent honor. Eucharist is for looking forward and back.

Both vegetarianism and meat-eating are logical in this world. Both follow the pattern of Christ; both try to make meaning of suffering. One participates in suffering (so Bulgakov on consumption) – one looks forward to its end. One acknowledges the creatureliness and implication and evolution of human beings in their environment – one imagines them better than their environment at the beginning and the end.

---

[11] Daniel Ullucci, *The Christian Rejection of Animal Sacrifice* (Oxford: Oxford University Press, 2011), 120.

[12] Mary Douglas, "The Bog Irish," in *Natural Symbols: Explorations in Cosmology with a New Introduction by the Author* (New York: Pantheon Books, 1982), 37–53.

Jesus joined us products of evolution, predation, and death; he joined us in eating, in meat-eating, in eating Passover lamb; he joined us also in death. If Christians eat meat, they should remember him; if Christians eat vegetables alone, they should remember his body as bread and his blood as wine. In either case, all blood is his. He uses it – to forgive. As even vegetarians love their animal companions, and may, some of them, feed them meat, so God too looks with love on humans even in our creaturehood. In the fall humans learned to scorn their bodies – which sleep and fuck and eat, even meat – but they scorn them because they tell the truth, that humans are not yet gods, but creatures still. And God loves humans as creatures, as finite, fallible creatures, vulnerable creatures, fallen creatures, the *lost* cause of whom God takes on, in taking on human bodies and blood. And God turns the blood of a human animal, the animal that God takes as God's own body, into the blood of new life – the blood that (so far from the blood of predation or the hunt) resembles the blood of menstruation that prepares new life.

But all this leads to a terrible paradox: shall humans shed blood that good may come? Shall humans shed blood, *O felix culpa,* that God may come? Two New Testament commands conflict: The prohibition in Acts 15:29, which Gentile Christians all but universally ignore, to refrain from eating blood; and the command in the Gospels to "Drink from it, all of you; for this is my blood of the covenant, which is poured out for many for the forgiveness of sins" (Mt. 26:27–28). Even though this is the blood of the vine, the wording, placed on the lips of Jesus, deliberately provokes and offends disciples or readers raised in kashrut. The offense implies that by divine irony God saves humans on the occasion of the worst they can do, of what they have done, and turns the blood of Abel, which cried out from the ground, into the blood of Christ, which is the cup of heaven.[13] The Welsh poet David Gwenallt Jones put it this way: we go "howling for the Blood that ransomed us."[14]

The whole panoply of evolution reflects this paradox: that God did not deny or bypass death; that God can dignify God's creatures to climb up even by means of one another, and bring ever greater finite goods (or so it looks to us), even if neither Eden nor heaven eat meat. God looks on evolved

---

[13] For more on this theme, see James Alison, *Raising Abel* (New York: Herder and Herder, 1996).

[14] I owe the translation to a remark by Rowan Williams in November 2014. It appears in Joseph Clancy, ed., *Twentieth Century Welsh Poems* (Llandyssul, Wales: Gwasg Gomer, 1982), p. 94. Williams published a different translation in *Headwaters* (Oxford: Perpetua Press, 2008): "Like wolves, we lift our snouts: Blood, blood, we cry, / The blood that bought us so we need not die." The Welsh is *udo am y gwaed a'n prynodd ni'*, in David Gwenallt Jones, "Pechod" ("Sin"), in *Cerddi Gwenallt: Y Casgliad Cyflawn* (Collected works), ed. Christine James (Llandyssul, Wales: Gwasg Gomer, 2001).

142   BLOOD THEOLOGY

creatures, even humans, and sees God's body in formation; and on their suffering, and sees God's blood.

Meat-eating more saliently than salad makes something good out of death, without making death good. Less successfully than the Eucharist, meat-eating figures as a cause for lament and thanksgiving at the same time.[15] It is pictured in neither Eden nor the Peaceable Kingdom, where death is not. Whether or not by humans, meat-eating will continue as long as death, even as evolution tries to outpace and outrace it. Vegetarianism approaches the God that did not eat; but Jesus both ate and gave himself for food.

If all blood belongs to God and thus to Jesus, then (as in kashrut) the blood of all animals is met in him, and in him Christians meet the blood of all flesh. This means that in animal predation and suffering they meet his sacrifice – whether they interpret animal predation as nature or sin, whether it counts as sin *and* suffering or suffering alone. Because God always intended to become vulnerable with creatures and bleed with them, God always intended to join with them to by giving Godself to them for food. "At what wedding feast apart from this did they break the body of the groom for guests in place of other food?"[16] In vegetarianism Christians bear witness to the innocence and hope of animals not to suffer, and in meat-eating they bear witness – they see and eat and take benefit from – the gift and willingness of God to suffer: take, eat, this is my body given for you. This is at evolution's heart, as Teilhard saw, that God uses eating to build up the many species and the whole body of life, that lives, like a multicellular organism, from the ingestion of many – and that God uses bleeding to share, esteem, and lift up their suffering, to honor their wounds and dignify their sacrifice as reflecting the sacrifice of God, for their blood is God's blood and God's blood is theirs.

Bulgakov seems to get both sides of that. Trained as an economist, he became the only theologian to allow *oikonomia* to mean both the pursuit of matter and the mercy of God. "Economy," he writes, "is the struggle of . . . life and death, freedom and necessity, mechanism and organism. . . . [E]conomy is the victory of the organizing forces of life over the disintegrating forces and deeds of death . . . . Economy is the struggle with the mortal forces of the prince of darkness, but is it capable of standing up to the prince himself? Is economy capable of chasing death from the world? . . . Is a new creative act of Divinity . . . required to 'destroy the final enemy – death'? . . . But if economy is a form of the struggle of life and death, and is a tool of life's self-affirmation,

---

[15] I owe this insight to a conversation with Lauren Winner.

[16] Jacob of Serugh, *Homily on the Veil of Moses*, 11.141–51, trans. in Sebastian Brock, *Studies in Syriac Spirituality*, Syrian Churches Series 13 (Poonah, India: Anita Printers, 1988), 95.

then we say with as much certainty that *economy is a function of death*, induced by the necessity to defend life. ... The distinguishing trait of economy is the re-creation or acquisition of goods, material or spiritual, *through labor*, as opposed to receiving them as gift. This human activity is the fulfillment of God's word – *In the sweat of thy face shalt thou eat bread* – and this includes all bread, that is, spiritual as well as material food."[17] Bulgakov's *Philosophy of Economy* dwells on what he calls the great *metabole,* both "change" and "metabolism," from death to life, which comes by eating, and by which God brings about what is distinctive to this economy, "the spiritualization of matter."[18] And yet the greatest change, which looks back to Eden and up to heaven, depends on something vegetable: bread. The curse on Adam, "in the sweat of thy brow shalt thou eat bread," becomes in the end the command that saves, the command to commune with the second Adam by eating the bread of heaven.[19]

An atonement theory that addresses sin alone overlooks mutability – the ability of creatures to undergo change, whether for the good, in growth, or for ill, in falling. Creatures, unlike the Creator, are made to change. God created them not static, but to grow; and in the absence of growth they show their creatureliness still by running down. The problem is not so much that of evil; the problem is that of suffering. Only a little evil can cause such disproportionate suffering, as when the touch of a button can deliver a shock in the Milgram experiments, or in drone warfare. So in Athanasius as in Chesterton the entire incarnation is pathos, patientia, suffering, and only God's answer, "Can ye drink of the cup that I drink of?" even begins to get God off the hook for creating a world in which suffering prevails: God shares it with us.

That does not answer the question. But it widens the atonement. Atonement is not only cure for sin. It is first of all solidarity in and companionship in growth.

Anselmian theories of the atonement think the problem Christ must solve is sin; Athanasian and Irenaean theories think the problem Christ must solve is mutability gone wrong, which includes suffering as well as sin. Sin-alone theories do badly by evolution, and suffering-theories do better. Sin theories define "us" narrowly: "we" are humans as distinguished from animals by our mortal souls. Suffering theories define "us" more broadly: "we" are animals united with humans by our *shared* suffering and growth.

---

[17] Sergei Bulgakov, *Philosophy of Economy: The World as Household*, trans. and ed. Catherine Evtuhov (New Haven, CT: Yale University Press, 2000), 71–6.

[18] *Philosophy of Economy*, 95–107.

[19] *Philosophy of Economy*, 75, 104–5.

144   BLOOD THEOLOGY

In any case, the Athanasian doctrine of salvation fares better than the vulgar
Anselmian one: the problem in evolution is not sin but corruptibility, the
capacity of flesh to run down and rot, the first sign of which is death, cured by
the resurrection, and of which sin is only the second sign, a distinctively
human way to die.[20] The Anselmian focus on sin can probably be saved from
the creationist reduction thereof by attending to its themes of gift, liberty,
communion, and joy: but that would be another task.

Earlier I said that creationists, like Gnostics, regard themselves as too good
for growth, and thus for the world – the world of growth is not good enough
for them. The problem is, how can a world of growth, necessarily imperfect,
count as "good"? Irenaeus has one answer: growth is good-for-our-state;
God is good absolutely. Our goal is to grow from one to the other, from
glory to glory. Creationists hardly consider the question, but they regard the
good of growth as second best: for them it detracts from God's power.

Aquinas, on the other hand, directs his argument squarely against the view
creationists would adopt. In Aquinas God makes creatures "intermediaries of
God's providence; not on account of any defect in God's power, but by the
abundance of God's goodness; so that the dignity of causality is imparted
even to creatures" (*ST* I.22.3, modified to avoid masculine pronouns for
God). The answers to the objections repeat and apply this reasoning:

> Inasmuch as we [creatures] execute [God's] orders, according to I Cor. 3:9,
> "we are God's coadjutors." Nor is this on account of any defect in the
> power of God, but because God employs intermediary causes, in order that
> the beauty of order may be preserved in the universe; and also that God may
> communicate to creatures the dignity of causality. (I.23.8 *ad* 2)
>
> Secondary causes cannot escape the order of the first universal cause . . .
> indeed, they execute that order. And therefore predestination [substitute:
> evolution] can be furthered by creatures, but it cannot be impeded by them.
> (I.23.8 *ad* 3)
>
> The effect of divine providence is not only that things should happen
> somehow; but that they should happen either by necessity or by contin-
> gency. Therefore whatsoever divine providence [substitute: evolution]
> ordains to happen infallibly and of necessity happens infallibly and of
> necessity; and that happens from contingency, which the plan of divine
> providence [evolution] conceives to happen from contingency. (I.22.4 *ad* 1)

Obviously Thomas had no modern theory of evolution to go by. But in the
context of his metaphysics, it is easy to place evolution as something that
providence ordains to happen contingently, which can be furthered by

---

[20] I owe the formulation of the last phrase to Greg Williams.

creatures and not impeded by them, with the beauty of order (read habitat) and the dignity of causality. On this view, creation is the more wonderful with "the dignity of causality" than it would be without, so that it is the perfect creationist machine that is not good enough, rather than the world we live in. The perfect creationist machine is not good enough, because it hobbles the causality of creatures and renders them imperfectible.

How Creationists Appeal to Blood

Although creationists distinguish themselves from one another in various ways, their self-distinctions attempt largely to make one more scientifically acceptable than another. No matter: it is not the purpose of this chapter to assess their scientific acceptability, but to apply theories of the social body to show how they rely on the language of blood. (For my own theology of evolution, see Chapter 9.) What is distinctive about Bryan and Ham is that, a hundred years apart, they draw out explicitly three features of blood language that other thinkers often leave to go without saying. They object to shedding blood as a necessary means; they object to sharing blood with various others; and they object to atoning blood before a human fall. That characteristic makes Bryan and Ham more sophisticated, in terms not of science, but of rhetoric, theology, and sociology. What's distinctive about Bryan and Ham is not that they share the three features – shedding, sharing, shriving blood – but that they use them reflectively to build staying power.

1. *Evolution red in tooth and claw.*[21] Predation, extinction, and death are self-evidently bad, according to creationists, when they become the ineliminable means by which God runs the universe. Here creationists claim a moral high ground. Even theologians and philosophers far removed from creationism are newly concerned, since Darwin, with the problem of animal suffering.[22] Hoggard identifies animal suffering, in her subtitle, as a "new problem for theodicy." Creationists credit themselves with treating the new problem consequently, seriously, and straightforwardly. Henry Morris, founder of the Institute for Creation Research, writes of evolutionist Christians that "They apparently

---

[21] Tennyson's "In Memoriam."

[22] For example, Nicola Hoggard Creegan, *Animal Suffering and the Problem of Evil* (New York: Oxford, 2013); Peter Singer, *Animal Liberation* (New York: HarperCollins 2007); Michael Murray, *Nature Red in Tooth and Claw: Theism and the Problem of Animal Suffering* (New York: Oxford University Press, 2008). You might argue that creationist concern for individual animals descends from nineteenth-century anti-Darwinian romanticism, and needs to deal with predators as keystone species enabling an entire habitat to flourish. That's the sort of argument Aquinas would make. But it's a topic for another day.

suppose that evolution may be God's method of creation, but this is a serious charge to bring against God. Evolution is the most wasteful, inefficient, cruel way that one could conceive by which to create man. If evolution *is* true, we certainly should not blame God for it!" (Instead we should blame the fall.) Liberal theologians thus "make God out to be a monster."[23] A raft of creationist children's books and a few creationist museums and theme parks show the issue's moral power. The most common and effective way of stating the new problem in theodicy is in terms of blood: "nature red in tooth and claw." Violence "itself" – redness, bloodiness, loss of bodily integrity – becomes self-evidently a moral problem. Thomas Aquinas would have asked (like a habitat scientist) what larger order, hierarchy, or structure was being "violated": referring violence to the individual would not have been automatic, but belonged to the order of the entire universe (*Summa Theologiae*, part I, question 47). I mention the contrast not to settle the matter, but to raise sociological questions: What bodies are being violated – individual, social, cosmic? And what are the relations among them?

2. The question of humans "sharing blood" with apes and other animals raises questions of "race." The fact that "blood" does duty for DNA and other markers only heightens blood's rhetorical power for disputing "them" and "us," a sociological issue right on the surface. Creationists divide according to what they find to be the moral high ground for their audience.[24] Bryan and a few late twentieth-century authors use blood language for racist purposes; Ham and his contemporaries use blood language to unite humans against other animals. In any case the language of sharing blood explicitly or implicitly raises the issue of who shares a social body with the audience.

3. Blood language to describe a substitutionary atonement wrought by Jesus for human sin on the cross is universal among fundamentalists, not just creationists.[25] Indeed, substitutionary atonement is one of *The Fundamentals* from which "fundamentalism" takes its name.[26] Creationists make human sin the cause of predation and death even in the nonhuman world: that's the theological reason why, for them, predation and extinction *cannot* mark

[23] Henry Morris, *King of Creation* (San Diego, CA: Creation-Life Publishers, 1970), 83–4.

[24] Extensive bibliography in Liz Rank Hughes, *Reviews of Creationist Books* (Berkeley, CA: National Center for Science Education, 1992) and Tom McIver, *Anti-Evolution: An Annotated Bibliography* (Jefferson, NC: McFarland), 1988.

[25] Peter J. Bowler, *Evolution: The History of an Idea* (Berkeley: University of California Press, 2009), 322–3 and Christopher P. Toumey, *God's Own Scientists: Creationism in a Secular World* (New Brunswick, NJ: Rutgers University Press, 1994), 105.

[26] Ray Ginger, *Six Days or Forever? Tennessee v. John Thomas Scopes* (Boston: Beacon Press, 1958).

RED IN TOOTH AND CLAW

evolution before the advent of humanity. The fall is our fault; therefore it (and predation) cannot predate us. The idea that Jesus's blood betters all who share it begs the question whether Jesus shares blood with nonhuman animals. A particular theory of the atonement dominates creationist texts in general – and in Bryan and Ham it explicitly underwrites both of the two preceding features. A few examples from other authors show how this is widespread.

> No Adam, no fall; no fall, no atonement; no atonement, no Saviour. Accepting Evolution, how can we believe in a fall?[27]
>
> If the first Adam is not real, . . . and if therefore the Fall did not really take place, then neither is the second Adam real and there is no need of a Savior.[28]
>
> If evolution is true, there was no Fall, and Christ's atonement is "utterly meaningless," a "complete hoax."[29]
>
> If evolution is true, then there was no created Adam and Eve, no Fall, no Atonement, no Christ as Redeemer and Saviour.[30]
>
> If men evolved from the beast, the sin nature is an inherited animal characteristic and cannot be due to the fall of man through disobedience. This denies the need of a Redeemer, and thus the atonement idea of Christ is foolishness.[31]

Creationists tend to share the three positions, even when they leave the connections to go without saying. But the most influential creationists then and now – William Jennings Bryan and Ken Ham – make the connections plain. Each of the three features of creationism is widespread and uncontroversial as a characterization of what creationists believe. But their deep connections go unanalyzed. It's the structural importance of the blood

---

[27] Quoted in Ginger, 63. Creationists took up this slogan so often that scholars have had trouble tracing its author. See Ronald L. Numbers, *The Creationists: From Scientific Creationism to Intelligent Design* (Cambridge, MA: Harvard University Press, 2006), 373, n. 32. The all-too-careful distinctions between "scientific creationism" and "biblical creationism" in, for example, Henry Morris, *Creation and the Modern Christian* (El Cajon, CA: Master Books, 1987), 298–300 only reassure creationist readers that the "scientific" arguments rest on biblical motives after all; they give away the code. "[M]any creationists' texts must be *revised* for public consumption" (Robert Root-Bernstein, "On Defining a Scientific Theory: Creationism Considered," in Ashley Montagu ed., *Science and Creationism* [Oxford: Oxford University Press, 1984], 64–94; here, 93 n. 52).

[28] Morris, *King of Creation* 57.

[29] McIver, *Anti-evolution* 204, quoting Herman J. Otten, *Baal or God* (New Haven, Missouri: Leader, 1965), 65.

[30] McIver 1988, 103 reviewing John Raymond Hand, *Why I Accept the Genesis Record* (Lincoln, NE: Back to the Bible, 1972).

[31] McIver, 46 quoting Charles Cook, *The Scope's Trial [sic]: A Nation Deceived* (Grand Terrance, CA: Center for Creation Studies, 1986).

148   BLOOD THEOLOGY

discourse in Christian contexts apart from evolution – atonement, communion, images of Christ on the cross, images from Leviticus to Revelation
about blood as a cleanser – that explains why blood critiques don't yield in
evolution's case.

Christian creationists' objections to evolution owe their persistence to
"the power in the blood" sociologically explained. As we saw in Chapter 1,
blood marks the bounds of the body.[32] Society interprets threats with images
of blood and defends against threats with spilling of blood. Society responds
to threats in blood's terms and by bloody means. In thinking of bodies, social
or individual, we imagine a bounded entity and hide from ourselves its
entrances, exits, permeations, and vulnerabilities: when blood gets out, it
gives those bounds the lie and paints the fiction red. Blood gives alarm by
revealing a leaky body, individual, animal, or social. Blood stains and exposes
the body's boundary. Therefore, society's work to maintain the fiction of
a bounded, secure, integral social body – the boundary between "us" and
"them," between security and danger – takes place in terms not of the body it
defends, but of the blood that marks it.

How Creationists First Appealed to Blood

The creationist appeal to blood falls into two stages. Both stages toggle
between blood of kinship and blood of Christ. That is, both use blood-talk,
as Bildhauer predicts, to define group (kinship) boundaries and, as Douglas
predicts, to lash their kinship boundaries to their cosmology – where founding
sagas (Genesis, atonement) meet accounts of how the world works (micro-
evolution, young-earth creationism). What distinguishes the two stages is the
way they use blood of kinship to claim the moral high ground. Both times the
high ground depends on "race." In the early twentieth century, creationist
rhetoric was implicitly *pro*-racist; by the early twentieth-first century creationist rhetoric had turned explicitly *anti*-racist.

At first creationists objected that humans and apes shared "blood." Thus
Williams Jennings Bryan railed against the "evolutionary hypothesis that
takes from man the breath of the Almighty and substitutes the blood of
a brute."[33] "These and all other creatures must be blood relatives if man is

---

[32] Bettina Bildhauer, *Medieval Blood* (Cardiff: University of Wales Press, 2006), 1–13.

[33] Bryan [1920]; similar in Bryan 1922, 60. William Jennings Bryan, "The Menace of
Evolution," 1920, pamphlet reprinted at law2.umkc.edu/faculty/projects/ftrials/scopes/
bryanonevol.html. A similar remark appears at Bryan, *The Menace of Darwinism* (1922),
reprinted at archive.org/stream/menaceofdarwinis00brya/menaceofdarwinis00brya_djvu
.txt

next of kin to the monkey" (Bryan 1922, 32). Bryan favored a cosmology of sharp separation over a cosmology of continuity. Mary Douglas has taught us to ask: What is the correlate in social structure of a separating cosmology?[34]

Bryan supported "declaring it unlawful for any teacher, principal, superintendent, trustee, director, member of a school board, or any other person exercising authority in or over a public school, college or university, whether holding office by election or appointment, to teach or permit to be taught in any institution of learning, supported by public taxation, atheism, agnosticism, Darwinism, or any other hypothesis that links man in blood relationship to any other form of life" (Bryan [1920]). In Bryan's closing statement for the Scopes trial, the language of blood joins the moral argument against evolutionary violence to the racial argument about apes and "men":

> Analyze this dogma of darkness and death. Evolutionists say that back in the twilight of life a beast, name and nature unknown, planted a murderous seed [that] throbs forever in the blood of the brute's descendants, inspiring killings innumerable, for which murderers are not responsible because coerced by a fate fixed by the laws of heredity. It is an insult to reason and shocks the heart.[35]

The composite blood-objection is that humans share blood with "brutes" – and the blood of the brutes throbs with violence. It's not too much to hear this as a racist argument in a South between Reconstruction and Jim Crow. A "brute" can be human or animal. The White audience thinks of Blacks as brutish and violent, fearing kinship and intermarriage with them: "When there is poison in the blood, no one knows on what part of the body it will break out, but we can be sure that it will continue to break out until the blood is purified."[36]

How Bryan correlates his cosmology with society he has now made plain. Separatist cosmology here belongs to segregationist society; White fear racializes sex and violence as Black and names them "blood." Even if the concerns for theodicy and morality are sincere, the power in the cosmology and ethics arises from the social correlates summed up as "blood." Having associated blood with violence, descent, kinship, and sex, Bryan has rung nearly all the changes on the word. What remains for him yet to speak of is the blood of Christ. Everyone is waiting for it. Bryan does not disappoint

---

[34] In Chapter 3 I treated the separations that God makes in creating the world, and tried to distinguish between good and bad separations.

[35] William Jennings Bryan, *Closing Speech for the Scopes Trial* (1925). Reprinted at www .wright.edu/~christopher.oldstone-moore/Bryan.htm

[36] Bryan, *Closing Speech.*

150   BLOOD THEOLOGY

them. He saves it for the peroration. Either Bryan again channels the almost
ineliminable Christian constellation of the term, or, if you believe with
Durkheim in social agency, the language of blood recruits him to complete
the pattern:

> Again force and love meet face to face, and the question, "What shall I do
> with Jesus?" must be answered. A bloody, brutal doctrine – evolution –
> demands, as the rabble did 1900 years ago, that He be crucified. That cannot
> be the answer of this jury, representing a Christian state and sworn to
> uphold the laws of Tennessee. ... If the law is nullified, there will be
> rejoicing wherever God is repudiated, the Saviour scoffed at and the Bible
> ridiculed.[37]

How Creationists Now Appeal to Blood

A critic might find Bryan no longer a worthy opponent, but a scarecrow. As
evolution becomes more accepted, the objection based on kinship has grown
more complex. To distinguish humans from "brutes" no longer commands
a high ground. If the objection depends on drawing a line, it's too easy to
draw it in the wrong place, on the human rather than the animal side and
reveal yourself a racist of the worst sort. Therefore the more recent version of
this argument claims the moral high ground of *anti*-racism, while continuing
to draw lines in the language of blood. The transformation goes to show that
societies have a limited fund of metaphors to think with and would rather
repurpose than replace them. "Blood of man – blood of apes" may be out.
But the exception once again proves the rule. Change of theory cannot avoid
but must still invoke the language of blood. The current creationist theory
depends on images of blood all the same. They abound in a book called *One
Race, One Blood* (Ham and Ware 2007)[38] and its predecessor, *One Blood:
A Biblical Answer to Racism* by young-earth creationist Ken Ham.[39]

  One Blood opens with the most embarrassing failure of original Darwinism:
racism tacit or explicit. As we saw in Bryan, however, racism united
Darwinists with their evangelical opponents. The author of the *One Blood*
books compares twenty-first-century evangelicalism to nineteenth-century
Darwinism. Similarly, creationists can hold Darwinists responsible for Nazi

---

[37] Bryan, *Closing Speech*.
[38] Ken Ham and Charles Ware, *One Race, One Blood* (Green Forest, AZ: Master Books), 2007.
[39] Ken Ham, Carl Weiland, and Don Batten, *One Blood: The Biblical Answer to Racism* (Green
  Forest, AZ: Master Books), 1999.

racism, while neglecting to hold Christians responsible for Nazi supersessionism. In short, they compare their ideal with the other side's real.[40]

Two other theological arguments animate the *One Blood* books, the argument from scripture and the argument from soteriology. By an argument "from soteriology," I mean a *reductio ad absurdum* of the form, "if you don't buy my argument, then salvation doesn't work anymore." The paradigm cases are the great Christological and trinitarian arguments. Why must Jesus count as human? Because if not, human beings are not saved. Why must Jesus count as divine? Because if not, human beings are not saved. Why must the Holy Spirit count as divine? Because if not, human beings are not saved. All of the great Christian controversies have been settled this way – especially the ones that seemed irreconcilable. Because arguments from scripture are brittle, arguments from soteriology are almost always more robust and interesting.

Here the argument from soteriology motivates the title of the book. The *One Blood* of the title is not only the one blood of the one human race. It is also the one blood of Jesus that saves the human race. The whole book depends on the soteriological argument: *If* there is more than one human race, then Jesus saves only his, leaving the rest unsaved. That contradicts Christian missionary practice, so it's absurd. Because the blood of Jesus saves the whole human race, the whole race *must* be of one blood. Everyone must descend from the one Adam. Everyone must descend from the one Adam, so that the Second Adam, of the same race, can save them.

Just because the claim of "one blood" is so central, arguments from blood can remain scattered, disconnected, and short. Meanwhile arguments from scripture are long, continual, and sophisticated. That's because the blood arguments remain powerful and primordial enough to go, not without saying, but with a wave and a nod, while scriptural arguments are left to support a weight they can hardly bear. The blood argument belongs so

---

[40] That doesn't mean that creationist racism is gone. You can find it still on Facebook. Here is an ugly example: "Ken Ham's 'Answers in Genesis' wrote a book called 'Darwin's Plantation: Evolution's Racist Roots,' which was retitled 'One Race One Blood; a Biblical Answer to Racism.' And to prove how much Ken Ham is a negro worshipper, the book was co-authored by an Africanus Americana, Dr. Charles Ware, who is president of Crossroads Bible College in Indianapolis and a leader in multicultural ministry and racial reconciliation that is, race mixing. On their website you can read about their partnering with the Indiana Blood Center 'To make a difference in the lives of many.' I bet it would, mixing black blood with White blood [sic]. But hey, we're all one race right? We'll be hearing more about these two antichrist characters when the trial resumes. . . . Yes, we have flesh like the other races, but the other races do not have the promise of a Kinsman Redeemer turning our mortality back into immortality." www.facebook.com/notes/ken-ham/a-racist-church-be-prepared-to-be-shocked/331613053550834/ linking to www.fgcp.org/content/universalism-trial-part-3.

152　　BLOOD THEOLOGY

deeply to the underlying, unspoken mythic picture – Jesus on the cross, shedding blood for all, the one sacrifice – that Ham can expound it in five sentences and a woodcut. The woodcut reminds us that what follows is not so much an argument as a picture:

> Christ suffered death (the penalty for sin) on the cross, shedding his blood ("and without the shedding of blood is no remission," Hebrews 9:22) so that those who put their trust in His work on the cross can come in repentance of their sin or rebellion (in Adam) and be reconciled to God.
> Thus, only descendants of the first man Adam can be saved.
> The Bible describes *all* human beings as sinners and as being *all* related: "And He has made all nations of men of one blood to dwell on the face of the earth" (Acts 17:26). The gospel only makes sense if all humans who have ever lived (except for the first woman) are descendants of the first man, Adam. Eve, in a sense, was a "descendant" of Adam in that she was made from his flesh.[41]

***

ANTICIPATE THE CRUCIFIXION WITH ANOTHER PICTURE: THE BAPTISM, IN which Christ commits himself to the mission of friendship and solidarity that comes to include his crucifixion. The baptism in the Jordan places the crucifixion in the wider context of God's descent. God comes down from heaven to be with us, but not only down to the sea-level surface of the earth.[42] In Christ, God goes further down, into the water. The water of the Jordan forms the lowest river on earth, descending past Jericho, at negative 846 feet the earth's lowest city, to debouche some 600 feet further down at the earth's lowest patch of land, the shore of the Dead Sea, by which point the Jordan has become seven times saltier than the ocean. God goes deep into the earth and further into the water: and the Jordan follows a crevice where the crust is thin and fragile and the earth sinks between two tectonic plates. The Jordan Valley Rift forms part of the concatenation or conceit of faults called the Great Rift, which angles southeast to follow the Red Sea, then southwest into the East African Rift, where among other places humans first evolved and the thinness of the earth gave up the bones of Lucy. In icons of the Anastasis we see Jesus raising Adam and Eve, for all the patriarchs, out of the depths of Sheol. In the Jordan likewise we may fancy to see God's descent

---

[41] Ham 1999, 21–2.
[42] I was inspired to write this paragraph by a conversation with Warren Woodfin in the occupied West Bank about descent into the Rift Valley, and one with Aminah Bradford about the water of the Jordan.

into the depths of Palestine's conflicted water politics and of evolutionary time to pick up the oldest humans – together with the primates from which they evolved, the burgeoning life of the Rift Valley, and all the creatures that dwell in salty water or flow with the blood that reproduces it. The very name of the Jordan comes from the Hebrew root ירד (*yarad*), to descend, to go down, to prostrate. God descended to the lowest place on earth; God went down into the water, into a place, the Rift Valley, that brought forth humanity out of the earth. Like the concept of blood, that of crucifixion is freighted with solidarity, descent, and prostration, God under water with the baptized. Because the crucifixion is of God, whom no category can capture, believers dare not confine it to one meaning.

Socio-theological Critique of Creationist Appeals to Blood

Ham's brevity sums up what the audience already knows. It can tap the power stored up in a common narrative. This brevity, almost credal, encapsulates the power of the blood. Like a pill or a potion, a little goes a long way. It works more like a premise than an argument: it is not yet subject to such questions as, "Is this a good Christology? Is it a good theory of sacrifice?" Theologically, three things go wrong in Ham's argument.

1. *Overcoming Evil*. Ham's God can only avoid evil, not overcome it. The creationist argument treats mutations as "mistakes," and these "mistakes" add no "new information" but cause "degeneration."[43] This fits in very well with the doctrine of the fall, by which life runs down. But it's quite a stretch to call mutations "evil." Most of them are maladaptive. A few are not. They are more a sort of trial and lots of error, or an amoral drift, than intentional evil. At worst they belong to what traditional Catholic theology calls, not moral, but "ontological evil," a harm to functionality. At best, they bestow the dignity of searching on things. Ham's theory addresses this problem of theodicy. But Ham's theory assumes a God so helpless in the face of evil that God's only choice is to prevent rather than use it. Ham's theory overlooks an important biblical pattern, according to which it marks God to bring good out of evil. Not that God causes evil, but God can *use* evil to bring good, not as a necessary means, but with dramatic irony. So if you regard mutations as "degenerative" or even "evil," the

---

[43] Ham 1999, 43–5.

154   BLOOD THEOLOGY

question remains, can God work with them, even bring good out of them? The central stories of the Bible, from Israel's enslavement to Christ's crucifixion, involve God's *dealing* with rather than preventing evil. Out of Egypt Israel reaches Canaan; out of death God brings salvation.[44] *Felix culpa quae tantum ac talem meruit Redemptorem.* It may well be that Ham's God, who keeps the divine hands clean by not treating with evil, is the more attractive God – the "morally superior" God. But the God of the incarnation is not "superior" in that sense, but "counts equality with God not a thing to be grasped, taking the form of a servant" (Phil. 2:7). The God of Ham's account is not the God that grants the dignity of causation to all creatures; and it is not the God that substitutes a ram for Isaac, leads Israel out of bondage and into Canaan, or allows Christ crucified to found the church.

---

[44] The claim that God can deal with evil does not mean, according to classical theology, that God creates evil that good may come; the classical claim is that God permits freedom and copes with the consequences. For Christian theology to take on board a scientific account of geology and evolution, it needs an analogical continuum of freedom that goes all the way down, such as prevailed in the Middle Ages. According to this, every created thing is created to seek its good by its proper movement. In the paradigm case, humans seek the good by reason, and this is called human freedom. Above them, God pursues the good without limit, and this is the divine freedom. Below them, animals move toward their good, such as Alpo, by instinct. Below animals, plants move toward their good, such as sunlight, by growing. The medieval theory went as far as rocks, which have their good in the center of the earth and seek it by falling. But we may extend the theory to say that among the proper movements or appropriate freedoms of genes is to vary or of tectonic plates to drift. John McPhee describes it this way:

> The Pacific Plate, sliding, weighs three hundred and forty-five quadrillion tons. Like a city planner, the plate motions have created Los Angeles. The plate motions have shaped its setting and its setting's exceptional beauty, raising its intimate mountains ten thousand feet. The mountains are such a phalanx that air flowing in from the west cannot get over them, and a result is the inversion layer that concentrates smog. Plate motions in Los Angeles folded the anticlines that trapped the oil that rained gold and silver into the streets. Plate motions have formed a basin so dry that water must be carried to it five hundred miles. Plate motions have built the topography that has induced the weather that has brought the fire that has prepared the topography for city-wrecking flows of rock debris. Plate motions are benign, fatal, ruinous, continual, and inevitable. ... Plate motions are earthquakes. (John McPhee, *The Patch* [New York: Farrar, Straus and Giroux, 2018], 105, paragraph boundary elided.)

If maladaptive mutations or volcanic eruptions should result, that is the price of freedom: the only alternative would be a static, unfree world in which, medieval Christians supposed, they would not choose to live. As the historian of Darwinism and religion Peter Bowler has written, "Perhaps an 'open-ended' form of evolution is the only way that God could create beings with free will" (Bowler 2009, 192).

Christianity, along with all other religions worth their salt, deals with evil and suffering rather than denying them. Indeed, to deal with evil and suffering is largely their point. The only alternative would be to have evil and suffering without point. A God who takes creatures out of this world without dealing with evil and suffering is well known to Christian theologians; that is the rejected God of Gnosticism. But it would be fitting for God to bring evolution from mutation: that would be in character for the God of the Bible.[45]

2. *The Trouble with Sin.* The second trouble with the creationist argument is that it depends on *human sin to account for ontological evil.* It troubles creationists less that animals are violent *after* the fall of Adam, than that, according to evolution, animals are violent *before* the fall of Adam. Without a theory of backwards causality (no problem for more sophisticated theologians!), violence *before* Adam doesn't make sense to them and so they deny it. But (according to Marilyn Adams), that mistakes the problem. Violence isn't the deepest part of the problem – vulnerability is. The problem is that hurting people is so *easy.* We "ought" to be more defended, and we're not. We are flesh, vulnerable to suffering *out of scale* with the harm others can cause to us, or worse, that we can (even innocently) cause others. If the problem is suffering (with sin as a subset), Christ solves the problem in a different way, as God's solidarity rather than God's payment.[46]

3. *Confining the Blood of Christ to the Bible.* The third trouble with the creationist atonement is that it confines itself to a single point at the crucifixion, failing to radiate backward and forward to give meaning to other sacrifices before and after it, as in other forms of Christianity. This comes from the Reformation's elevation of scripture over Eucharist, or writing over ritual. In a book called *One Blood,* the blood of the crucified Jesus may be telegraphic, but the blood of the Eucharistic

---

[45] As Hoggard has written, "God in Christ suffers with all that suffers, human and non-human alike. ... But this is ... less helpful for non-human creatures. ... Humans can contemplate ... and be comforted. The lamb or the giraffe torn apart by a horde of lions [or sacrificers] has no such comfort, that makes sense to us, at least" (Hoggard, 60). We humans before our medical review boards now think morally so much in terms of informed consent that we don't know how to think about animals. We are not privy to their ways of knowledge and resignation, and so we expect too much or too little and use them to think with either way. They do not seek death, but romantically we comfort ourselves that they accept it gracefully. Perhaps the Aristotelian concept of flourishing works better, but that is a chapter for another day. Or perhaps it is enough for us to explain suffering to ourselves: as far as we know, animals do not try to explain or suffer from a lack of explanation.

[46] Marilyn McCord Adams, *Christ and Horrors: The Coherence of Christology* (Cambridge: Cambridge University Press), 2006.

156 BLOOD THEOLOGY

Jesus is absent. That's odder still because it's the office of the Eucharist, in other forms of Christianity, to create and maintain the kinship of the group. Young-earth creationists pile so much weight on pseudobiological kinship in Adam that none falls on Eucharistic kinship in Christ. If you must avoid Eucharistic kinship as catholicizing, then kinship hangs on exegesis, even exegesis that misreads Genesis as a textbook. Even if kinship in Adam is more universal than kinship in Eucharist, the signaling is too costly: this peacock keels over. The costs limit scripture's capacity truly to nourish the community and absorb the world. Mark Twain makes fun of the fall as a cause for animal predation in his *Extracts from Adam's Diary*: "About an hour after sun-up, as I was riding through a flowery plain where thousands of animals were grazing, slumbering, or playing with each other, according to their wont, all of a sudden they broke into a tempest of frightful noises, and in one moment the plain was a frantic commotion and every beast was destroying its neighbor. I knew what it meant – Eve had eaten that fruit, and death was come into the world."[47]

What Christian Accounts of Evolution Require

The sociological result is that blood language is ineliminable, but can be used in different ways. The narrow usage of blood to atone only for sin bespeaks a tight, narrow boundary around the social body: one that limits it in theory to human beings and in practice to a small, embattled social group. Social groups in theory defining themselves to include human ancestors and in practice more secure in their intellectual, economic, and political power find themselves free to expand the role of blood language to encompass human and animal suffering. To remain both theologically adequate and sociologically robust, Christian accounts of evolution need more blood, not less. With this remark, I am not trying to repair creationism, but to prefer alternatives. Christian accounts of evolution need, that is, a more adequate theology of the atonement – one that need not reduce suffering to sin. One example is Marilyn Adams; another is Teilhard de Chardin, much too brief, but still suggestive. *In "The Mass on the World," as we have seen, he interprets the whole world as an altar, on which animals preyed upon and species extinguished suffer and die, and on which the successes of evolution are lifted up. Christ the Logos presides over the whole. Upon every achievement of*

---

[47] Mark Twain, *Adam's Diary* (New York and London: Harper Bros, 1904 [1893]), 43.

development or growth, Christ pronounces "This is my body." Upon every death and extinction, Christ pronounces "This is my blood."[48] More ancient examples would include Irenaeus of Lyon and Athanasius of Alexandria.

In either case, the Durkheimian structure that I call "the analogy of blood" causes that connection, the connection between blood and Blood, to *persist,* however we explain it, and although it waxes and wanes. The analogy of blood marks the whole social structure *within which* theological debates play out. Quite apart from non-creationist Christians, evolutionary scientists and other citizens concerned for the health of public discourse, public funding, and public education therefore gain an interest in wider blood discourses that treat sin as a form of suffering because they are better able to use the ineliminable blood rhetoric to accommodate evolution. Orthodox Christology makes every creature a companion, gives every creature a share in the divine body, and, for the sake of the divine body, in the divine blood.[49]

In Chesterton's *The Man Who Was Thursday,* human beings participate in the battle between being and nothingness, fragile on the frontier, and receive – as also in Julian of Norwich – honor for their wounds. Sunday, the God-figure, says to the disciple-figures, "you were always heroes – epic on epic, iliad on iliad, and you always brothers in arms. Whether it was but recently (for time is nothing), or at the beginning of the world, I sent you out to war. ... You did not forget your secret honour, though the whole cosmos turned an engine of torture to tear it out of you."

Syme, the Peter-figure, one-ups Sunday in applying the heroism not just to humans, but to the whole created world:

> "Why does each thing on the earth war against each other thing? Why does each small thing in the world have to fight against the world itself? Why does a fly ... [or] a dandelion have to fight the whole universe? For the same reason that I had to be alone in the Council of the Days. So that each thing that obeys law may have the glory and the isolation of the anarchist. So that each [one] fighting for order may be as brave and good ... as the dynamiter. So that ... by tears and torture we may earn the right to say to this [accuser], 'We also have suffered.'"
>
> He turned his eyes so as to see suddenly the great face of Sunday, which wore a strange smile.

---

[48] Teilhard, 123.
[49] Paraphrasing Karl Barth, *Church Dogmatics* II/2 (Edinburgh, T. and T. Clark, 1957), 142.

158   BLOOD THEOLOGY

"Have you," he cried in a dreadful voice, "have you ever suffered?"

As he gazed, the great face grew to an awful size, grew larger than the colossal mask of Memnon, which had made him scream as a child. It grew larger and larger, filling the whole sky; then everything went black. Only in the blackness before it entirely destroyed his brain he seemed to hear a distant voice saying a commonplace text that he had heard somewhere, "Can ye drink of the cup that I drink of?"

When the Accuser asks, "Have you, have you ever suffered?" this God allows every creature to say "Yes" – because this is the God who, when the Peter figure asks, "Have you, have you ever suffered?" can answer with another question, "Can ye drink of the cup that I drink of?"[50]

In Chesterton, evil may be an illusion, but suffering is real: a wound to be honored and a solidarity to be shared.

---

[50] G. K. Chesterton, "The Accuser," in *The Man Who Was Thursday* (London and New York: Penguin Books, 1986), 179–83.

Excursus: Brittleness in Scripture and Community

A word that captures many features of creationists' appeal to *sola scriptura* is "brittleness." Brittleness is a technical term in geology, opposed to "ductility." Brittle rocks are inflexible; under stress they easily shear. That's what Protestant groups do: they shear under pressure; they are liable to schism. Brittle rocks do not lack strength, but enjoy it only in the dimension perpendicular to the layers. They do well under pressure, or when squeezed. They do not stretch well or (to put "stretching" into Latin) respond well to tension. In short, certain pressures can make them stronger. But under tensions from different directions, they simply break. Sociologically, the metaphor implies that groups with brittle boundaries or authorities are fissiporous, subject to division. Imagine your foundations built upon shale. You have bedrock; you can apply weight; the foundation is not subject to any softness; it will not bend, bow, or flow; but you can build only with delicacy and difficulty. The friability in bedrock provokes anxiety. It cannot shift, compress, rebound, or flow under pressure; it tends to crack or even shatter. So it is that the cry of "*sola scriptura*" is in practice anxious rather than confident: groups fear that if the shale gives in one direction it will not give at all, but fly into pieces: the whole house will fall. Such appeals make scripture a foundation that cannot give.

"Brittleness" bears not only a technical sense in geology, but a popular sense in psychology. A personality can also be "brittle." The brittle person, like the brittle shale or the brittle appeal to scripture, also does not lack strength, but possesses it in one direction rather than another, like a piece of glass; straight, transparent, upright, but rigid and subject to shattering. A brittle personality "shows little adaptive flexibility when encountering novel or stressful situations."[51] The brittle personality wears a self-confident mask to cover anxiety. It is low in resilience, quick to anger on slight provocation.

Theologically, brittle groups are marked by appeals to purity (according to insiders) rather than charity (according to outsiders). This diagnosis was classically applied by Augustine in the Donatist controversy. In this case, brittle groups have little "give" in another sense: they subordinate charity to purity.

Historically, the "literal sense" of the Bible is flexible, not brittle under premodern conditions, where it means "what the author intends." Since the

---

[51] S. J. Huey, Jr. and J. R. Weisz, "Ego Control, Ego Resiliency," *J. Abnormal Psychology* 106 (1997): 404–15; here, 404.

author can be read to intend more than one thing, especially with authorship ascribed to God, the literal sense can be capacious.[52] Two features distinguish that account from more familiar ones. 1. It's premodern (i.e., pre-fundamentalist), so the literal sense is not univocal, but supports spiritual senses, because literal includes whatever the Author intends. And that requires a whole class of readings that are true and accord with how the words go (*salva litterae circumstantia*). 2. It accepts historical criticism on theological grounds, because God (a) does not violate human agency and (b) subjected Godself to historical circumstance in the incarnation. Yes, it still holds that God's providence rules the world, but that now means that historical criticism helps reveal God's intention rather than denying it.

Scripture is brittle, like an old piece of paper. Even vellum is blood-less and grows brittle with time.[53] Blood, however, is ductile. It flows. These two principles of unity have opposite strengths. Brittle groups are high-group and low-grid, although not all high-group, low-grid denominations are brittle. Baptists and Quakers are both high-group, low-grid, and even high-tension, but Baptists are brittle and Quakers are not. That's because the totemic principle of community has different characteristics. For Quakers, the principle of unity is the Spirit, which is highly ductile and blows where it wills. For Baptists, the principle of unity is scripture, which is subject to tearing. Better for the Spirit to write on the heart than on paper.

---

[52] Hans Frei, "The 'Literal Reading' of Biblical Narrative in the Christian Tradition: Does It Stretch or Will It Break," in Frank McConnell, ed., *The Bible and the Narrative Tradition* (Oxford: Oxford University Press, 1986), 36–77.

[53] I owe this conceit to conversation with Lauren Winner.

7

BLOOD PURITY AND HUMAN SACRIFICE
Castilians Meet Aztecs in War

Usually, the ceremony peaked when splendidly attired captors and captives danced in procession to the various temples where they were escorted (sometimes unwillingly) up the stairways to the sacrificial stone. The victim was [arched over] the sacrificial stone (*techcatl*) [to expose and distend the chest], held down by a group of four priests, and the temple priest cut through the chest wall with the ritual flint knife (*tecpatl*). The priest grasped the still-beating heart, called "precious eagle cactus fruit," tore it from the chest, offered it [one source specifies, steaming] to the sun for vitality and nourishment, and placed it in a curved circular vessel called the *cuauhxicalli* (eagle bowl). In one case, the body, now called "eagle man," was rolled, flailing, down the temple steps to the bottom where it was skinned and dismembered. In several rites the corpse was decapitated, the skull was removed, the brains taken out, and, after skinning, it was placed on the Tzompantli (skull rack), which consisted of long poles horizontally laid and loaded with skulls. In Tlacaxipehualiztli, the Feast of the Flaying of Men, the captor ... together with his relatives ... celebrated a ritual meal consisting of "a bowl of stew of dried maize called tlacatlaolli ... on each went a piece of the flesh of the captive."[1]

Beyond intra-Christian disputes, blood debates fuel civil ones. In the late 2010s, a presidential candidate shamed his interviewer as "bleeding from her wherever," and neo-Nazis marched in Charlottesville chanting "blood and soil." Yale sociologist Philip Gorski argues that such blood references are "knit together by a hidden logic" so that "[t]he metaphor of blood connects white racism (blood purity), unrestrained militarism (blood conquest), and no-holds-barred anti-terrorist policies (blood sacrifice)." Gorski sees a secularized (I would say blasphemous) religious nationalism, stripped of Christian language, ethics, and transcendence, which doubles down on apocalyptic conflict and national salvation,

---

[1] Davíd Carrasco, *City of Sacrifice: The Aztec Empire and the Role of Violence in Civilization* (Boston: Beacon Press, 1999), 83–4. The internal quotation is not identified.

161

often invoking the language of blood. The appeal of a familiar framework "not only explains why so many evangelicals rallied to Trump," Gorski points out, but also which ones: those who go to church less often.[2] Misuses of blood language, both civil and theological, repeat the question of this Part: Given that blood language is not going to go away, how does blood-language go *wrong*? Especially in contexts of nationalism and its bloodiest consequence, war?

Although both Bush administrations revived "just war" arguments in terms of "blood and treasure," other wars lie far enough away or long enough ago to generate more light than heat. During and after the *Reconquista*, Christian warfare against Muslims in the Iberian peninsula and then against indigenous peoples in Mexico preoccupied Spanish Christians with real blood and sacrifice. In *Reconquista* Spain, Ferdinand's barely united state turned its anxieties inward with anti-Semitic laws on *limpieza de sangre* (purity of blood) among Christian converts from Judaism and Islam. The same state turned those anxieties outward to conquer Mexico, where Franciscans, sensitized by blood-purity debates, spent fifty years recording Aztec human sacrifice in drawings and codices dominated by red. Both Castilians and Aztecs signaled their external bounds and internal hierarchy with blood.[3] Distinctively Christian or Christianist ethnicizing ideas of blood purity crossed the Atlantic to rubricate Christian perceptions of Mesoamerican sacrifice. In the conquest of Mexico, Gorski's three bloods come together with a vengeance: Castilian blood purity, Aztec blood sacrifice, and two traditions of blood conquest. Warfare remains the greatest danger of summoning blood through image and language, however we try to sublimate or subvert it. Yet this chapter is not ethics, but an attempt to analyze and channel the symbols.

How did the contemporaneous Spanish accounts of Aztec blood and sacrifice show the influence of the Spaniards' own preoccupations with blood and sacrifice? In the recent past, everyone thought they knew that the Aztecs did not *really* sacrifice their victims – like cannibalism, human sacrifice was less a reality than an accusation against one's enemies. But the new consensus, based on archaeological and skeletal evidence that aligns

---

[2] Phillip S. Gorski, "Why Do Evangelicals Vote for Trump?" in *The Immanent Frame: Secularism, Religion, and the Public Sphere* (Oct. 4, 2016) at tif.ssrc.org/2016/10/04/why-do-evangelicals-vote-for-trump/. See also Gorski, "Why Evangelicals Voted for Trump," *American Journal of Cultural Sociology* (2017), doi:10.1057/s41290-017-0043-9.

[3] "Aztec" was never the native term for any ethnic group, but few English-speaking theologians would recognize the others (Mexica, Nahua, Colhuah, Tenochca). Scholarly consensus is evolving, and Aztec remains the most common term.

with Aztec statues, carvings, and inscriptions, as well as with Spanish descriptions, is that human sacrifice did take place.[4] The authors of our earliest descriptions of Aztec sacrifice were Spanish Franciscan friars and priests. They arrived in the New World with extensive experience of both the sacrifices of war and of *limpieza de sangre,* or "purity of blood," from *Reconquista* Castile. Franciscan priests who performed "the sacrifice of the mass" every day depicted Aztec priests who performed ritual killings atop the pyramids every month. How did Spaniards' prior preoccupation with blood and race influence their account of Aztec sacrifice? Did it cause them to see connections between their blood rituals and those of the Aztecs? Were those connections real or projected? Having perceived them consciously or subconsciously, did the observers acknowledge or deny them? What form did their denial take? Did they perceive a rival? To the extent that rivalry or denial infected their encounter, did they reenact in Mexico the rivalry and denial that in Castile they had felt against Jews? Jews and Aztecs do not seem much alike. But they both became *near others* – both neighbors and objects of inimical projection – to Castilian Christians. Jews, who shared blood and scripture with Jesus, were too close for comfort; and Aztecs, who shared blood and sacrifice with the Catholic priesthood, suggested disturbing comparisons. To what extent did Franciscan priests intentionally or unwittingly inflect their accounts of *Aztec* sacrifice with their commitment to *Christian* sacrifice – did they attempt to differentiate and distinguish an image disturbingly alike? We will not answer all these questions, but they overshadow the account that follows.

Blood Purity

The most important book about blood purity in Reconquista Spain was written by an American, in French, and only then translated into Spanish: Albert A. Sicroff, *Los estatutos de limpieza de sangre: Controversias entre los siglos XV y XVII.* According to Sicroff and his sources, "blood" in Reconquista Spain is about class, which is to say, about lineage and privilege.[5] Recent scholarship, on the other hand, has focused almost entirely on the extent to which blood purity anticipates modern discourses of race. Much of that scholarship argues about what the word "race" means now, in order to

---

[4] Davíd Carrasco, *The Aztecs: A Very Short Introduction* (Oxford: Oxford University Press, 2011), 61–3.
[5] Trans. Mauro Armiño, revised by the author (Madrid: Taurus, 1979), 9–24, 307–48.

164   BLOOD THEOLOGY

apply or trace it then.[6] Only stray sentences of that discussion are remotely
theological. It never seriously connects its disputes about race to disputes about
Paul on Jews and Gentiles, or the Christology of Christ's Jewishness, or the
significance of baptism. This chapter, therefore, tries to throw a different light.
It asks about the untheology in favor of blood purity; the real theology against
blood purity; and the reasons why the real theology so fecklessly failed. Yet in
raising the last question – why the real theology remained of little effect – this
remains a theological, not a historical analysis. My conclusion will be as
historically simplistic as it is theologically profound: The real theology failed
because of sin. It lost not in the intellect but in the heart.

But first we need enough details, if not to prove, at least to color such
a claim.

Popular uprisings without royal authority forced huge numbers of Jews to
convert beginning in 1391, "grasping despairingly at Christianity to escape
death" (Sicroff, 46); a hundred years later, in 1492, royal authority expelled
those unconverted. Vicente Ferrer, called in his own time "the angel of the
Apocalypse," and afterwards a saint, was said, by his death in 1419, to have led
some 35,000 Jews into baptism. In Valencia alone, where Ferrer was active,
lower estimates of the numbers converted cluster between 7,000 and 11,000 –
and range as high as 100,000. One of his converts, Jerónimo de Santa Fe, coerced
numerous rabbis to attend a "disputation" a hundred miles south at Tortosa,
attempting to prove from the Talmud that Jesus was the Messiah, at which all
but two converted, bringing their congregations with them.[7]

The conversions maintained social class. Jews of high class became
Christians of high class.[8] In Aragón, the family de la Caballería traced its

---

[6] Perhaps the most judicious is David Nirenberg, "Was There Race Before Modernity? The
Example of 'Jewish Blood' in Late Medieval Spain," in *The Origins of Racism in the West*, ed.
Ben Isaac, Yossi Ziegler, and Miriam Eliav-Feldon (Cambridge: Cambridge University
Press, 2010), 233–64, with references to more recent literature. "All racisms," he writes,
"are attempts to ground discriminations, whether social, economic, or religious, in biology
and reproduction. All claim a congruence of 'cultural' categories with 'natural' ones" (235).
"What if . . . we treat race as but one chapter in the long history of the conviction that culture
is produced and reproduced in the same way that the species procreates itself?" (239).
"But . . . real biological differences have no obvious or natural relationship to the cultural
work they are asked to do in systems of racial discrimination, systems which are products of
culture, not of nature" (236). "We cannot solve this difficulty by cutting ('race did not exist
before modernity'), by stitching ('race has always already existed') or by refusing to talk about
what cannot be clearly defined ('races do not exist, and race does not have a history')" (262).
"We cannot reject [theorizations of race] without impoverishment, but neither can we
accept their suggestions without suspicion" (263). That conclusion goes in spades, of
course, for theorizations of blood.

[7] Sicroff, 46.

[8] Sicroff, 48.

nobility to King David to place itself in the line of Christ. Alfonso de Aragón y Escobar, half-brother of King Ferdinand II, married Estenza ha-Cohen, daughter of a rich Jewish merchant, one of whose sons (another Alfonso) became Archbishop of Tarragona.[9] Hernando de Talavera, whom Sicroff (13) identifies as a *converso*, studied theology at Salamanca, became bishop of Ávila, archbishop of Granada, and confessor of Queen Isabella. Another of Jerónimo's converts, Andrés Beltrán, became bishop of Barcelona. In still another case, the chief rabbi of Burgos, Solomon ha-Levi de la Caballería, became Pablo de Santa María – its bishop (Sicroff, 48–50).

Such examples show that – despite expulsions – episcopacy, nobility, and even royalty coursed with ineliminable "Jewish blood." In Sicroff's analysis, elites accepted the realities and complexities of conversion and intermarriage, but non-elites (in reality or imagination) saw their mobility blocked. Their anxiety affected everyone, and, to agitate them further, intermarriage and integration meant that expulsion – what we would now, by a similar metaphor, call "ethnic cleansing" – could never "succeed." There could be no unmixing, but centuries of suspicion.

On January 10, 1449, the northeastern Iberian kingdom of Aragon invaded the central kingdom of Castile. At that time, the kingdoms were ruled by two Juans II, who were not the same. These were the two kingdoms that Ferdinand II (of Aragón) and Isabella I (of Castile) would unite to form the nucleus of modern Spain when Ferdinand's father died in 1479.[10] Thirty years earlier, that solution was not yet in sight. On January 26, Álvaro de Luna, constable of Castile (the king's enforcer), arrived in Toledo to demand a loan from the city, to be raised as a tax, of 1,000,000 maravedís, for Castile's defense. But the conflict was far to their north, and the people of Toledo resisted. Their resistance found a place to overflow: The municipal treasurer, Alonso Cota, would collect the tax; Alonso Cota was a rich *converso*; therefore, the people supposed, Alonso Cota must secretly have instigated the sudden tax, somehow to profit thereby. On January 27, after the king's enforcer had left town, cathedral officials rang the bells to gather the people in the *plaza*, who then sacked the neighborhood of the richest *conversos* and killed one of its defenders. It was a short step to pass an ordinance that *conversos* might no longer serve as city officials. In sum: two Gentile Christian states went to war and blamed Jewish Christians for what it cost.

---

[9] Sicroff, 48. Of the many Alfonsos of Aragón, the father is the one who lived 1417–85, the son, the one who served as Archbishop of Tarragona 1512–14.

[10] Distinguish Juan II, king of Castile (1405–54), father of Isabella, from Juan II, king of Aragón (1398–1479), father of Ferdinand.

166   BLOOD THEOLOGY

But the unrest didn't stop there: others saw how to use it for wider purposes. The same king who imposed a new tax had also imposed a new mayor. The king and his taxes becoming unpopular, the new mayor, Pedro Sarmiento, found his position insecure. His duty was to restore order, but his interest was to lead the rebellion. So he joined "the people," fortified the city with the rebels, denied reentry to the king's enforcer, and enriched himself from the businesses of the New (Jewish) Christians. Under those circumstances, he proclaimed the first ordinance of blood purity in Spain.[11]

His ally Esteben García defended the ordinance. Previous kings had conceded various *privilegios* for the well-being of Toledo. The current king had confirmed them all. Among those privileges, Garcia claimed, was that of expelling *conversos* of Jewish origin from public office. The Old Christians of Toledo were merely asserting that ancient privilege. Anyone who opposed them was eroding the ancient privileges of the city.

References to such a "privilege" became popular from that moment. But before that moment, historians have found no documentation of, or even references to such a privilege. Sicroff calls it a *"privilegio fantasma."*[12]

It was, in short, the familiar but ungranted privilege for some Christians to be better than others – as Orwell would put it, "more equal." In the past, Gentile Christians had been "better than" Jews, and it was that ungranted but undoubtedly ancient "privilege" that they sought to maintain. It was that privilege that they remembered with a familiarity that seemed to make it true. To defend that privilege they adopted the language of blood. That cannot be a good use of Christian blood-language. It is one of the evil ones. Can we take the negative example as a principle, the principle that the defense of privilege – real or imagined – cannot be a proper use of Christian blood-language? Christ, after all, considered equality with God *not* a privilege to be grasped, but humbled himself, taking the form of a slave (Phil. 2:6).

(In the English American colonies, the form of a slave, according to the legal principle *partus sequitur ventrem*, followed the blood of the mother; in Christian Spain, the form of a Jew should have followed the blood of Mary.)[13]

When the mayor and "old Christians" of Toledo see their "privileges" eroded and resist the king's war taxes, they looked for money-lenders, in

---

[11] The ordinance (*"Sentencia-Estatuto"*) appears in Fritz Baer, *Die Juden im christlichen Spanien*, 2 vols. (Berlin: Akademie-Verlag, 1936), vol. II, #302, pp. 315–17. You might suspect a book about Jews published in Berlin in 1936. The editor, however, took the name Yitzhak Baer, began to teach at Hebrew University in 1928, and won the Israel Prize in 1958.

[12] Sicroff, 53–4, n. 33. See Benzion Netanyahu, "Did the Toledans in 1449 Rely on a Real Royal Privilege," *Proceedings of the American Academy of Jewish Research* 44 (1977): 93–125.

[13] I owe this remark to Gregory Williams.

a time-honored way, and blamed them as Jews. Here is a paradox: the elites – royalty, nobility, hierarchy – accepted New Christians, often with fanfare; non-elites suspected them. But the nobility found it terrible to have their pedigree investigated. After Toledo, they could not beat back prejudice. At least, that's the version of the story kindest to the Old Christians.

David Nirenberg describes another defense of the statute by the Bachelor Marco García de Mora:

> "baptised Jews and those proceeding from their damaged line" were waging an implacable and cruel war against Christianity. Their conversions were motivated only by ambition for office and "carnal lust for nuns and [Christian] virgins." *Marrano* physicians even poisoned their Christian patients in order to get hold of their inheritance and offices, "marry the wives of the old Christians they kill" and stain their "clean blood" (*sangre limpia*). Arguing that all those "descended from the perverse lineage of the Jews" were, like their ancestors in ancient times, "enemies" who sought above all "to destroy all the Old Christians," the Toledans set about confronting the danger, first with violence, and then with a "Sentencia-Estatuto" banning descendants of converts from holding public office for at least four generations.[14]

How, I wondered, could a Christian society so lose sight of baptism? Did they not destroy confidence in baptism through their own act, their own most grievous act, of imposing it by force?[15] By what twist of theology could they justify *limpieza de sangre*? I expected – perhaps I even hoped – to find some weird and crooked arguments. I didn't. I found no arguments that qualified as theology at all. I found instead excellent theological arguments *against limpieza de sangre*. We might mine them for anti-racist theology today. The Confessing Church against Nazi Germany and the South African churches against apartheid might have used them with profit.

On the one hand, good theology fought back. On the other hand, it manifestly failed. It failed for three hundred years. It was feckless, if not entirely impotent. The resistance of popes, kings, bishops, and abbots fairly quickly gave way and showed itself of no effect.

Although – telling weakness – even the *anti*-purity arguments reassured their opponents that they did not oppose social class. Both sides, *for and against* "blood purity," sought to preserve privilege from one generation to the next.

---

[14] Nirenberg, 254–5, quoting Eloy Benito Ruano, "El Memorial del bachiller Marcos García de Mora contra los conversos," in *Los orígenes del problema converso* (Barcelona: El Albir, 1976), 95–132; here, 103, 111, 113.

[15] I owe this question to Greg Williams.

168   BLOOD THEOLOGY

Thus blood purity and not the theology of baptism was the theory that, as Marx put it writing on Hegel's *Philosophy of Right*, became a "material force" because it had "gripped the masses."[16]

Here is one of the good theological arguments. It comes from a Jewish-Christian family. In the same year, 1449, Alonso de Cartagena, archbishop of Burgos (son of the former-rabbi-turned-archbishop Pablo de Santa María), responded to the blood-purity statutes in Toledo with his *Defensorium Unitatis Christianae* (*Defense of Christian Unity*). It became "the manual from which *conversos* took the majority of their arguments" (Sicroff, 62). It begins, as the title indicates, not with pleas for justice, or testimonials about what good Christians *conversos* were, but with Christian unity, which had always been a matter of solidarity in difference; and it was directed to the king, whose office it was always to seek the unity of the realm.

God's plan of creation, Alonso argued, had always included difference in unity: there was one flesh from Adam, and many peoples. Among them, God chose one to be ministers of God; why that one belongs to the mystery of God's election lies beyond human examination (Sicroff, 64).

God is the same in both Testaments, and the New Testament contains much of the Old. It is therefore converted *Gentiles* who encounter the New Testament as strange (65). "The Gentiles who receive Christianity can be compared to sons who after a long absence return to their father's house, whereas the Jews would be the daughters who never abandoned the hearth" (Sicroff's paraphrase, 65–6). When Christ arrived to reunite the peoples in a New Jerusalem, it was Gentiles who had to be integrated into the Church (66). In baptism there was "no Jew or Greek . . . but you are all one in Christ Jesus" (Gal. 3:28–29).

If Christ were another savior, distinct from the Old Testament promise, and excluded Jews, Alonso continues, how to explain Paul's numerous exhortations to Jews in the New Testament?[17] Even if in a new sense an "Israelite" belongs to the New Israel, the Church, then how to justify rejecting an Israelite who is that in a double sense, in the flesh *and* in the Church? If Israelites (of both types!) have sinned, how (citing Isaiah 43:27–44:3) does that take away God's repeated renewals of the promise? As Paul reminds his Gentile followers, "it is not you that support the root, but the root that supports you" (Rom. 11:18; Sicroff, 67).

---

[16] I owe the remark to Greg Williams.

[17] The rhetorical questions that follow are a translation or close paraphrase of Sicroff's version of Cartagena.

BLOOD PURITY AND HUMAN SACRIFICE   169

Alonso does not hesitate to apply the word "heretic" to those guilty of the ordinances in Toledo. "Who can deny that this error sows discord among brothers and teaches a grave schism in Christianity?" (Sicroff, 81).

Against such arguments, how could blood-purity rules prevail in an environment of theologically educated and virtuously committed people – in a monastery?

The Iberian Hieronymites were founded in 1373 as strict followers of the Augustinian rule. (Called *jerónimos* in Spanish, they commemorated St. Jerome, the translator of the Vulgate, not Jerónimo de Santa Fe, the anti-Jewish *converso*, whom they preceded.) They accused *conversos* among their ranks of keeping the Jewish Sabbath and fasting on Yom Kippur (Sicroff, 104) – observances that Jesus also kept.

In 1485, the order came into "dishonor" with the Inquisition, due in part to a certain fray Diego de Marchena, whose observances go unrecorded (Sicroff, 105). In 1486 the Inquisition ordered an investigation "to avoid disorder and enable good Catholics to enjoy the love and mutual esteem prescribed by the Gospels by living in harmony, without attending to differences of descent" (Sicroff, 105). "Conscious that some *conversos* had entered the order simply to avoid inquisitorial inquiries, the Hieronymites ended by decreeing that no New Christian could take the habit of Saint Jerome, before the kingdom should be clean of all heresy" (Sicroff, 106). The prior of Guadalupe asked Pope Innocent VIII to confirm a rule to exclude Hieronymite *conversos* from the offices of prior, vicar, or confessor, on account of "the recent, bitter experiences 'from which the Order received greater dishonor than it had ever received since its foundation.'"[18] (Of course, Jesus received dishonor without self-defense.)

A reaction against that move began in San Bartolomé, where fray García de Madrid petitioned to have the Superior General annul the rule. García produced a bull of Nicholas V excommunicating the authors of blood-purity regulations as schismatics, and, closer to home, "invoked the Synod of Toledo (1483), which had denounced as contrary to the Christian faith any demand that a monastery, college, or confraternity submit their members to an examination of their descent as a condition of admission." The Archbishop, Alonso Carrillo, applied those authorities against the monastery by ordering them to repeal the rules of blood purity within a month (Sicroff, 106). The Superior General, fray Rodrigo de Orenes, "fell to his knees

---

[18] Sicroff, p. 106, quoting from fray José de Sigüenza, *Historia de la Orden de San Jerónimo*, 2nd ed., 2 vols. (Madrid, 1907–9), vol. 2, p. 33*a*.

begging absolution for his sin" and excommunicated two priors who opposed his decision (107).

But later that year Orenes' term as Superior General came to an end. Three hours before the chapter to elect his successor, Orenes tried to detain the excommunicated as schismatics to prevent them from participating. They produced letters of absolution from the bishop of Palencia. They remained to elect a new, anti-*converso* Superior General.

The New Christians then produced royal charters in which the Catholic Monarchs begged the Order to renounce the policy of blood purity.

At that point the prior of La Sisla, fray Juan de Corales, made a long speech.[19] He admitted that discriminating against converted Jews went against the Christian faith. The Order could deny them, as converts, none of the spiritual and temporal benefits of Christians. The letters of Paul, the decrees of popes, and the decisions of councils prohibited such discrimination and justly excommunicated its authors.

Furthermore, everyone was equal in sin, children of wrath and perdition, whom the mercy of God alone could save, so that no one could claim special privilege. That was the Creed, confessing one church indivisible.

The Hieronymites intended to exclude no one on the basis of descent, Jewish, Moorish, Arab, pagan, or Turkish. The Order had established blood purity as a condition for entering the Order not out of contempt for Jews, but for other grave reasons altogether. The text itself of the rule "expressed its desire to avoid the dishonor that fell upon the Order from admitting those with no intention beyond saving themselves from the Inquisition. Those refugees constituted a turbulent element in the Order, where they formed factions, insinuated themselves ... into high positions, and even more gravely, taught their false doctrines to the ignorant."

"Given the role of the *conversos* within the Order of San Jerónimo, fray Juan found the statute necessary, salutary, and in conformity with the authority of Saint Paul and the Holy Scripture." His argument, according to Sicroff, "promptly convinced vacillators that they should ratify the statute of blood purity."

Nevertheless, they did not. Against their conviction, they acceded to the will of the monarchs, and ended by revoking the statute.

Yet the Order kept seeking ways to adopt the statute until they benefitted from the election of a new pope. Alexander VI was Spanish. On December 22, 1495, he wrote that although many New Christians enjoyed excellent reputations, others bore the guilt of apostasy and heresy. To protect

---

[19] The exposition of this speech translates, abridges, and paraphrases Sicroff, 109–11.

the honor of the Order, the new pope consented to the rule that the Order might admit no one until the fourth generation after conversion. Current New Christian members of the Order could neither exercise any office nor receive the priesthood (Sicroff, 113).

After that, other orders adopted statutes to purify their blood (Sicroff, 116–22), and defenders of inclusive Christian orthodoxy began to publish their arguments anonymously. Arguing in the *conversos'* favor became a pretext to investigate an author's orthodoxy and parentage (177–90). The investigations drove true theology into spirituality – as in Teresa of Ávila, herself rumored to have Jewish forbears – or anonymity. Its authors were the real "anonymous Christians."

The controversy over blood purity supports Aquinas's claim that the intellect must remain less affected by sin, precisely to locate sin more firmly in the will (even if – or just because – an evil will can also misdirect the intellect). Is it possible to draw lessons about the use of blood-language from the example of blood purity? Perhaps so. Here are some candidates: The language of blood must not be used to protect privilege or honor. The languages of "purity" and "order" are suspect from long abuse and must bear the burden of proof.

$$***$$

TIMOTHY RADCLIFFE INTERPRETS THE LETTER TO THE HEBREWS TO commend the reverse: the subversion of privilege and purity. He calls its rhetorical technique "cultic irony."[20] He means that the letter plays on tropes of purity – which relate to those of honor – to release the energy contained in the sacred or taboo. In Mary Douglas's analysis, now familiar, purity and danger mark two countries that meet in social lines – and the energy of maintaining their boundary does not confine itself to maintaining the lines, but can creatively break out when a figure, like Jesus or the pangolin, transgresses them. The book of Hebrews, according to Radcliffe, undams the power of purity and danger, not by invoking, but by ironizing them. Radcliffe does not mean to privilege a Christian strategy over a rabbinic one; he notes that "All [the] groups that could no longer take part in the liturgy of the Temple went on using cultic, priestly language. ... The liturgy was not just the specialized activity of a few hereditary families butchering sheep and goats, but a metaphor for God's making and sustaining of the cosmos. So even when the cult finally ceased in Jerusalem, one still had to go on talking about God, the creator of heaven and earth" (495).

---

[20] Timothy Radcliffe, O.P., "Christ in Hebrews: Cultic Irony," *New Blackfriars* 68 (1987): 494–504. I owe my attention to this article to Janet Soskice.

172   Blood Theology

In that shared context, "[The book of] Hebrews transformed what it meant to talk of God as creator, and so subverted the meaning of cultic language. Hebrews is faithful to the proper reference of sacrificial and priestly language but it transforms its meaning by seeing God's creative act as being not, most typically, [disclosed in the great cosmic separations of the beginning: of light and darkness, day and night, the waters above and the waters below,] the great conquest of chaos in Genesis 1, but in the death and resurrection of Christ."[21] Therefore, Hebrews releases the language of purity from maintaining the divisions that created the cosmos. Rather, it is now Jesus the great high priest, rather than the separations of Genesis, through whom God "also created the world," and Jesus who "upholds the universe by his word of power" (Heb. 12:1). In this new interpretation of Genesis, it is Jesus who "makes purity" (*katharismon*) not by maintaining distinctions, but by crossing them: by passing from life to death and back – doing so not by keeping and containing but by sharing and shedding his blood (Radcliffe, 496) – by transgressing a border.

According to Radcliffe, "the author of Hebrews turns [the principle of separation] on its head and bases the priesthood of Christ on his solidarity, closeness, to others. The OT priest was such by virtue of his separation from others [like the priesthoods of many other religions, including the Catholic, Radcliffe should add!]; Jesus is the great high priest by virtue of his solidarity" (499): "Therefore he had to be made like his brethren in every respect, so that he might become a merciful and faithful high priest ... for the sins of the people" (Heb. 2:17).[22]

Above all, according to Radcliffe, it is Christ's solidarity with the dead that drives this reversal. "God had been perceived as the source of all life and holiness precisely in his separation from death. The purity regulations aim at creating the maximum distance between the corpse and the Holy of Holies. The corpse was the ultimately impure object, 'the father of the fathers of impurity'" (499). This corpse is what the dead Christ becomes, the source rather than the denial of his power, so that "through death he might destroy him who holds the power of death" (Heb. 2:14). Radcliffe concludes: "So [the author of Hebrews'] use of cultic language is ultimately ironic ...

---

[21] Radcliffe, 496; I bracket his language from the following line.
[22] We must avoid interpreting Hebrews in terms of supersessionism. In his own life, Jesus critiques not Temple sacrifice as such, but only its commercialization; the words of Jesus at the Last Supper before his death do not replace animal sacrifice but intensify it into self-sacrifice. After the Second Temple was destroyed, both rabbinic Judaism and the Jesus movement had to deal with the actual end of animal sacrifice: Judaism sublated sacrifice into the words of Mishna Yoma on Yom Kippur; Christianity sublated it into what it calls the Word in Jesus.

a subversion made possible by a new theology of creation; God the creator is the one [who] raises from the dead" (499). It is that greatest crossing of the lines that, Christians believe, unleashes not only the power of taboos broken, but frees the power of life from death. By a further cultic irony, Christians cross more lines to celebrate and remember this: their cult claims to drink, at his command, the one thing Jesus's own cult forbade: blood.

Jesus says, "This is my blood, given for you." "This is my blood, poured out for many." How far from this is the discourse of blood-purity *Reconquista* Catholics. Theirs says, "This is my blood; I keep it for myself. If I don't have Jewish blood, I keep it pure; if I do have Jewish blood, I keep it secret; whatever I do I do not let it out. I practice purity as a politics of containment. I contain blood and I contain its secrets."

The blood of Abel cries out for Christ's, and the blood of Christ is Jewish blood, which exposes blood libel as a projection. Here is another irony. "Blood libel" is the canard that Jews desire Christian blood to make their matzos with – whereas in fact, Christians desire the blood of Jesus, a Jew; they desire and they drink it. Scholars have written shelves of books on blood libel; it needs no chapter here.[23] But just here is where we glimpse that blood purity is the libel's mirror image, the negative that prints it out. I don't mean that historically but conceptually. Libel and purity follow the same logic. Better than purity is the re-enclosure in a larger whole (see the end of Chapter 3).

If all blood is the blood of Jesus – because all blood belongs to God, and the blood of Jesus is the blood of God – then both the blood of communion is the blood of Jesus, and the blood of Jesus is Jewish blood – so that the blood of communion is Jewish blood. But Gentile Christians are afraid of Jewish blood as the blood of the other, and their feet have run to do evil. They project their fear and blame Jews: this is blood libel, their gravest and guiltiest misprision of blood. Here they hate the source of their savior and fear the transfusion, the adoptive kinship that his blood effects. The blood of Mary, which according to Maximus founds the world, is Jewish blood.

And if Christians followed the Aztec line (as indeed sometimes they have) and sought to sacrifice human beings, the victims would be Jews.

And that's because Christians fetishize or magic Jewish blood, anti-Semites and philo-Semites both. When I spent a year in Tübingen in 1984–5, many students, especially students of theology, went to Israel to work on

---

[23] Among a vast literature, see the recent theological account of Lauren Winner, *The Dangers of Christian Practice: On Wayward Gifts, Characteristic Damage, and Sin* (New Haven: Yale University Press, 2018).

174   BLOOD THEOLOGY

kibbutzim. When I asked why so many (presumably to make amends), a young theologian added another reason: she wanted "to know the people who bewitched our parents." That is the danger even from friends who see that the blood of communion is the blood of a Jew.

It is easy to see continuity between the Reconquest of Iberia, which by convention had lasted continually if intermittently and seasonally for some 800 years since 718 or 722 until 1492, and the Conquest of the Americas, which in some ways began in the same year, 1492. Although neither Cortés nor Pizarro had had military experience before the New World, and their soldiers were often too young, the father of Cortés had been an infantry captain and Pizarro's father had served in Navarre and Italy. Diego Velázquez, colonizer of Cuba, had served in Seville. Isabella met Columbus just to the north – in the Alcázar of Córdoba, where she had moved to direct the campaign – and in the very month that the Emirate of Granada, the last Muslim state in Iberia, surrendered on January 2, 1492. By April 17, Isabella and Columbus reached an agreement; in August he sailed. The Castilian war of reconquest didn't end on the Iberian Peninsula, but in 1497 took Mellila on the northern coast of Africa (claimed by Morocco, still a part of Spain today) and, in 1510, Tripoli. Alexander VI – the same pope who would approve the Hieronymite statute against *conversos* in 1495 – in 1493 commanded Spain to conquer the New World for the sake of converts. Standard texts assume that the treatment of *conversos* in Spain provided a template for the treatment of converts in New Spain, and that the pattern of conquest as expansion into an already populated area provided a template for the conquest of Mexico.[24] With 1492 as a hinge, the Reconquest and the Conquest look continuous.

Blood Sacrifice

In Mexico, "A quail was beheaded for the [sacrificial victim] and cast away."[25]

In Leviticus, "The priest shall command that two living clean birds . . . be brought for the one who is to be cleansed. The priest shall command that one of the birds be slaughtered . . . and he shall let the living bird go into the open field" (Lev. 14:5, 7).

[24] James Lockhart and Stuart B. Schwartz, *Early Latin America: A History of Colonial Spanish America and Brazil* (Cambridge: Cambridge University Press, 1983), 10–11, 61–2.
[25] David Carrasco, *City of Sacrifice: The Aztec Empire and the Role of Violence in Civilization* (Boston: Beacon Press, 2000), 144.

During the feast of Toxcatl, a man became a god, Tezcatlipoca, in order that in him the god might sacrifice himself and renew creation; the man became the god's living image.[26]

He is the image of the invisible God. (Col. 1:15)

Other humans owed the gods for the gods' own sacrifice in creating, caring for, and renewing the earth, and they repaid the debt by imitating the gods' sacrifice. Priests accompanied the victim to the top of the temple in Tenochtitlan, bent his back over a rock to arch his chest up, cut it open with an obsidian knife, and drew out his heart with their hands.

> [W]e do all things out of love rather than fear – love to him who has shown us such grace that no greater can be found, as he himself asserts, saying, 'Greater love than this no man hath, that a man lay down his life for his friends' (Abelard, *Commentary on Romans*).[27]

> 'First, the blood of the victim is carried to many temples in the city .... The blood is spread, touching the stone, wooden, and perishable images of gods.'[28]

> 'This is my blood of the covenant, poured out for many' (Mk. 14:24).

The fragmented body of a sacrificed God-man was skinned and divided "in order to eat him. There they portioned him out. They cut him to pieces and they distributed him,"[29] with "one thigh going to the palace for Moctezuma and one piece of flesh eaten by the blood relatives of the captor in a bowl of dried maize stew."[30] Those who ate "would be considered gods."[31] But the captor himself may not eat the flesh of the sacrificed God-man, for he says, "Shall I perchance eat my very self?" as he had said "He is my beloved son," with the one to be sacrificed answering, "He is my beloved father."[32]

"'How can this man give us his flesh to eat?' So Jesus said to them, 'Very truly, I tell you, unless you eat the flesh of the Son of Man and drink his blood, you have no life in you. Those who eat my flesh and drink my blood abide in me, and I in them. Just as the living Father sent me, and I live because of the Father, so whosoever eats me will live because of me'" (John 6: 52–57).

---

[26] Davíd Carrasco, *The Aztecs: A Very Short Introduction* (Oxford: Oxford University Press, 2011), 65–7.

[27] In Eugene Fairweather, ed., *A Scholastic Miscellany: Anselm to Ockham* (Philadelphia: Westminster John Knox, 1956), 284.

[28] *City of Sacrifice*, 159.

[29] *City of Sacrifice*, 160.

[30] *City of Sacrifice*, 142.

[31] *City of Sacrifice*, 145.

[32] *City of Sacrifice*, 145.

BLOOD THEOLOGY

"The flesh of all those who died in sacrifice was held truly to be consecrated and blessed. It was eaten with reverence, ritual, and fastidiousness – as if it were something from heaven."[33]

"Just as we have borne the image of the man of dust, we will also bear the image of the man of heaven" (1 Cor. 15:49).

Statues of Aztec gods show one body in two skins. The second skin hangs off the first. The effect is vivid at the wrists, where the second skin drapes over the arms, but hangs off the hands, a second set of fingers over the first, degloved. This represents no mere metaphor, according to historians, but the practice of Aztec warriors who displayed, put on, wore, and paraded in the skins door to door around the city. In mock battles those would-be warriors who did not qualify to impersonate a god by putting on his skin could grab at the skin worn by a god-wearer, especially around the navel, and "gain social status by acquiring some of the skin under their fingernails."[34]

"Instead, put on the lord Jesus Christ" (Rom. 13:14). "As many of you were baptized into Christ have clothed yourself with Christ" (Gal. 3:27).[35] Such passages prompt Tyler Joseph, of the band Twenty One Pilots, to sing to Jesus, "Here I come, come to you in the very clothes, that I killed, killed you in."[36]

The Aztec sacrifice is a human being. The sacrifice is also, at the same time, a god. The sacrifice takes the god's identity; later the young men use the skin to "put him on"; they clothe themselves in him. They revere and manipulate his blood. And they eat his flesh. The god returns in every sacrifice; he lives on. Can God – the real God, whoever that may be – can God use such a form of thought and practice? Christians seem to think so.

In juxtaposing descriptions of Aztec sacrifice with passages from the Bible and Abelard I do not mean either to commit blasphemy or to present a synthetic theory of religion. I merely mean to make an ad hoc, bilateral comparison that throws a peculiar light on Christian blood language, to make it strange. Or maybe a bit more: to suggest, with Wittgenstein, that there is something deeply, disturbingly human about the tropes of communion and absorption that Aztec religion and Christianity share and that, if Christianity does have anything to do with God, God takes up and deals with and seeks to use for purposes of salvation: taking the worst humans can do, and turning it to good.

---

[33] *City of Sacrifice,* quoting Diego Durán, a Dominican priest who grew up in Mexico immediately after the conquest.

[34] *City of Sacrifice,* 155.

[35] See also Job 29:14, Eph. 4:24, Col. 3:10 and 3:12.

[36] I owe the reference to my student Arthur Blankinship. The song is "Drown," the album "The Early Years," New Albany Music and Tyler Joseph, 2007.

Or perhaps those things resonate only because the likes of Sahagún and Durán first saw them that way and infected everyone who came afterwards.

***

WITTGENSTEIN HAS BEEN READING FRAZER'S *GOLDEN BOUGH*. HE comments on Frazer's attempt to explain a tradition of human sacrifice (the priest-king in the grove at Nemi). "Compared with the story of what happened," notes Fergus Kerr, "the explanation is banal. The rationalistic attempt to find [a] deeper psychological or evolutionary significance of the ceremony only distracts us from the deep significance *that a description of the event already communicates*."[37] Something of the same fecklessness and distraction afflicts commentators on Hebrews, where too the explanation of the thing pales beside what the description, like Wyschogrod's, already communicates. Kerr collects several examples of things Wittgenstein says escape language – not that we could never generate more language about them; we could, but that's not the point. The point is rather that generating more language about them would distract us from other ways of knowing. Among Wittgenstein's examples are the sound of music, the aroma of coffee, and the sense of ceremony. The coffee exists to be smelled, not described; the music exists to be heard; the ceremony exists to be practiced.

What would it mean to say, "Human sacrifice exists to be practiced"?

Wittgenstein says the practice of human sacrifice can only mean something "terrible, impressive, horrible, tragic." It means something, that is, that "we find in ourselves. ... We could almost say, the human being is a ceremonious animal. ... When we watch the life and behavior of people all over the earth we see that apart from what we might call animal activities, taking food, etc., etc., people also carry out actions that bear a peculiar character and might be called ritualistic. ... there is something in us too that speaks in support of those observances by the savages."

"What makes human sacrifice something deep and sinister anyway? Is it only the suffering of the victim that impresses us in this way? All manner of diseases bring just as much suffering and do *not* make this impression. No, this deep and sinister aspect is not obvious just from learning the history of the external action, but *we* insert it [the deep and sinister aspect] *from an experience in ourselves*."[38] From something that we know or recognize about ourselves.

---

[37] Fergus Kerr, *Theology after Wittgenstein* (Blackwell Publishers, 1986), 160.

[38] Ludwig Wittgenstein, *Bemerkungen über Frazers Golden Bough/Remarks on Frazer's Golden Bough*, German and English on facing pages, ed. Rush Rees, trans. A. C. Miles (Atlantic Highlands, NJ: Humanities Press International, 1979), 8.

Now I do something else illicit. I compare the reality of one thing with the ideal of another. I compare the reality of Castilian blood purity with the ideal of Aztec sacrifice. Since I am comparing a reality with an ideal, the ideal naturally comes out better. I do this as a corrective and a provocation. It is a provocation, because the Aztecs come out ahead. But it is a corrective, because, historically, it was the Spaniards who recorded the Aztecs; it was the Spanish who consciously or unconsciously compared the Aztec reality with the Christian idea. What would happen if the asymmetry were reversed? What would happen, that is, if it had been Aztecs who crossed the Atlantic, conquered Spain, and discovered an indigenous religion somewhat as blood-obsessed as their own? What if Aztecs had discovered and described Spanish Christianity?

Both Aztecs and Christians sacrifice a god or gods become human, put on his identity, and eat his flesh. The "only" difference is that Christians do it metaphorically while claiming that it is ontologically real (true God and true man; real transformation; transubstantiation). Aztecs practice on human flesh where Christians substitute. But what does this say about what Wittgenstein calls the "deep and sinister" side of ourselves? It says whatever blood says, when we admit we still think in its terms. And it says we have to be careful how we express that side of ourselves. The Aztec practice is a politics of abundance, an abundance of blood, even in a Bourdieusian sense of terrible waste. It is costly signaling magnified.

The sacrificial economy of Spain did not penetrate class: that privilege was not to be sacrificed, neither by the advocates nor the critics of blood purity. You wonder if the Aztec economy of blood was more alive, for all its cult of death. Aztec priests and royalty also sacrificed themselves; scholars call it "autosacrifice"; it was "the most common form of sacrifice":[39] they drew sharp, serrated maguey blades – spiked on the end and spined on the edges – to transfix and perforate their ears, thighs, arms, tongues, and penises, to ream out the holes, to draw and collect the blood onto blotters and into bowls in order to offer it up. Senior priests would bleed their tongues until they lost the power of speech. Their cult of blood was not self-serving, except, perhaps, as costly signaling.[40]

Even theologians and humanists know a simple version of costly signaling. Peacocks grow tails and antelopes antlers at a high cost to signal their evolutionary fitness. Their ornaments supposedly help them compete within one gender for the favors of another. Religion, meanwhile, seems hard for evolution to explain: religious people do things that sacrifice their reproductive fitness, like joining a monastery, taking a vow of celibacy, or martyring themselves. Instead

[39] Carrasco, *The Aztecs,* p. 65.
[40] I owe my attention to costly signaling theory to Rich Sosis.

of dying out, even martyr-religions seem to flourish. But a more sophisticated application of costly signaling tries to explain that. Costly signaling explains not only sexual selection, but how social animals gain fitness by sacrificing themselves *for their group*. The monk or martyr loses his own children but secures social cohesion. Jesus was a martyr without children; Paul advised celibacy; but between them they founded a successful and cohesive group, Christianity. Aztecs and Christians both know that among humans, the costliest signaling takes place in blood. Blood is meaning made with bodies on the line. *For that reason both "without shedding blood there is no forgiveness" (Heb. 9:22) and suicide bombings continue.*

Some animals even seem to deliberate on cost. Is this display worth it, or does the animal withdraw? Other animals mislead with signaling that appears more costly than it is. Christians do something more distinctive than count or counterfeit the cost. They use gesture and ritual, image, symbol, and language to magnify blood's power to signal while lowering its cost, racheting their cultural niche to increasingly subtle and effective signaling. The Eucharistic ritual is powerful – many Christians find it more powerful than biological blood, because it is the blood of God. But in evolutionary terms, it's a whole lot cheaper. The Eucharistic wine is no counterfeit: no one is misled by it, even if they disagree on what theory makes it God's blood. It is something else, which marshals humans' distinctive ability to imagine and live into alternate futures and virtual worlds.[41] Multiple societies have constructed their own environmental niches in which blood matters in more ways than one. Because they construct their cultural environment, they can also reflect on it; they begin to identify wisdom and folly. Despite its ties to oppression and war, blood-signaling, in our cultural niche, also fosters goods of virtue, cooperation, and gratitude – and therefore persists.

The Spanish chronicler Toribio de Motolinía had already admired the Aztec autosacrifice of one's own blood. First he condemns it, because he perceives the offering as bleeding upon an idol. But even so he can't help but compare the Nahuas to the Spaniards ("who often bleed themselves and others"), concluding that "Nahua bloodletting shows a certain superiority to Spaniards'."[42]

---

[41] Augustín Fuentes, *Why We Believe: Evolution and the Human Way of Being* (New Haven: Yale University Press, 2019).

[42] Pete Sigal, *The Flower and the Scorpion: Sexuality and Ritual in Early Nahua Culture* (Durham, NC: Duke University Press, 2011), 124, citing Toribio de Motolinía (Benevente), *History of the Indians of New Spain*, ed. Elizabeth Andros Foster (Albuquerque: Cortés Society, 1950), 124. The first quotation is from Motolinía, the second from Sigal.

180 BLOOD THEOLOGY

Aztec sacrifice is better, because it is self-sacrifice. Spanish sacrifice is worse, because it is self-seeking. Both sides regarded war as noble. Self-sacrifice was noble; the taking of captives for sacrifice involved them in a noble pursuit: it not only ennobled, it deified them. And Spanish self-seeking was noble, too; it provided gold for the Catholic Monarchs, glory for the Christian kingdom, and converts for the Christian faith. Stanley Hauerwas critiques both motives in his essay "Sacrificing the Sacrifices of War." He asks, why does war persist, when we know (constructing the reader as a pacifist) that war is wrong? Because, he admits, war seems to bring unique solidarity among soldiers and cultivate virtues of courage and self-sacrifice.[43] Those goods are so glorious – so noble – that it is a real sacrifice to give them up. Just as we must suspect blood used to defend honor, we must suspect it again when it falsely – or even truly – ennobles us.

***

THROUGHOUT THIS BOOK, I HAVE REPEATED THAT WE MUST expose, investigate, contain, rechannel, and chastise the language of blood – because it isn't going away. I could, of course, be wrong about that. The chronicles, the psalms, the gospels, and above all the prophets include disavowals of offerings and of blood:

Has the Lord as great delight in burnt offerings and sacrifices, as in obedience to the voice of the Lord? Surely, to obey is better than sacrifice, and to heed than the fat of rams. (1 Sam. 15:22)

Sacrifice and offering you do not desire, but you have given me an open ear. Burnt offering and sin offering you have not required. Then I said, "Here I am; in the scroll of the book it is written of me. I delight to do your will, O my God; your law is within my heart." (Ps. 40:6–8)

Not for your sacrifices do I rebuke you; your burnt offerings are continually before me. I will not accept a bull from your house, or goats from your folds. For every wild animal of the forest is mine, the cattle on a thousand hills. (Ps. 50:9–10)

The sacrifice of the wicked is an abomination to the Lord, but the prayer of the upright is his delight. (Prov. 15:8)

All deeds are right in the sight of the doer, but the Lord weighs the heart. To do righteousness and justice is more acceptable to the Lord than sacrifice. (Prov. 21:2–3)

What to me is the multitude of your sacrifices? says the Lord; I have had enough of burnt offerings of rams and the fat of fed beasts; I do not delight in the blood of bulls or of lambs, or of goats. (Is. 1:11)

---

[43] Stanley Hauerwas, "Sacrificing the Sacrifices of War," *Criswell Theological Review N.S.* 4 (2007): 77–95.

Of what use to me is frankincense that comes from Sheba, or sweet cane from a distant land? Your burnt offerings are not acceptable, nor are your sacrifices pleasing to me. Therefore thus says the Lord: See, I am laying before this people stumbling blocks against which they shall stumble; parents and children together, neighbor and friend shall perish. (Jer. 6:20–21)

Thus says the Lord of hosts, the God of Israel: Add your burnt offerings to your sacrifices, and eat the flesh. For in the day that I brought your ancestors out of the land of Egypt, I did not speak to them or command them concerning burnt offerings and sacrifices. But this command I gave them, "Obey my voice, and I will be your God, and you shall be my people." (Jer. 7:21–22)

For I desire steadfast love and not sacrifice, the knowledge of God rather than burnt offerings. (Hos. 6:6)

I hate, I despise your festivals, and I take no delight in your solemn assemblies. Even though you offer me your burnt offerings and grain offerings, I will not accept them; and the offerings of well-being of your fatted animals I will not look upon. Take away from me the noise of your songs; I will not listen to the melody of your harps. But let justice roll down like waters, and righteousness like an ever-flowing stream. (Amos 5:21–24)

Oh, that someone among you would shut the temple doors, so that you would not kindle fire on my altar in vain! I have no pleasure in you, says the Lord of hosts, and I will not accept an offering from your hands. (Mal. 1:10)

So when you are offering your gift at the altar, if you remember that your brother or sister has something against you, leave your gift before the altar and go; first be reconciled to your brother or sister, and then come and offer your gift. (Mt. 5:23–24)

Go and learn what this means: "I desire mercy, and not sacrifice." (Mt. 9:13)

But if you had known what this means, "I desire mercy and not sacrifice," you would not have condemned the guiltless. (Mt. 12:7)

I appeal to you therefore, brothers and sisters, by the mercies of God, to present your bodies as a living sacrifice, holy and acceptable to God, which is your reasonable worship (*logike latreia*). (Rom. 12:1)

And of course Paul's description, *logike latreia,* soon becomes the even more pointed "bloodless sacrifice," a common Christian term for the Eucharist and the Christian life.[44] What interests me, however, is how blood persists, in different usages and more metaphorical forms, despite those disavowals and

---

[44] Benedikt Eckhardt, "'Bloodless Sacrifice': A Note on Greek Cultic Language in the Imperial Era," *Greek, Roman, and Byzantine Studies* 54 (2014) 255–73; Eleonora Tagliaferro, "Ἀναίμακτος θυσία – λογικὴ θυσία: a proposito della critica al sacrificio cruento," in *Sangue e antropologia nella liturgia* III, ed. Francesco Vattioni (Rome 1984), 1573–95.

absences. Jesus does something more transformative than to deny or avow blood practices: he at once subverts and reclaims them, "removing them," as Judith Butler would say, "from the contexts of oppression and violence and mobilizing the signifier for an alternative production."

David Nirenberg (writing about something else) suggests a more cautious formulation: "We cannot reject [blood's] power without impoverishment, but neither can we accept [its] suggestions without suspicion."[45]

A book about blood must include a chapter on war. This one was meant to be it. I had a great idea for it. It was to be about how some uses of blood language must go wrong. It is about that still. But it leaves plenty of room for others to write about blood in war, because it has turned out differently. Not about how war misuses blood – although it does. But about how two cultures who both loved blood and met in war misused blood differently, even as, in other respects, they understood it profoundly. The Spanish went wrong in trying to keep blood pure, which is to say, in trying to keep it, full stop. The Aztecs went wrong in trying to take blood from others, that is, from captives. Keeping and taking both abuse blood: it can only be given.

---

[45] "Was There Race Before Modernity?" 263. His antecedent is "histories and theorizations of race."

Part IV

The Blood of God at the Heart of Things

Causality Sacramental and Cosmic

8

HOW THE EUCHARIST "CAUSES" SALVATION
The Physiology of the Eucharist, or Virtue and Blood Chemistry

P ART OF ME WOULD LIKE TO RE-ENCHANT THE EUCHARIST, SO that matter itself becomes saving. Why not? Doesn't the incarnation work that way? Aquinas objects to this idea. By the end of the chapter we get part of it back. But that will require reframing the question.

It would seem, writes Thomas Aquinas, entertaining in an objection a view he *does not hold*, that "this sacrament is a kind of spiritual food. As bodily food is requisite for bodily health, so also is this sacrament [necessary] for spiritual health." But Aquinas will answer in his reply, "the comparison does not hold."[1]

I have a taste for nutritive theories of the Eucharist, but they are hard to swallow.

Nevertheless, let's see, in the manner of Aquinas, why the view he rejects might be attractive.

It would seem that the Eucharist ought to work on the body. *Christ gave his blood that ours might change.* Primate studies show that the emotions circulate chemically in the blood.[2] Aquinas argues that virtues moderate passions and habituate – even rationalize – the body. The Gospel of John places on the lips of Jesus the warning that "unless you eat the flesh of the Son of Man, and drink his blood, you will not have life in you."[3] Anselm thinks that the way you accept Jesus is not into your mind but into your mouth. Many

---

[1] Thomas Aquinas, *Summa Theologiae* Part III, question 73, article 3, objection 2, and the reply to objection 2. Henceforward in the text like this: *ST* III.73.3 obj. 2 and *ad* 2. Translations are my own or modify the "Benzinger" edition: *Summa Theologica: First Complete American Edition, Literally Translated by Fathers of the English Dominican Province*, rev. ed., 3 vols. (New York: Benziger Brothers, 1920). Reprint in 5 vols. Allen, TX: Christian Classics, 1981. The "Fathers of the English Dominican Province" are principally Laurence Shapcoate.

[2] For a hilarious version, see Robert Sapolsky, *A Primate's Memoir: A Neuroscientist's Unconventional Life among the Baboons* (New York: Scribner, 2001), 37–40.

[3] John 6:53.

186 BLOOD THEOLOGY

Eucharistic theories figure it medicinal. The Eucharist ought to work on the body, because the works of love are done in the body, the love of neighbor is done in the body, the salvation of Jesus is wrought in the body. The body, according to Susan Harvey, is the means of salvation and the place in which it is done; it is where we know God and experience God's presence.[4] The soul is, of course, always involved, the subject of the body's virtues and the body's very form: but the soul (according to the Vulgate) is in the blood: *anima enim omnis carnis in sanguine est.*[5]

"The soul is in the blood." Blood reaches in two directions. It reaches out to include animals with blood like ours – primates, mammals – and further to include creatures that live from or in salty water. We live from blood or in its salty predecessor. The soul – the force of life – is in the blood.

Blood reaches out also in another direction. It is that medium in which emotions, borne on chemicals, circulate. Adrenaline, testosterone, corticosteroids throng the blood. Fear and desire, love and anger circulate by means of blood. The soul – not only in Leviticus, but even now as the emotions that move and check us – also swims in the blood. The soul's renewal therefore, must involve the blood. The retraining of the amygdala and the discipline of the neocortex, the endocrine system, the communication of cerebrospinal fluid with the rest of the body, the habituation of our emotions and the materialization of our virtues, animate or ensoul us with and through the blood.

The sacrifice and feast of Christ's body and blood claims to heal and elevate the soul by means of blood. In some traditions, that idea is more than a flight of fancy. In Gregory of Nyssa's *Great Catechetical Oration*, it implies a physiology:

> [S]ince human nature is twofold, a composite of soul and body, those who are being saved must grasp Him who leads the way toward life by means of both. . . . For the union with Life involves a sharing of life. [And "the life is in the blood."]
>
> Those who have through treachery received poison neutralize its destructive force by means of another drug. But the antidote, like the poison, must enter the vital organs of the person, in order that the effect of the remedy may, by passing through them, be distributed through the entire body. So, when we had tasted of that which brought destruction to

---

[4] "Embodiment in Time and Eternity: A Syriac Perspective," in *Theology and Sexuality: Classic and Contemporary Readings*, ed. Eugene F. Rogers, Jr. (Oxford: Blackwell Publishers, 2002), 4, 10, 18.

[5] Lev. 17:14.

our nature, of necessity we needed in turn something to restore what was destroyed . . . .

What is this, then? It is nothing else but that body which was shown to be mightier than death and which inaugurated our life. For just as a little leaven, as the Apostle says (I Co. 5.6), makes the whole lump like itself, so the body which was made immortal by God, by passing entire into our body, alters and changes it to itself. For just as when a deadly drug is mingled with a healthy body, the whole of what it is mingled with becomes as worthless as the drug, so also that immortal body, passing into him who receives it, changes the entire body to its own nature.

But it is not possible for anything to enter the body, unless it is mingled with the vital organs by way of food and drink. Therefore the body must receive the life-giving power in the way that its nature permits.[6]

In Romanos the Melodist, the effects of the Eucharist horrify Hell: "the dust has been deified; drawn to the table, he dared to eat, and did not fear to drink the One who Himself created him."[7] Cannot the Creator, swallowed down, recreate from inside out?

Multiple Christian traditions claim that the greatest of spiritual gifts — gratitude, community, reconciliation, heaven — come by drinking as if by transfusion to circulate in salty liquid.

Are such theories just pious fiction, "mere" symbols, moored only to implausible metaphor and antique association? Or can the association become intelligible again? Does contemporary Christianity enjoy any resources for recovering this biblical, patristic, and medieval claim? Can it become no more a sink of intelligibility, a dark place that absorbs any light thrown on it, but again a source of intelligibility, a place that generates its own light to illuminate other things?

On two occasions I've traveled in Malaysian Borneo, once in Sarawak and once in Sabah, looking at curly-tailed macaques and proboscis monkeys and hoping to see an orangutan. Perhaps it's inappropriate to do theology in the jungle, but I can't help it. The thought comes unbidden, "98% chimpanzee." I know the quantification is highly misleading.[8] But as a rhetorical device for expressing continuity, it is impressive. What percent macaque? What percent

---

[6] Gregory of Nyssa, *The Great Catechetical Oration* 37, ed. and trans. J. H. Strawley, revised in Daniel J. Sheerin, *The Eucharist*, Message of the Fathers of the Church, vol. 7 (Wilmington, DE: Michael Glazier, Inc., 1986), 59–61. My comment in brackets.

[7] Romanos the Melodist, "On Baptism," strophe 4, in *Kontakia of Romanos, Byzantine Melodist*, trans. and ed. Marjorie Carpenter (Columbia, MO: University of Missouri Press, 1970), vol. 2, 227–36; here, 230, words omitted without ellipses.

[8] See Jonathan Marks, *What It Means to Be 98% Chimpanzee: Apes, People, and Their Genes*, with a new preface (Berkeley: University of California Press, 2003).

188 BLOOD THEOLOGY

orangutan? God became human, therefore God became a primate. The syllogism (unlike the percentage) is impeccable. Deep in the jungle, I find myself deep into the incarnation, imagining Rahner's evolutionary Christology fleshed out. I reformulate Anselm's question: Why did God become simian?

Frans de Waal's *Chimpanzee Politics* shows how scapegoating becomes a politically effective strategy for chimps.[9] It reduces stress in leaders measured by glucocorticoids in the blood. Scapegoating circulates in our blood since before we were human. If God became human, then God became a primate and took on scapegoating with God's body. It might not be in the semen, as for Augustine, but it's measurably in the blood. Girard does not solve everything, but has his place.

The Eucharist – the Great Thanksgiving – practices gratitude through blood. For primatologist DeWaal, peacekeeping (charity) and peacemaking (forgiveness) both show up in blood. They make the Eucharist both love feast and atonement sacrifice. Medievals and moderns both see blood as a medium to circulate emotions. Anselm sees atonement in communion, so that Christians participate in their redemption by eating and drinking, by an exchange of bodily fluids. Redemption comes to modify blood chemistry. *Christ gives his blood that ours may change.*

Anselm's *Why God Became Human* is at bottom a communion meditation. It's about body and blood. That it's even more about blood appears in the shorter, prayed version reproduced as *Meditation on Human Redemption.* Speaking to his soul, he admonishes it to "Consider again the strength of your salvation and where it is found."

> *Taste* the goodness of your Redeemer . . . . *Chew* the honeycomb of his words, *suck* their flavour which is sweeter than sap, *swallow* their wholesome sweetness. Chew by thinking, suck by understanding, swallow by loving and rejoicing. Be glad to chew, be thankful to suck, rejoice to swallow.
>
> Chew this, bite it, suck it, let your heart swallow it, when your mouth receives the body and blood of your Redeemer. Make it in this life your daily bread, your food, your way-bread, for through this and not otherwise than through this, you will remain in Christ and Christ in you, and your joy will be full.[10]

---

[9] Frans de Waal, *Chimpanzee Politics: Power and Sex among Apes* (Baltimore: Johns Hopkins University Press, 2007).

[10] Anselm of Canterbury, *Meditation on Human Redemption*, in *Prayers and Meditations of St Anselm*, trans. Benedicta Ward (New York: Penguin, 1973), 230–7; here, 230, 234–5. Emphasis added.

I ask my students how Anselm expects Christians to participate in this redemption, and inevitably they answer "faith." But when I ask them to look to the text, they have trouble finding the word. Occasionally someone will see that Anselm thinks Christians participate in their redemption by eating and drinking, by an exchange of bodily fluids. (There are sexual as well as eating metaphors here.) Redemption turns out to be a matter of modifiable blood chemistry. *Christ gives his blood that ours may change.*

Aquinas ought to be a good guide for this. Like Aristotle, he believes that human beings are moved by emotion and habit. They are rational all the way down – no part unaffected – and yet rationality has to grow, or be trained, over time. So, we now say, the prefrontal cortex moderates the amygdala. For Aristotle and Aquinas, as well as for modern neuroscience, emotion and habit have to be rational*ized*. It is a process that takes place over time. For Anselm, it is also a process that takes place in the body and the blood. Is it also a matter of blood chemistry for Aquinas?

The Eucharist – the Great Thanksgiving – celebrates and inculcates gratitude: and its means is blood. What if blood is not (primarily) a symbol, but is a chemical transmitter, a hormone conveyance device? Then it doesn't so much *symbolize* as it actually works: it conveys emotion, tension, anxiety, gratitude, ecstasy.

Christ does not have to be incarnate in other creatures because human beings *already are* those other creatures. We relate to them by evolution, and we live by them in our microbiome. Maximus expresses that in terms of macro- and microcosm. Vulgar biology expresses it in terms of percentage. Bulgakov expresses it in terms of matter divinized by being hominized.[11] God became flesh and blood, that the whole world might be saved that way; God became flesh and blood, that the world might become divine.

How Aquinas Slaps Me Down

What follows is an argument among several parts of myself, which are also several parts of Christian traditions, and may represent different books on your shelf or different parts of yourself. There is the part where I was raised Presbyterian, and grew up eating soft white bread and drinking grape juice at communion, and therefore sought for more for the Eucharist to mean. In authors like Schmemann and Aquinas I did find more. Then there is the part where I have always been educated and have almost always taught in departments of Religious Studies, which is interested in material substances,

---

[11] See Chapter 6.

such as blood. I have received the gift of Christian blood-language made strange, and I want, in some romantic or exotic or orientalist way for it to become stranger still. I went looking for a nutritive theory of the Eucharist. I came to Aquinas hoping to find a theory according to which the Eucharist *changes human beings by physical means*, a metabolic theory. But he resists me at almost every turn.

Aquinas quotes, for example, Augustine's famous remark that ordinary food changes into us humans, but divine food changes humans into God. But he draws the unexpected conclusion that while ordinary food is necessary for the body, spiritual food is not, precisely because it depends on God, who can work directly and omit the means.[12] God can save, if necessary, without food.

So in this chapter there is constantly the part where I pose my questions, and the part where Aquinas changes them. In what follows I proceed by theses. Some are about Aquinas; some depart from or supplement Aquinas; and one I borrow from my book about the Holy Spirit and put here to different use. Along the way I observe how Aquinas uses the rhetoric of Aristotelian logic to do something quite un-Aristotelian: illuminate how God moves creatures. I know it's hard to hear tone in Aquinas. But over the years I have come to think that Aquinas allows himself a tone of irony and delight when he uses Aristotle this way, and I invite you to hear it too. When Aquinas explains how the Eucharist "causes" salvation, he is entirely serious, but he makes Aristotle do theological things, and sometimes, I think, he winks – not because it isn't true, but because the truth is marvelous.

1. When Thomas says the Eucharist causes salvation, what does "cause" mean? Aquinas uses "logical" words in senses far wider than modern philosophy: *demonstrare, via, demonstratio Patris, deducitur, propositio* range far beyond logic. Such words occur in both Aristotle and the Vulgate. It is Aquinas's duty as a theologian not to distinguish, but to keep those occurrences together, so that theology can discipline philosophy, and Aristotle can talk to the Vulgate. By the time Aquinas is through, the primary Aristotelian demonstration is the Son's *demonstratio patris*, his "demonstration of the Father," which is no theistic argument, but Christ's entire life. The primary

---

[12] "The difference between corporeal and spiritual food lies in this, that the former is changed into the substance of the person nourished, and consequently it cannot avail for supporting life except it be partaken of; but spiritual food changes man into itself, according to that saying of Augustine (*Confess.* vii), that he heard the voice of Christ as it were saying to him: 'Nor shalt thou change Me into thyself, as food of thy flesh, but thou shalt be changed into Me.' But one can be changed into Christ, and be incorporated in Him by mental desire, even without receiving this sacrament. And consequently the comparison does not hold" (*ST* III.73.3 *ad* 2).

via, or Way, as in the notorious Five Ways, is "Jesus Christ our Savior, who as a human being is the Way stretched out for us into God" (proemium to *ST* I.2). A "proposition" is an offering – of a bargain, a riddle, or a mystery – so that the Vulgate's most common use of the word is in the phrase *panis propositionis*, the bread of offering, or the show bread. In Thomas Aquinas, to accept a proposition, you do not first of all agree to a sentence; you first of all take the bread. In this context, Aquinas's use of causal words like "effects," "causes," and so on concerns *how God moves creatures*. The same set of words gets used, analogically, for how God moves planets; how God moves creatures by their nature; and how God moves creatures by grace, including by the sacraments. This is all seamless. Therefore: Aquinas's remarks that the Eucharist is the cause (*causa*) of action, or that it effects (*efficit*) salvation, are to be taken literally. But, as we shall see, Aquinas fails to answer, or implicitly rejects some of our questions, because "literally" does not work from the bottom up. "Literally" works from God down.

2. Consider Aquinas's Commentary on John 6:50–52.[13] The Vulgate reads:

> 47 Amen, amen, I say to you:
> Whoever believes in me has eternal life.
> 48 I am the bread of life.
> . . .
> 50 This is the bread that comes down from heaven,
> so that if anyone eats of this
> he will not die.
> 51 I am the living bread
> That has come down from heaven.
> 52 If anyone eats of this bread,
> he will live forever.
> And the bread which I will give is my flesh,
> for the life of the world.
> . . .
> 54 Amen, amen, I say to you,
> unless you eat the flesh of the Son of Man, and drink his blood,
> you will not have life in you.

---

[13] Thomas Aquinas, *Super Evangelium s. Ioannis lectura*, ed. R. Cai (Turin: Marietti, 1952), *lectio* 6 on chapter 6, §§949–82. English adapted from James A. Weisheipl and Fabian R. Larcher, trans., with introduction and notes by Daniel Keating and Matthew Levering, *Commentary on the Gospel of John*, 2 vols., with parallel Latin text and the Greek text of the gospel (Lander, WY: The Aquinas Institute, 2013) and online at aquinas.cc/la/en/~Ioan. Further references by section number in the text. The section numbers originate with the Marietti edition.

Now, what fascinates me is *spirit in matter*. That's the topic of my book on the Holy Spirit, where I propose that the Spirit characteristically comes to rest on the Son, and because the Son takes a body, the Spirit, as a gift to the Son, comes to rest on bodies, too – the body of Christ in Jesus, in the Eucharist, in the people, and in holy places and things. The Spirit in matter also animates this book, since ancient *pneuma* circulates and boils out of the blood, as it is the fire in the wine.[14] What I want from Aquinas – and from Aquinas I expect – is more detail about *how* this bread is life-giving insofar as it is taken. Even better if he would tell me about the wine. I want to know, what is the physiology, what is the metabolism of bread in the human body so that it divinizes. And Aquinas doesn't give me that.

How, with his interest in causes, can he avoid a nutritive theory of the Eucharist? Why doesn't he treat bread and blood separately, given that *pneuma* circulates in blood? But my frustration means he's trying to answer a different question altogether.

He's trying to understand the Eucharist on the model, not of nutrition, but of incarnation: *not from human metabolism up, but from divine metabolism down*, where by "divine metabolism" I mean the great *metabole* by which God becomes a human being. Aquinas would specify here that God does not "become" a human being by changing the divine nature; technically, God *assumes*, that is, takes up or elevates a human nature to join it to Godself. *We* do not change God into ourselves by our metabolism: *God* changes us into God by joining humanity to Godself: both in the incarnation, when the Word joins a human nature to itself by the grace of union, and in the Eucharist, when the Word joins other human beings to itself by the grace of healing.

So Aquinas's question is not "how do we digest the bread so as to become divine?" but "how does the Word become bread and wine so as to reach and involve us?" Not, how does our digestion work, but how does God's incarnation work? Not from us up, like the tower of Babel, but from God down, like Pentecost.

3. Aquinas answers that question in his *Commentary on John*:

> Since this is the sacrament of the Lord's passion, it contains in itself the Christ who suffered [*continet in se Christum passum*]. Thus whatever is a [causal] *effectus* of our Lord's passion *is an effect of this sacrament*. For this sacrament is nothing other than the application of our Lord's passion to us. ... Hence it is clear that the destruction of death, which Christ

[14] See Excursus 3 to Chapter 4. For more, see Eugene F. Rogers, Jr., "The Fire in the Wine: How Does the Blood of Christ Carry the Holy Spirit?" in *Third Article Theology*, ed. Myk Habets (Minneapolis, MN: Fortress, 2016), 251–64.

HOW THE EUCHARIST "CAUSES" SALVATION   193

accomplished by his death, and the restoration of life, which he accomplished [*efficit*] by his resurrection, are (causal) effects of this sacrament [#963].[15]

4. Thus the body of Christ acting is God acting; and as a corollary, the bread acting is God acting.

5. Main thesis: The logic of the incarnation works for the bread and wine. This entitles us to ask certain questions that would not otherwise occur. But in principle, what you believe about the incarnation should go for the Eucharist. In the incarnation,

> even [Christ's] flesh is life-giving, for it is an instrument of his divinity [*organum divinitatis*]. Thus, since an instrument acts by virtue of the agent [*cum instrumentum agat virtute agentis*], then just as the divinity of Christ is life-giving, so too his flesh gives life (as Damascene says) because of the Word to which it is united. Thus Christ healed the sick by his touch. So what he said above, **I am the living bread,** pertained to the power of the Word; but what he is saying here ["If anyone eats of this bread, they will have eternal life"] pertains to the sharing of his body [*communionem sui corporis*], that is, to the sacrament of the Eucharist. (#959)

That passage models God's use of the Eucharistic elements on God's use of Christ's historical human body, quoting John of Damascus, that the body of Christ (in Jesus or in communion) is God's "instrument." Aquinas uses first "*organum*," speaking in his own voice, and then "*instrumentum*," quoting Aristotle about how an agent expresses their power or *virtus*. This remark is helpful *above* the level of Eucharistic theory – transubstantiation is not in the context, and the language of instrument can explain memorial theories as well. On this account, the Eucharist extends the pattern of God doing divine things humanly and human things divinely in the body of Christ. The pattern extends up and down the analogical series that runs on Christ's body and blood. We don't need to choose a (transubstantiating or memorial) theory about *how* this happens. We only need to admire the conjunction. As a theological matter, "the blood of Christ is the blood of God" has to be a true statement on various analogical levels, even if we don't know *how* the statement is true, as if it were written in x's and y's.

Christ's incarnation causes salvation in his Eucharistic body and blood, that is, in the same way that it causes salvation in his historical body and blood.

---

[15] Thomas Aquinas, *In Ioannem* 6:56, in *Commentary on the Gospel of John*, trans. by Fabian Larcher and James Weisheipl (Washington, DC: Catholic University of America Press, 2010), paragraph 963, modified in accord with the Latin texts at www.corpusthomisticum.org/.

The body and blood are not only God's instrument, but God's *own* instrument, joined to God by a union that is closer than that of body and soul, since it is the union of the creator to the creator's own humanity. Thus: not like a hammer, but like a hand; indeed, closer than a hand.

6. Main thesis restated: The incarnational principle applies, that Christ does divine things humanly and human things divinely. Therefore: the elements of the Eucharist do divine things humanly and human things divinely.

7. Question. Does that mean the elements *act*? Only in the sense that a body acts – that is, when moved by an intention. The elements act, therefore, not robotically, automatically, mechanically, or magically, but because God acts through them. In the Eucharist as in the incarnation, blood acts because God's intention acts through it. If you think medievally, that question is easier. The idea that blood acts is even more intimate because, for the Vulgate, *anima omnis carnis in sanguine est*, the soul of all flesh is in the blood.

8. Corollary. God does things of the Spirit by blood and things done by blood have results in the Spirit. This is because the Spirit rests on the Son *as on his blood*, for his blood is the very matter of the Son (*ST* III.31.5 *ad* 3; see more about this in Chapters 4 and 9). Christ is made up of the Spirit and blood. We know this from the theory of his conception, the efficacy of his death, and the manner of his supper. The close relation, by which the Spirit travels in the blood (as in anger), is hidden from us only by the impediment of modern medicine. God forms Adam from a clot of blood in the Koran; the Holy Spirit forms Christ from a clot of blood in Aquinas; menstruation shows that a woman makes a clot of blood every month, which either forms into a fetus or not. The thesis of Leviticus that "The life is in the blood," and the thesis of Aristotle that the mother's blood makes up the fetus, coincide for Aquinas. Thus *pneuma* travels in the blood.

9. Theses 5 and 6 show how the Eucharist works from *God's* side. God can do what God likes without means, and God can do what God likes with means, even with bread, although God need not. (God need not: that's why the comparison fails between ordinary and spiritual food.) But *why* does God do things with means, without need? For human benefit. What is the human benefit?

10. Aquinas says the human benefit is twofold: faith, which joins the intellect to God as to One Unknown; and love, which "tends" or stretches out into God. Love is different from faith and hope, in that it *moves* one into

another and *joins* them. This is underlyingly an erotic and incarnational metaphor. Christ is, *as a human being, via nobis tendendi in Deum*, a way for us stretching into God. Therefore: The bread is, *as the body of Christ*, also a way for human beings stretching into God. That's why Aquinas repeats the language of a love that "tends" or stretches into God.

11. From God's point of view again: why does God use eating to do God's business? Because God *wants* to become human, as in Christ, so in us. By digestion, God is made human again. (Note: this works like yeast – both bread and wine are fermented – and not by quantity.) In this way, God gets inside human beings, closer to us than we are to ourselves, this time *physically*, or at least paraphysically.

12. Christ heals the sick, Aquinas reminds us – channeling Athanasius in *Against the Arians – by touching*. Therefore he says, the bread and wine can heal us *by the eating and drinking*. I would like for this to work physically or paraphysically. But Aquinas refuses me a nutritive theory. I would like for the digestion and circulation of the Eucharist to produce effects, in the way that we now think of adrenaline or oxytocin. But this, as I said, is where Aquinas slaps me down.

13. Here in another way is what I *wanted* him to say. Love is the virtue, the right use, of the concupiscible passion. This takes the animal energy of desire and trains it, first by reason and then by grace (or the other way around), into charity. Justice is the virtue or right use of the irascible passion. This generates extra animal energy when desire meets an obstacle. So, the love and justice that are the fruits of the Eucharist *begin*, in us animals, as bodily passions that circulate in the blood, just as oxytocin and adrenaline do.

14. But *Aquinas does not take this route*. Return to the incarnation as model. When Jesus heals by the touch of his hand, he graces a human thing and humanizes an act of grace. The principle of *non-violation* holds the key to why Aquinas avoids the nutritive route. It is a principle of Aquinas that grace desires not to violate but to elevate human nature. And that means that grace engages the will, not as an obligation, but as its inevitable result. I do not "have to" move my will any more than a tree has to fruit or a shadow has to follow a body. The paradox is soft: the language of obligation is out of place, but for human acts the language of voluntariness is necessary. Human acts come *suaviter*, "sweetly," because grace moves the heart more interiorly than we are to ourselves, like romantic love: grace lures and attracts our desires, so that what we do, including the movement of our will, accords both with our willing and with grace. Love, in short,

moves the heart; and grace brings us to "love God and do what you will." The trouble with nutritive or humoral theories is not quite that they work like magic – that would be a false dichotomy. The trouble is that they seem to work by human movements like digestion and responses to adrenaline that are autonomic rather than voluntary. Digestion and adrenaline shots bypass the will. A human action without intention does not count, technically speaking, as a human *act*; it is not something-having-been-done of a human agent. Aquinas makes a terminological distinction neglected by translators: human actions are raw movements; human acts are intentional. So *taking* the Eucharist voluntarily (an act of the will) differs from *digesting* the Eucharist involuntarily (an action of the intestines). In his own terms Aquinas is right to make something depend on eating and not on digestion. He makes it depend on the willed act, the voluntary act, the *human* act. The Creator, swallowed down, *can* recreate from inside out – but also from outside in. The point is not where (from inside) but by what means (by invitation).

15. Aquinas's theory works like intercessory prayer.[16] God *takes* my prayer as the cause of someone else's good. God need not do so; in a way my prayer is superfluous, gratuitous in the good sense; but God can set the chains of cause and effect so that my prayer counts as the cause even of what God would do anyway, because that is more fitting, and because that *involves me* in charity toward others, which is good for both of us: it is good for me to have such agency, and good for others to benefit from my involvement. *If* I pray, God takes the occasion of my prayer to be a cause of good to others. This is how God draws God's creatures Godward. Similarly, God takes my reception as the cause of my salvation. (Aquinas insists: God may also take my intention as the cause of my salvation. Intention matters whether the wine and wafer are present or not.)

16. Just as in the incarnation, the voluntary act sets up a blessed exchange. *If* I eat, then God takes the occasion of my eating, by a kind of divine irony, to be the cause of my salvation. This is also how God draws creatures Godward.

---

[16] "Human beings do certain actions, not that thereby they may change the Divine disposition, but that by those actions they may achieve certain effects according to the order of the Divine disposition: and the same is to be said of natural causes. And so is it with regard to prayer. For we pray not that we may change the Divine disposition, but that we may obtain that which God has disposed to be fulfilled by our prayers; in other words 'that by asking, men may deserve to receive what Almighty God from eternity has disposed to give,' as Gregory says (*Dial.* i, 8)" (*ST* II-II.83.2).

17. In Thomas Aquinas, as we have seen, faith both prepares and results from the reception of the sacrament, because the reception must count as a human act. Now, intentions are evident in human acts, whether we consciously thematize them or not. Aquinas just picks out the voluntary aspect of a completed act, so that digestion doesn't count, but reception does. He can assume that reception is intentional and voluntary, whether we are thinking about it or not, when the bread is received as the Eucharist (no particular theory required, just recognition).

18. What does not work is from the bottom up, from nutrition to heaven. Something else can work from the top down, if what we have to do with here is "the bread of heaven" come down. Here is where Thomas to some extent gives back what he took away.

> The usefulness of this sacrament is universal because the life it gives is not only the life of one person, but so far as concerns itself, *the life of the entire world* [*totius mundi*, cf. Schmemann, Teilhard]: and for this the death of Christ is fully sufficient. "He is the offering for our sins; and not for ours only, but for those of the entire world." (1 Jn 2:2)
>
> We should note that this sacrament is different from the others: for the other sacraments have individual effects: as in baptism, only the one baptized receives grace. But in the immolation of this sacrament, the effect is universal: because it affects not just the priest, but also those for whom he prays, as well as the entire Church, of the living and of the dead. The reason for this is that it contains the universal cause [namely Christ's passion] of all the sacraments. (964)

This universality effectively rejects my question – and satisfies my attraction. It's not a question of human metabolism at all – but it is universal. Obviously, Thomas is thinking about *totius mundi* as "all human beings," but nothing prevents us from considering an even wider application. When Teilhard directs his intention to all of life, and takes his altar as the whole world, that's in line with this bit of Thomas's thinking. In "The Mass on the World," he interprets the whole world as an altar, on which animals preyed upon and species extinguished suffer and die, and on which also the successes of evolution are lifted up. Christ the Logos presides over the whole. Upon every achievement of development or growth, Christ pronounces "This is my body." Upon every death and extinction, Christ pronounces "This is my blood" (Teilhard 1979, 123). The salty sea and the primate blood included.

19. Alexander Schmemann thinks the Eucharist from the top down in another, more inclusive way. Just if God created the world for covenant, to bring us to Godself, then God made the world capable of grace, capable of God-

198   BLOOD THEOLOGY

bearing, a sacramental material. We are to offer it back to God. In so doing, we receive it as God-leading. If creation has this Godward power, it feels the Spirit moving over the waters and participates in God's original intention. This is a superball-theory of the sacraments. If they have any power, it can only be the power of bouncing back up. Their power to elevate, if any, can only rebound from God come down. All creation participates in the great V-shaped structure by which the Word descends into the uttermost depths of the earth, even to the Jordan or the dead, there to push off again and bring us up, like Adam and Eve in the great icon of the Anastasis, by the hand. In such a picture it comes not amiss if even the command "in the sweat of thy brow shalt thou eat bread" contains a crumb of grace, for in Bulgakov it prefigures the command to eat bread "in remembrance of me." The bread, that is, was always already made to nourish the human being with what her life was meant for, life with God: and it comes not amiss, therefore, if the Eucharist finally re-enables bread to do what it was always meant for.

> In this eucharistic offering in Christ of all things to the One to whom they belong and in whom alone they really exist, this movement of ascension has reached its end. We are at the paschal table of the Kingdom. What we have offered – our food, our life, ourselves, and the whole world – we offered in Christ as Christ because He Himself has assumed our life and is our life. And now this is given back to us as the gift of new life, and therefore – necessarily – as *food*.
>
> The world as human food is not something "material" and limited to material functions, thus different from, and opposed to the specifically "spiritual" functions by which the human being is related to God. All that exists is God's gift to the human being, and it all exists to make God known to the human being, to make human life communion with God. It is divine love made food, made life for the human being. . . . "O taste and see that the Lord is good." . . . The world was created as the "matter," the material of one all-embracing eucharist.[17]

20. From Schmemann's perspective we can reformulate Bulgakov's thesis from above.[18] Bulgakov says, "Food is *natural communion* – partaking of the flesh of the world."[19] That statement is intelligible only as an inference from Eucharistic communion. Food, like nature, is a "remainder concept," one

---

[17] Schmemann, *For the Life of the World* (New York: St. Vladimir's Seminary Press, 1998), 41 and 14–15, paragraph boundary elided, modified for gender inclusiveness.

[18] I repeat this paragraph for a different purpose from Eugene F. Rogers, Jr., *After the Spirit: A Constructive Pneumatology from Resources outside the Modern West* (Grand Rapids, MI: Eerdmans Publishing, 2005), 44.

[19] Sergei Bulgakov, *Philosophy of Economy: The World as Household*, trans. and ed. Catherine Evtuhov (New Haven, CT: Yale University Press, 2000), 103.

formed (logically, not historically) by subtraction from the context in which God intends it. In this perspective, breadwinners are like the disciples who take up "what was left over, twelve baskets of broken pieces";[20] the laborer only seeks to go like Ruth "to the field, and glean among the ears of grain after him in whose sight [she] shall find favor."[21] Even the manna of the Israelites falls, like the crumbs of the Syrophoenician woman, from the Lord's table.[22] The Psalm (145:15) speaks of surplus, the merciful remnant of the Creator's bounty, when it proclaims that wine makes glad the human heart, and bread sustains it. Food and drink become a sacrament in reserve.[23]

21. My initial question, which Aquinas rejects and Bulgakov transforms, was this: how do we metabolize the Eucharist? What's the physiology? How do we digest it? My question cannot be answered except as recast. The Eucharist is not ordinary food with heavenly effect: Rather, ordinary food is left over from the Eucharist. Everything whatsoever is intended to join us to God; the virtue of the Eucharist is to make that clear. This means that primate blood and salty seas come back. Not because the Eucharist is magical, but because all creation is sacramental. Not sacrament as such, but sacrament in waiting, waiting to join creatures to God, as creation was always intended.

If it is the Logos that structures and inscribes itself in the world at creation, and the Logos that repairs and elevates the "whole world" at the Eucharist, then it makes sense to compare the division of the elements at creation with the division of the elements at the sacrament. At the sacrament, for sure, the Logos divides – multiplies – in order to unite. So too, then, at creation. God divides, after all, *to make a world* – to make which, it takes, as the saying goes, "all kinds."

22. "The virtue of the Eucharist is to make that clear." Unless of course we misuse it. Eucharists like all things human can go awry. Cavanaugh remarks on the "failure of excommunication" that allowed Chilean torturers to receive the sacrament.[24] Lauren Winner remarks on "the curious optimism, almost magical thinking – of the postliberal Eucharist."[25] She reminds of us of waves of violence against Jews, supposedly for "host desecration": Röttingen, 1298; Korneuburg, 1302–5; St. Pölten, 1306; Pulkau, 1338;

---

[20] Luke 9:17.
[21] Ruth 2:2.
[22] Mark 7:28.
[23] Quoted with some omissions and an addition from my *After the Spirit* (Grand Rapids, MI: Eerdmans, 2005), 44.
[24] William T. Cavanaugh, *Torture and Eucharist* (Oxford: Blackwell Publishers, 1998), 240–64.
[25] Lauren Winner, *The Dangers of Christian Practice Practice: On Wayward Gifts, Characteristic Damage, and Sin* (New Haven, CT: Yale University Press, 2018), 40.

200   BLOOD THEOLOGY

Breslau, 1350s; Brussels, 1370; Salzburg, 1404; Vienna, 1421; Regensburg, 1470; eventually killing three thousand people.[26] Even at the time, some people doubted whether any host desecration had actually taken place: the chronicler of the Pulkau episode blamed it on a local priest who "had sprinkled a wafer with blood and tossed it near a Jew's house." That episode killed some 150 people.[27] Until the 1920s, a Carmelite church celebrated the Eucharist with an alternative *Kyrie*: "Oh Jesus, unsurpassed in your goodness, Stabbed by Jews and soaked in blood again, Through your new wounds And spilled springs of blood Have Mercy on Us."[28] The very boundary-marking function of the Eucharist, Winner argues, tends to cause "characteristic damage." The proximity of Jewish flesh, *in the wafer itself*, alarms the community that others and mistakes it. And the betrayal of its ideals began at the beginning, when Jesus dipped a morsel for Judas.[29]

23. Isaac of Nineveh returns us to an account where love and blood do not conflict:

> When we have found love, we eat the heavenly bread and we are sustained without labor and without weariness. Heavenly bread is that which has descended from heaven and which gives the world life; this is the food of angels. He who has found love eats Christ at all times and becomes immortal from then onwards. Blessed is he that has eaten from the bread of love which is Jesus. Whoever is fed with love is fed with Christ, who is the all-governing God. John witnesses to this when he says: "God is love." Thus he who lives with love in this creation smells life from God; he breathes here the air of the resurrection. Love is the kingdom of which our Lord spoke, when symbolically he promised the disciples that ... "you shall eat and drink at the table of my kingdom." What should they eat, if not love? ... This is the wine that gladdens the heart of the human being. ... This is the wine which the debauched have drunk and they become chaste, the sinners have drunk and they forgot the paths of stumbling, the drunk and they became fasters, the rich and they became desirous of poverty, the poor and they became rich in hope, the sick and they regained strength, the fools and they became wise.[30]

---

[26] *Dangers*, 30.

[27] *Dangers*, 50; I quote Winner, not the chronicler.

[28] *Dangers*, 32–3.

[29] *Dangers*, 34–5, 52–6. For more on blood language gone wrong, see the chapters in Part III on family, truth, and tribe.

[30] Isaac of Nineveh, in *Mystical Treatises*, trans. A. J. Wensinck (Amsterdam: Koninklijke Akademie von Wetenschapen, 1923), 211–12, reprinted in Rogers, *The Holy Spirit: Classic and Contemporary Readings* (Oxford: Wiley-Blackwell, 2009), 111–212.

9

THE BLOOD OF CHRIST
AND THE CHRISTOLOGY OF THINGS
Why Things Became Human

Adam and Eve

"Who then were Adam and Eve? They were the first hominid group that in whatever form of religion or language used some expression that we might translate 'God,' as a vocative."[1] Robert Jenson's *Systematic Theology* parallels four descriptions of the form "Adam and Eve are the first ones who . . . ": the first to call upon God; the first ritually present to God; the first obligated to God; and the first to disobey God.[2] Those firsts bespeak standard theological topics: prayer, sacraments, command, sin. They demark the human being as a praying animal, a ceremonious animal, a moral animal, and a failure. In line with his dictum that "if the Father of Jesus Christ is the Creator of the world, you ought to be able to tell,"[3] Jenson enlarges each topic to absorb details from secular anthropology: Adam and Eve become the "first hominid group" to do these things.

At first glance, that seems a dangerous opening: In evolutionary science, firstness changes every week, not least because scientists get press for identifying a form as earlier or more distinctive.[4] Jenson avoids the pitfall by specifying also the kinds of firstness theology may ignore. Because "[i]n

---

[1] Robert W. Jenson, *Systematic Theology*, 2 vols. (New York: Oxford University Press, 1997–99), 2:59.

[2] Ibid., 2:59, 60, 61, 63, 150.

[3] Repeated orally to me by David Yeago.

[4] Terminological case in point. When Jenson wrote his *Systematic Theology,* the correct term for humans and their extinct ancestors was "hominid." As of 2016 (to distance orangutans from gorillas, bonobos, chimps, and humans), the Linnaean classification has moved "hominid" one degree upstream, coining "hominin" for humans and their closest ancestors. Culturally, theologians may dislike such novelty as out of conformity with tradition, while scientists may accept it as in greater conformity with reality. When Jenson's *Systematic Theology* says "hominid" and this chapter says "hominin," they mean the same thing.

Genesis, the specific relation to God is *as such* the peculiarity attributed to humanity," it need not coincide with specific human developments, which, however, God remains free to use. Human intentionality or awareness of other minds need not amount to prayer, but at some point God can use it. Human ceremony may resemble that of bower-birds, but God may make more of it. Human self-sacrifice may develop out of animal cooperation, before it makes offerings to God. Human failure may be animal behavior, before it counts as sin. "Theology need not share the anxious effort to stipulate morphological marks that distinguish prehumans from humans in the evolutionary succession. If there is no ontological difference between us and our hominid progenitors, the effort is pointless; if there is, the development may not coincide with the establishment of our species."[5] Otherwise, grace would become a necessity rather than a gift, and humans could extort it. Or there could be other animals with a destiny to fellowship with God: otherwise, humans would bind God's love. As Lauren Winner has written,

> Traditionally, the church has attributed sin only to those things Jesus assumes and can redeem; thus, the church has not attributed sin to non-human animals. The reasoning whereby some non-human primates might be included in the category of creatures-with-agency-who-sin would have to go something like this: if non-human primates (or extra-terrestrials, or any other living creature) share something with us that means they can sin, then they share that thing with Jesus, too.[6]

For Jenson, Adam and Eve are hominids whose species remains irrelevant unless Christologically disciplined. They are first a group, and then, as they encounter their obligations to one another, a community. They call upon God; they come before God in ritual; they hear God's commands in their relations with one another; and they fall short.

Blood

All of those features appear in the following three verses:

> Cain brought to the Lord an offering of the fruit of the ground, and Abel brought of the firstlings of his flock and of the fat portions. And the Lord had regard for Abel and his offering, but for Cain and his offering he had no regard ... And when they were in the field, Cain rose up against his brother

---

[5] Ibid., 59.
[6] Lauren Winner, *The Dangers of Christian Practice: On Wayward Gifts, Characteristic Damage, and Sin* (New Haven, CT: Yale University Press, 2018), 181 n. 1.

Abel, and killed him . . . And the Lord said, "What have you done? Listen; the voice of your brother's blood is crying out to me from the ground."[7]

"The human being," says Wittgenstein, "is a ceremonious animal." And among the first ceremonies Genesis describes outside Eden is one involving blood: the tacit blood of a lamb, and the screaming blood of a human being. The human distinctions that Jenson names attract many symbols, but one symbol covers them all and rises to salience in both the Hebrew Bible and the New Testament: blood, without the shedding of which, as if to explain Cain's rejection, there is no forgiveness of sin (Heb. 9:22).

Tool Use

The stone remains that come down to us – and vastly predate, say, paintings in caves – happen to be knives. Perhaps the earliest tools were ropes or skins. Perhaps hominins first used knives to make clothes or shelter. We know they used knives to chop vegetables.[8] Because the bones of nonhuman animals survive, we know that hominins used knives to kill animals and carve meat.[9] Whatever their users thought, the artifacts remind us moderns of animal sacrifice, including that of Abel.

Many of our earliest artifacts (stone tools) show generations of imitation, and many of them (knives, spearpoints, arrowheads) imply violence, toward animals if not other humans. There is also that great example of the oversized, larger-than-life stone knife, the striped "Excalibur of Atapuerca," thrown as an offering (archaeologists suppose) into a grave, in a great gift-sacrifice of someone's work and wealth.[10] Even before Cain tilled fields or Abel kept herds, hominins made knives, gave gifts, and drew blood.

Early humans came to turn over tools in their hands and in their heads, create images on their walls with red ochre, invest landscape with meaning, and use it for ritual. Their knives and spears drew blood; their pigments stayed red; they observed menstruation and childbirth; they shared meat; they began to ritualize death; they enlarged and decorated their knives and donated them to their dead. They had already performed the acts that at some

---

[7] Gen. 4:3–5, 10, NRSV.

[8] Sonia Ragir, "Diet and Food Preparation: Rethinking Early Hominid Behavior," *Evolutionary Anthropology* 8 (2000): 153–5.

[9] Shannon McPherron, et al., "Evidence for Stone-Tool-Assisted Consumption of Animal Tissues before 3.39 Million Years Ago at Dikika, Ethiopia," *Nature* 466 (2010): 857–60.

[10] E. Carbonell and M. Mosquera, "The Emergence of a Symbolic Behaviour: The Sepulchral Pit of Sima de los Huesos, Sierra de Atapuerca, Burgos, Spain." *Comptes Rendus Palevol* 5 (2006): 155–60.

204 BLOOD THEOLOGY

point they would invest with the meanings of religious sacrifice; at some point they began to think with blood.

Secular Thing Theory

While social construction illuminates the way I look at blood, a critic might observe that the social constructive and structuralist anthropological approaches – which identify humans individual and collective as the agents of blood's work – are foreign and anachronistic to many of the Christian texts, images, and attitudes I study. In those sources, blood itself does things. Blood is itself an agent. A recent movement in anthropology, philosophy, and politics – "thing theory" – may prove truer to those sources. It may do more justice, in fact, to another preoccupation of this book: blood's uncanny ability to persist across periods, to reappear when repressed, to seep in where it seems not to belong. Thing theory seeks to recover the agency of things, to query the anthropocentrism in which only humans act in their lordly isolation.

Blood is both a fluid to think with, and, for a creature, a life to live. Or even, from Abel to Christ, a life poured out. How can Christians keep the symbol of blood together with the life that Leviticus places in it? In many cases it is clear that they construct or conscript blood to do cultural work: but what of its materiality that fills the veins of Jesus or cries out from the ground? We are in old territory: words and things, realism and nominalism, social construction and theory of things. But to think about blood between Eden and Abel it does not do to think about blood as such, which does not survive; to think about blood, you have to think about tools that draw it. This is an advantage, because words and stones are both tools.

The philosopher of language, Ludwig Wittgenstein, and the philosopher of things, Jane Bennett, concur: words work like tools, and the things we think with work like tools, too.[11] Evolutionary psychologists speculate that language emerges with tool use in two ways. Making stone tools gets especially complicated if you fashion cores or blanks to be turned into various tools later, and language would certainly help the teaching of such complex methods. But more than that, some evolutionary psychologists speculate the brain treats language itself as if it were a set of physical tools. Making and using tools over millennia develops potentials in the brain for manipulating objects, turning them over in our heads, and *words piggyback on this process.*

[11] Jane Bennett, *Vibrant Matter: A Political Ecology of Things* (Durham, NC: Duke University Press, 2010).

We think with words as a special case of how we think with tools.[12] Or better, we have only tools, some manual and some linguistic. Blood is both: we recognize it as a thing and as a word of power; we manipulate it manually and mentally; we handle and invoke it.

The thinker constructs the tool, but the materials resist and inspire the maker. They inspire us, if the shape of a stone suggests an idea, or escape us, if the shape of a stone lets it scoot from a blow; and they gain further agency in unexpected ways when they work together with a whole assemblage of other things – from knapstones to iPhones – to exert a hold: observers of Israel saw this in October 2015 as knives came to fascinate Palestinian teenagers who watched loops of knife-attacks and Israeli overresponse on continuous replay in social media. In such videos as well as in painting, history, sacrament, and text, blood, too, can escape or captivate us. It will not stay put. Not only that: we are conflicted about blood, and we express our conflicts in blood's own terms. Blood escapes and persists also because we contend among ourselves who counts as "us," and use blood-language to express and enact our cross-purposes. We use blood-language the way we use other tools like knives: to nourish, defend, and define ourselves. This makes clear that blood itself, like other tools that draw blood, turns back on the agent with an agent-like capacity of its own; it is itself, says Bennett, an actant. "It is because of the creative activity *within* actants that the agency of [things and their] assemblages is not best described in terms of social structures, a locution that designates a stolid whole whose efficacy resides only in its conditioning recalcitrance or capacity to obstruct."[13]

Bennett asks how our thinking would change "were we to take seriously the vitality of (nonhuman) bodies" – "the capacity of things – edibles, commodities, storms, metals – not only to impede or block the will and designs of humans but also to act as quasi agents or forces with trajectories, propensities, or tendencies of their own."[14] As Michael Saler notes, "enchantment" has meant, at least since the Middle Ages, two things: both the human capacity to "delight in wonderful things," and "the potential to be placed under their spell, to be beguiled."[15] Although to fall under a spell

---

[12] Peter Hiscock, "Learning in Lithic Landscapes: A Reconsideration of the Hominid 'Toolmaking' Niche," *Biological Theory* 9 (2014): 27–41; John McNabb, Francesca Binyon, and Lee Hazelwood, "The Large Cutting Tools from the South African Acheulean and the Question of Social Traditions," *Current Anthropology* 45 (2004): 653–77; Lyn Wadley, "Recognizing Complex Cognition through Innovative Technology in Stone Age and Palaeolithic Sites," *Cambridge Archaeological Journal* 23 (2013): 163–83.

[13] Bennett, *Vibrant Matter*, 35.

[14] Ibid., viii.

[15] Ibid., 124 n. 10, citing Michael Saler, "Modernity, Disenchantment, and the Ironic Imagination," *Philosophy and Literature* 28, no.1 (2004): 137–49; here, 138.

reduces human agency, the capacity for delight can empower it. As Augustine wrote to Simplician, only delight can move the will.[16] So our earlier ancestors delighted in rocks that might take shape, that showed their potential to our own. *Homo faber, homo sapiens* record in their names their capacity to take delight from the shapes and qualities of things – for hundreds of thousands of years, to take delight in stones, their shapes, their hardness, their friability, their cooperation with the toolmaker.

"Tool-use," Bennett observes, "engendered a being with an inside, with, that is, a psychological landscape of interiority. Stiegler contends that conscious reflection in (proto) humans first emerged with the use of stone tools because the materiality of the tool acted as an external marker of a past need, as an 'archive' of its function. The stone tool (its texture, color, weight), in calling attention to its projected and recollected use, produced the first hollow of reflection."[17]

Speaking of "the creative activity *within* actants" Bennett admits to anthropomorphizing. "But anthropomorphizing," she insists, "has its uses."[18] Furthermore, if God has become human, Christian theology has more categories to offer than anthropomorphizing or reifying, construction or agency. God can work in humans and in things; agency is already analogical up and down the chain of being; Augustine and Aquinas already hold together love and gravity as two versions of the one way God moves creatures, each appropriate to that creature's own good. Bennett's "spectrum of agentic capacities"[19] is just one corollary of the way creatures participate in the agency of God. Bennett helps willy-nilly to recover the wider reaches of theology; theology gives us a context in which to see Bennett as more than a mere contemporary.[20]

A larger question hangs here: which is it to be, the social construction of blood, in which it has a cultural history, or the thingly agency of blood, in which it seeps beyond that history to constrain, inspire, and escape its manipulators, to slip between their fingers and bring about effects that they do not intend and can hardly contain?

---

[16] Peter Brown's paraphrase of *Ad Simplicianum* I.ii.13 in *Augustine of Hippo* (Berkeley: University of California Press, 1967), 154–5.

[17] Ibid., 31, citing Bernard Stiegler, *Technics and Time*, vol. 1, *The Fault of Epimetheus*, trans. Richard Beardsworth and George Collins (Stanford: Stanford University Press, 1998).

[18] Ibid., 25.

[19] Ibid., 30, quoting from Diana Coole, "Rethinking Agency: A Phenomenological Approach to Embodiment and Agentic Capacities," *Political Studies* 53 (2005): 124–42; here, 128.

[20] Bennett's rejection of souls seems tone-deaf when she considers no mineral movements or vegetable souls and when she reads Leon Kass (who argues in favor) as an "evangelical Christian" rather than a philosophical Jew. Ibid., 56.

The answer is, we must have both. Humans construct blood according to their own interests and purposes, and blood also resists and escapes them. This was less of a mystery to pre-Cartesian thinkers who had softer dualisms to go by – as well as to makers of stone tools, who needed to respect both the stones themselves and the apprenticeships that socialized them.

Aquinas and Maximus on Things Created

Thomas Aquinas, in the thirteenth century, gives us some basic principles, and Maximus, in the seventh, leads us deep into the heart of things.

The things of nature, Aquinas writes, are "constituted between *two* intellects": *Res naturalis inter duos intellectus constituta est.* The one intellect, of course, is the human, by which we natively and necessarily construct things. We must do this. Our things are "constituted" this way, even in the thirteenth century. Known as a moderate realist, Aquinas, student of forms in the mind, acknowledges and insists upon the mind's role in "constituting" reality.

On the other hand, Aquinas also acknowledges and insists that things (as Judith Butler says) call forth more language, even if that language is the "ouch" that we utter when we stub our toes on them. He also knows that things resist, inspire, and escape us. That feature, too, he seeks to explain, when he writes that "a natural thing is constituted between *two* intellects." Aquinas takes so seriously what Bennett calls the "agentic capacity" of things that he ascribes it to a "nature," which Jonathan Lear defines as an "internal principle of *change.*"[21] For Aquinas, the gravity that attracts things and the love that attracts humans are rationally related, similar phenomena emerging on different levels, because all things seek their good (*ST* I-II.26.2). Thus material things seek their good, the center of the earth; that's why they fall; and this movement of theirs is their own, natural movement, product of their internal principle of change, in short, their material soul. This is not yet a rational soul, or even an animal or vegetable soul: it is merely the principle of movement of material things. Plants, however, enjoy another, superimposed principle of movement; they move by growing; that is the desire of their nature and the movement of their vegetable soul. Animals move by instinct; they seek their good, which is Alpo; it is the desire of their nature and the movement of their animal soul. And humans move by reason; they seek their good, which (in this life) is understanding; that is the desire of their

---

[21] Jonathan Lear, *Aristotle: The Desire to Understand* (Cambridge: Cambridge University Press, 1988), 15–19.

208   BLOOD THEOLOGY

nature and the hallmark of their soul. Because of their desire to understand, humans must construct the world: but things have movements of their own, and failing to understand the movement of things would also frustrate our human nature. To explain the movements of things, it would be inadequate to refer to the human intellect alone. Things also have an "understanding," that is, an appropriate participation in the formal relationships that become understanding in us. The structure of things is understanding waiting to happen. To understand bird flight is Bernoulli's principle; but Bernoulli's principle is embodied in the wing of a bird, and that structure participates in what understanding will be.[22] So a structural or formal proto-understanding animates the natures of things, and there a similar understanding animates our minds, and these understandings, under the name "form," emerge as one unitary thing under two aspects, material and intellectual.

But Aquinas goes two steps further to secure the independence of the thing, and the charter of the mind. He saves the thing from human possession by a negation and a name. The thing is independent because the human being has not created it. And he protects that negation by giving its source a name, the intellect of God. This *other,* second intellect, which is not ours, also constitutes things, and grants their agentic capacity, he calls the intellect of God in part so that we may not usurp it. To deny the agency of things is to deny God. Aquinas thus protects the agency of things by naming its source and calling it God. Aquinas never meant his famous Five Ways to prove the existence of God, but to tell us something about how God-language works: at the end of each Way Aquinas remarks, "and this everyone calls 'God.'"[23] Each of the Five Ways, that is, names a way in which things escape our grasp and point beyond themselves.

It is God's creative fashioning of things which makes them finitely knowable by us and finally unfathomable to us.[24] "Things have their intelligibility, their inner clarity and lucidity, and the power to reveal themselves, because God has creatively thought them. This is why they are essentially intelligible [in themselves, not necessarily to us]. . . . . [T]hings are knowable because they have been created."[25]

---

[22] Terence Irwin, *Aristotle's First Principles* (Oxford: Clarendon, 1990), 4.

[23] Eugene F. Rogers, Jr., *Thomas Aquinas and Karl Barth: Sacred Doctrine and the Natural Knowledge of God* (South Bend, IN: University of Notre Dame Press, 1995), 20–73.

[24] This paragraph and the two that follow modify three paragraphs, embedded in a more technical discussion, from my *Aquinas and the Supreme Court: Race, Gender, and the Failure of Natural Law* (Oxford: Wiley-Blackwell, 2013), 33–4.

[25] Josef Pieper, *The Silence of St. Thomas* (New York: Pantheon, 1957), 53–6.

And things are unfathomable for the same reason. Because we cannot create them, we cannot possess, constrain, or enclose them. Their God-relation, their createdness, their capacity for revealing themselves to us, remains rooted in God. This is part of why Aquinas insists that not just some things but all things whatsoever (*omnia quaecumque*) are *divinitus revelabilia*, divinely revealable precisely in their createdness (I.1.6).[26] This does not mean that things are mean or stingy in their knowability: it means their knowability participates *divinitus* in God's capacity to reveal, so that we cannot get to the bottom of them. They outrun us. We never exhaust their light. Aquinas's language for this is that we cannot know their essence. "The essence of all things (as creatures) is that they are formed after an archetypal pattern which dwells in the absolutely creative mind of God."[27] "We can never properly grasp this correspondence between the original pattern in God and the created copy."[28] To do so would be to stand in God's place, and to know that correspondence – how things stand in God – is to know their "essence," the most intimate place where God comes closer to a thing than it is to itself. Aquinas's statements of this sort are frequent and strong: *Principia essentialia rerum sunt nobis ignota*, the essential principles of things are unknown to us. *Formae substantiales per se ipsas sunt ignota*, the substantial forms are unknown through themselves (but through their effects or through the beatific vision by which God shares God's own vision with us). *Differentiae essentiales sunt nobis ignotae*, essential differences are unknown to us.[29]

In short, our minds are made to know things in the world, but not how they correspond to the mind of God. Aquinas calls this unknown correspondence the truth of things. Pieper puts it like this: "We can of course know things; we cannot formally know their *truth*."[30] But in this system it is their truth – their God-relatedness or essence – that first makes knowledge possible. Aquinas turns the usual relation around: *Cognitio est quidam veritatis effectus.* As Pieper writes, "this again is a revolutionary sentence . . . that stands our more normal formulae on their heads: 'Knowledge is a certain effect of truth' . . . indeed of the truth of things!"[31] We can know *that* something is true by inference from its effects, but not by deduction from its essence, not from the inside as if we had created its mechanism. We cannot know what *makes* things to be themselves. Aquinas reveals and re-veils a realm more

---

[26] See the index entries for *revelabilia* in Rogers, *Thomas Aquinas and Karl Barth.*
[27] Pieper, *The Silence of St. Thomas*, 61.
[28] Ibid., 63.
[29] Ibid., 65; quoting *In de anima* I.1.15, *De spiritualibus creaturis* 11 *ad* 3, and *De ver.* 4.1 *ad* 8.
[30] Ibid., 59.
[31] Ibid., 58; quoting *de Ver.* 1.1.

intimate or haram than all our quarks and quantum foam, in which, for all
that our prying is fair and decent, all things strip naked (*panta gymna*) for God
alone (Heb. 4:13). Inventing a realm of intentionality incomprehensible to
Aristotle, Aquinas beholds a *mystery*, which is not first of all what we cannot
know, but first of all their God-related fullness. There remains always more
light from God's things. That is their unfathomability. If we regard our
knowledge as certain, if we close things off, we impugn the Creator.
"According to the doctrine of St. Thomas, it is part of the very nature of
things that their knowability cannot be wholly exhausted by any finite
intellect, *because* these things are creatures, which means that the very
element which makes them capable of being known must necessarily be at
the same time the reason why things are unfathomable."[32]

Aquinas's reference to God is not, therefore, meant to mystify the world
and call a halt to human understanding. For the mystery and the understanding both come from *the same source*. God creates *both* things to escape us
and the mind to grasp them. This is not a paradox. This is the place of the
human in the world. That is why things are constituted not by one but
between *two* intellects. Their constitution by the intellect of God explains
both their luminosity and our insight, their clarity and our perception, their
structure and our understanding. Things receive both their independence
and their intelligibility from the same source. The unfathomability and the
knowledge of things belong together, because both arise from their participation in God. We have to give ourselves over to things to understand them,
and they give themselves to be understood. Our place in the world is to
practice with all things a mutual self-donation.

That is, of course, a Christological remark. To learn more about our place
in the world of things, we turn to Maximus the Confessor, who presents
a compatible theory in the language of Christology.

"For the Logos of God (who is God) wills *always and in all things* (*aei kai en
pasin*) to effect the mystery of his embodiment."[33] Things can be naked
before God as before a mother that gave them embodiment. "God will be *all
in all*, wholly penetrating all who are his in a way that is appropriate for each
(cf. 1 Cor. 15:28)."[34] This certainly gives agentic capacity to all things. Nor
does it reduce them to objects in the hands of God, which would remove
their agency even more effectively than the hands of humans. Rather, God's

[32] Ibid., 60.

[33] Maximus the Confessor, *Ambigua*, translated as *On Difficulties in the Church Fathers* by
Nicholas Constas, English and Greek text on facing pages, 2 vols. (Washington, DC:
Dumbarton Oaks Press, 2014–15), cited by Migne number. Here, vol. 1, 1084C-D.

[34] 1076C.

Word grants them the dignity of their own agency, willing to effect the mystery of God's embodiment in *them*. "This is evident in the incomparable differences among created things. For each is unmistakably unique in itself and its identity remains distinct in relation to other things."[35] This is "evident in" things that can be observed, but that's not the underlying *reason* for their differences. The reason, as the Greek reveals, is Christological. Because the divine and human natures must remain united but "unconfused" (*asungchtos*) or (as translated here) "distinct" in the Logos, so that all the things participating in the Logos must anticipate its love of distinction. This is not the creationist doctrine that every species must remain unevolved because God distinguished it in the beginning. This is the much richer teaching that infinite distinction and variation – as possibly represented by evolution – is willed by God and through God's Logos, plan, or word, who wills always to accomplish the mystery of God's embodiment. The accomplishing unfolds or proceeds (*energesthai*); it takes time (*aei*); it remains a *mysterion*, a word that implies something not so much unknown as a wondrous change or becoming, like the *mysterion* of the Eucharist.

Indeed, the whole principle is Eucharistic, as the word "*mysterion*" makes plain. Everything created by the Logos participates in what the Logos does with flesh, which is to become a human being in the Incarnation and bread and wine in the sacrament. This principle of Maximus's says that all becoming is, if not exactly a sacrament, at least sacramental, a sacrament-in-waiting.

What's wrong with creationism, therefore, is that it's static; in effect it denies the ongoing presence of the Logos in created things and removes him to a realm apart; and in effect it denies that God can represent God's infinity with creation by endlessly multiplying creatures as the miracle stories multiply loaves and fishes according to need, the divided bread endlessly multiplies the body, and every drop of wine contains enough of the savior's blood. If the Logos multiplies this way in the New Testament stories and in the Eucharist, it would hardly befit the Logos *not* to multiply in the creatures.

Thus Aquinas writes (as we saw in Chapter 3), "the distinction and multitude of things come from the intention of the first agent, who is God. For God brought things into being in order that God's goodness might be communicated to creatures, and be represented by them; and because God's goodness could not be adequately represented by one creature alone, God produced creatures many and diverse, that what was wanting to one in the representation of the divine goodness might be supplied by another. For goodness, which in God is simple and uniform, in creatures is manifold and

---

[35] 1077C *asungchutos*.

divided and hence the whole universe together participates the divine goodness more perfectly, and represents it better than any single creature whatever" (*ST*, I.47.1). Or, as Maximus puts it, "[F]rom the one from whom we have received being we long to receive being moved as well."[36] Maximus's language for this is that every thing has its own *logos*, its own internal word, reason, rationale, form, structure, argument, or story. This resembles Aquinas's doctrine of essences: everything has a God-relation to make it luminous, both knowable in its form and unknowable in its depth. The difference here is that *logos* anticipates Christology.

The context of Maximus's doctrine is a remark of Gregory Nazianzen that for human beings our "very limitations are a form of training."[37] We are made to need the world and one another, not to be alone. As part of creation we all – humans, animals, and other things – have movements of our own; but we are not *un*moved movers, like God; we are *moved* movers.

God incarnate in Jesus is God's own argument or story, but all things have arguments (conative capacities) of their own, through which also God makes God's reason known. This vision is anthropocentric in a technical sense: God the human being stands at the center, and the other things are analogous or lead up, *logoi* in the *Logos*. And yet in this case, "humanity's central position actually serves to highlight rather than obscure our connections with other creatures ... a creature that stands at the intersection of the many aspects of created reality that give shape to the universe as a whole." It can "support a theology that sees the wider creation as the defining focus of (as opposed to a more or less dispensable background to) humanity's vocation as a creature."[38] This vocation is to play "a kind of natural bond mediating between extremes ... in order to bring all things together with God."[39]

Tools and the Blood of the Logos

In a flight of Evagrian fancy, Maximus even remarks that "The logoi of intelligible beings may be understood as the blood of the Logos."[40] Blood, in other words, carries meaning; the meaning of things is a Christological

---

[36] 1076B.

[37] *Oration* 14.7.

[38] Ian A. McFarland, "Microcosm and Mediator: Humanity and the Destiny of Creation," *Clergy Journal* 87 (2010), 9–11.

[39] 1305B.

[40] Lars Thunberg, *Microcosm and Mediator: The Theological Anthropology of Maximus the Confessor* (Chicago: Open Court, 1995), 76–7.

WHY THINGS BECAME HUMAN

matter: they are or even seek to be understood in terms of Christ's blood. (See Chapter 4.)

We don't know how far back blood goes, in human history and prehistory, as a carrier of meaning. We know that it has a history of varying, changing, inflecting, and we know that it persists across histories and borders. We know that Anidjar's efforts to pin it to one event (the Inquisition) look anachronistic and arbitrary; we know that Bynum's *Wonderful Blood* is a case study; we know that Bildhauer has identified anthropological structures; and we know that David Biale's *Circulation of a Metaphor* is one of the right approaches.[41] Blood has a history of circulation. But I would like to complete this meditation by associating blood with the oldest set of hominin artifacts that we have. They do not show that blood goes all the way down or all the way back. They do not tell us what blood meant in prehistoric times. They do not pinpoint the origins of sacrifice. But they give us concrete artifacts to ponder: stone knives, blades, hand axes that could and did draw blood, in their use and in their production, and despite other uses such as eating food, scraping skins, cutting cane, and chopping vegetables. And they tend to prove that the agency of things and construction of meaning do belong together, all the way down and all the way back.

Studies of hominin stone toolmaking argue that attention to the material does not diminish but distinguishes the human. Here, the agency of things goes together with the agency of hominins — remembering, transporting, learning, planning.

Toolmaking, which formed hominins for 2.5–3.5 million years, relies upon the agency of things.[42] Not only the procurement and selection of material require that the rock show itself and inspire the maker. The manufacture of artifacts also takes cues from the will and spell of the thing. "[S]trategies for constructing and maintaining viable platforms [for flaking further pieces effectively from a partially worked stone] often involve projecting at least five to ten actions ahead"[43] – a level of planning like bridge, chess, or poetry. It requires "mental projections of both future actions and predicted outcomes."[44] This needs development of both

[41] Gil Anidjar, *Blood: A Critique of Christianity* (New York: Columbia University Press, 2015), reviewed by David van Dusen, "Red Cells and Grey," *Times Literary Supplement*, no. 5818 (October 3, 2014), 32; Caroline Bynum, *Wonderful Blood* (Philadelphia: University of Pennsylvania Press, 2007); David Biale, *Blood and Belief: The Circulation of a Symbol between Jews and Christians* (Berkeley: University of California Press, 2007); and Bettina Bildhauer, *Medieval Blood* (Cardiff: University of Wales Press, 2008).

[42] Hiscock, "Learning in Lithic Landscapes," 27.

[43] Ibid., 33.

[44] Ibid., 34.

214 BLOOD THEOLOGY

"conceptualization and memory" and of social learning and apprenticeship. A "capacity for developing extended narratives, recalling past examples and projecting detailed imagined ones into potential future situations is likely to have been a key transformation in human cognition .... [N]eural circuits implicated in language were increasingly employed during knapping in the Lower Paleolithic, especially as knappers began to produce thinner bifaces."[45]

"Knappers" fracture rock with blows exceeding the elasticity of the material. Convincing a rock to give up its elasticity and sacrifice one form for another is "unforgiving in two senses. Physically it is dangerous ... because [flying shattered pieces,] ... sometimes sharper than scalpels," can cut hands, laps, and eyes. Technically it is difficult, because "at any point in the *chaîne opératoire* a poor strategic choice ..., a mis-struck blow, a flaw or inclusion in the rock, a failure of the hammer stone ... might [raise ridges running down the center of the stone] that make it substantially more difficult or even impossible to transform the object into a specific form."[46]

On the other hand, this toolmaking involved far more from humans than attention and respect for the stone, even the utmost attention from a master sculptor working alone. For toolmaking was a profoundly social activity. "[B]oth competency and expertise in knapping comes at a high learning cost for ... the social group to which [apprentice knappers] belong," including "the cost of learning necessary technical skills, of developing sensitivity in diagnosing the physical properties of rocks, of creating and maintaining shared knowledge about the distribution of knappable rock within the landscape."[47]

"[O]nce lithic artifacts were regularly made they ... created a context which selected for physical and cognitive capacities that facilitated the technology, producing a feedback loop ... for social learning that could be transferred to other tasks."[48]

Blood and Divine Intimacy

Thus: social construction also goes all the way down – and the agency of things develops alongside the social construction of reality. They belong together, not apart. Stone toolmaking fails without both stones to inspire it and apprenticeships to practice it.

[45] Ibid., 34–5.
[46] Ibid., 33.
[47] Ibid., 27, 30.
[48] Ibid., 36.

The example of stone toolmaking shows that over very long periods of time, indeed during the time in which we became human, from as long ago as 3.5 million years, social practices of attention, apprenticeship, and communication developed from and with the inspiration of things. Human virtues of patience, persistence, planning, sequencing, and sheer doggedness – the very characteristics of responsible, long-term change – arose in deep cooperation with others and the stones themselves. Even language, which is hard to trace because brains and vocal chords do not fossilize, may reveal itself in the persistence and beauty of tools that show long apprenticeship and the handing down of culture for even longer generations. More than that, some neuroscientists speculate that the long selection for brains that can turn over tools in the mind and plan long sequences in advance selected also for using words as abstract tools and creating strings of syntax to make sentences. There must have been other, softer developments in human toolmaking – when did we begin to make clothes or tents? – but abundant remains testify that it was in cooperation with stones that we became human.

In Maximian terms, the *logoi* of the stones themselves strove to participate in God's embodiment, if the accounts of toolmaking and the incarnation are both correct. The stones first humanified us, so that God could humanify Godself. In both movements, the Logos was "always and in all things seeking to effect the mystery of his embodiment." Not in the evasion of human responsibility, but in its very development under the Spirit who moves the stones, so that the saying comes true, that "God is able from these stones to raise up children for Abraham" (Mat. 3:9). The very "stones would cry out" (Luke 19:40), as the earth under Abel, because the Logos shares God's voice with all things.

Indeed, the mystery is better than that: seeking a stone, the human being finds bread (Luke 7:8–9). In bread too, along with the wine that becomes his blood, the Logos seeks to accomplish the mystery of his embodiment. Blood, which seeps in where it hardly seems to belong, resembles the Logos that resides in the *logoi* of all things, because both get to the heart of things. That's why the blood of Christ seeps everywhere: the Logos is everywhere already in the *logoi*. The pattern and revelation of this is the sacraments that multiply and contain holiness in every part, like the miracle of loaves and fishes and the contagious holiness of relics. The blood is the fluid, living, material, biohazard version of the Logos. Thus the Gospel of John makes blood the principle of divine intimacy: "Those who eat my flesh and drink my blood abide in me, and I in them" (John 6:56).

If we look into the profoundest thinkers of the Christian tradition, from Jenson back to Aquinas and then Maxiumus, we find the same confidence about the divine intimacy. We learn from them to find it in a Christological reading of creation, indeed of things *tout court,* a Christology of created things. Traditions of biology, sacrifice, the words of Jesus, and the practice of the Eucharist make blood a principle of divine intimacy.

Thus without comment – and so at arm's length – Maximus repeats a tradition that the whole matter of the incarnation arises from the Virgin's blood: "Some among the saints say that the soul is sown by the Holy Spirit in the manner of the man's seed and that the flesh is formed from the virginal blood."[49] (See also Chapter 4.) We glimpse through a dim mirror why Maximus might want to speak of blood here, to make it the sign of intelligible things. The Logos relates to created things not only in the divine pattern, but particularly and concretely and intimately in his blood. The blood of the Logos is creaturely blood, and the blood (here glossed as the intelligibility) of things is their participation in the Logos. But since all creaturely blood belongs to God, Maximus also makes blood signify "the future divinization" or "eternal wellbeing" in which humans belong to God forever.[50] Maximus expands upon the Athanasian pattern, by which the Logos became human, that humans might become logified. Here we see that the Logos became blood – not just in Mary, not just in human beings, not just in higher animals, but in all things intelligible – so that blood, in all things, might coagulate to embody the Logos and take part in its divinity.

---

[49] Maximus the Confessor, *Questiones et dubia,* #50 (complete), trans. Despina Prassas as *St. Maximus the Confessor's Questions and Doubts* (DeKalb: Illinois University Press, 2010), 72. Cf. Bettina Bildhauer, *Medieval Blood,* 84–132.

[50] *Ad Thalassium* 35 in Maximos the Confessor, *On Difficulties in Sacred Scripture: The Responses to Thalassios,* ed. and trans. Fr. Maximos [Nicholas] Constas, The Fathers of the Church, vol. 136 (Washington, DC: Catholic University of America Press, 2018), 212–14.

APPENDIX

REVIEW OF GIL ANIDJAR'S *BLOOD: A CRITIQUE OF CHRISTIANITY*

For further reading, I commend Bettina Bildhauer's *Medieval Blood,* the book that influenced me the most; Ruth George's *Nine Pints,* which overlaps little with this book but is a great read; and David Biale's *Blood: The Circulation of a Metaphor,* on the relation between Christian and Jewish discourses of blood. My own book began with the three presentments of the first chapter (simians, sex, and sacrifice) that made Christian blood-talk, usually so familiar and domesticated, strange to me. It did not begin with other books; in fact, when I read Bildhauer, I had to think whether I had other things to say. The oldest chapter dates to 2002, and the next impulses date from 2008 and 2009. The main themes of my book were settled by 2014, when Gil Anidjar's book, *Blood: A Critique of Christianity,* came out, and my book is not intended as a reply to it. Nevertheless, readers of grant proposals regularly asked about it. We both push far beyond our training; I hope for better luck with evidence. We both think blood is dangerous, but he wants blood, I think, to go away. I think blood, like gender, is hardly going away but would cause more damage underground and needs to be queered. His book links blood with violence; mine links it also with fertility. His book thinks in binaries; mine tries to subvert or sublate them. His follows Nietzsche, mine Wittgenstein. His sings an aria; mine tries to play a fugue. His pursues critique; mine nourishes a hope for repair. For those who have read both, here follows my review of his book.[1]

---

[1] First published as Eugene Rogers, "The Genre of This [that is, Anidjar's] Book," in *Syndicate: A New Forum for Theology* 2 (2015): 145–54. Online at syndicate.network/symposia/theol ogy/blood/.

218   APPENDIX

The Genre of a Handel Aria

Your whole reading of Anidjar's book depends on how you perceive its tone and genre. If you expect reasoned detachment and persuasive argument, you're only going to frustrate and irritate yourself. It lacks – or spurns – the usual academic virtues, which are Aristotelian (measure, moderation, the rhetoric gauged to its audience), in favor of what might be called a noble vice or Nietzschean virtue. His book designs to provoke, not persuade. It uses history not to make arguments, but to pose questions. It free-associates not to escape rigor but to expose sedimented verities. It adopts an angry tone, which can be the seed of virtue, if anger shows a desire for justice rather than the vice of irascibility.

But the way to really enjoy the book is to think about opera, where the important thing is not that an emotion be trained as fuel for reason, but that it be forcefully, even beautifully expressed, with extra notes that run away and digressive cadenzas that try or delight the patience. The genre of Anidjar's book is not argument but aria. Think of your favorite anger arias. I think of Handel's in Italian: *Traditore! Gelosia! Crudeltà!* The book set the first line of one running through my head: *Vivi, tiranno! Svenami, ingrato!* from Handel's *Rodelinda*. Loosely, he sings, "Live on, tyrant; go ahead and kill me!" The tone is caustic and full of rebuke; the metaphor is one of blood. Literally, *Svenami, ingrato, sfoga il furor* is "Dis-vein me, ingrate! Unleash your fury!" "Sarcasm" lacks the requisite bravado and magnificence. The book, like Handel's singer, protests the power of those who (like the tyrant) should have no power. Like the aria, it is full of defiance, baroque in notes that sound briefly and flee away. The singer of the book, like that of the aria, is a hero who disclaims agency, or a victim who exercises agency by taunting the tyrant. By "the singer of the book," I don't mean Anidjar any more than I mean that Handel is his singer Senesino: the author is not a victim, but (with tenure at Columbia) resembles a court composer. Rather, in writing the book, the author has created a persona who, like a Handelian character, marshals the power at the margins to deploy, not reasoned argument or careful qualification – when does Handel do that? – but contrast, exaggeration, suspicion, and hauteur. If you read Anidjar's book, you must make up your mind to enjoy it.

Or another way. Many figures begin in a polemical stage. *Enfant terrible.* The early Karl Barth, for example. The question is whether they will develop a constructive stage. Barth did. Milbank? The constructive Nietzsche we

APPENDIX 219

never saw. Certainly Anidjar has one thing in common with the theologians. He has caught their eponymous disease, the *rabies theologorum*.

Anidjar's is not so much a book *about* blood, as a contribution to one of its native literatures, the polemic. It aims not so much to describe as to draw blood; it re-taliates. As Christian anti-Semitism has tarred Jews with charges of carnality and blood-obsession, Anidjar's book seeks to turn the tables and describe those charges as projecting attitudes internal to Christianity and only blamed on the victim. This is a good question. But Anidjar doesn't answer it. His power of association – his method – is conceptual and phenomenological: Freudian and (as I've said) Nietzschean. It only masquerades as history. It does not carefully disentangle continuities and discontinuities, but deals in identities and binaries. Here is Anidjar's series of identities: Blood=violence=death=capitalism=Christianity. Here is its binary: No-blood=peace=life=Judaism. The continuity is unbroken in each identity, the discontinuity completes between the binaries. They are constantly elaborated, complicated, and detailed, but not disturbed, crossed, blued, or queered. The first identity is realistic; the second is idealistic. Identities and binaries can be quite heuristic; phenomenology is not wrong; one might profitably compare reality with ideals – but not when reality is univocally assigned to one group and ideality to another. Anidjar brilliantly generates and elaborates hypotheses. Historical facts are recruited for this construct; they are not allowed to gray the chiaroscuro effect or muddy the music. Blood must always mean death; it is not allowed to mean life. Magisterially he refuses to see (as we do in class when we have to make the best of a dumb student) when others he cites present evidence and argument at odds with his own. (Those Anidjar treats as dumb students whose arguments I prefer to his own: Biale, Eilberg-Schwarz, Mary Douglas, Nancy Jay.) He tests these hypotheses by exposing them to readers.

There is much to admire in Anidjar's book. In my own book about blood, now underway, I thought I had rung all the changes on blood vocabulary, but Anidjar composes much more elaborate variations. The bibliography alone is prodigious (it would help to have one apart from the notes, and to list the authors in the index). The sheer number of surprising hypotheses will generate some brilliant ones. The idea that blood is not an anthropological given, but must have a history, has to be right, even if its history turns out to be much more complicated and quite different from the identities and binaries that Anidjar proposes. The idea that Christians project their own obsessions onto Jews must also of course be true, even if others are not immune to the fault.

220   APPENDIX

Improvements for the Second Edition

It is pointless to criticize the argument of such a book, if its point is not stepwise moderation but the heuristic and provocative power of contrast. Rather I suggest improvements for the second edition: not to sap its energy, but to keep it from missing so many notes. The second edition that surpasses or overturns the first has some important exemplars in theology. For example, the most influential Christian protest against World War I is not the first edition of Karl Barth's famous *Epistle to the Romans* but the preface to the (much changed) *second* edition. It was important the first time, but much more important the second time.

The Treatment of the Evidence

A number of small things add up to undermine the contrast and reduce the effect by seeding doubt in the mind of the reader.

   1. For example, why refer to the Hebrew Bible as the Old Testament without so much as a scare quote? Wouldn't it be more effective to contrast the Christian with the Jewish interpretation of these texts, or at least point out the hegemonic name, largely avoided by Religious Studies scholars?

   2. Genesis 9:4, Lev. 17:11 and 14, and Deut. 12:23 all say that the life is in the blood. Anidjar tells us the Hebrew word is *nefesh,* which means person or soul, and is not the same as "life." But how do we get from there to the conclusion that blood means death? Certainly there are no comparable verses that say the death is in the blood. To most readers, "the soul is in the blood" will reinforce, not undermine the idea that blood means, not life alone, but life *and* death: that is part of its power. Anidjar has read Walter Benjamin before he turns to the biblical evidence, and draws the conclusion that blood equals violence; but this misleads him when he comes to the biblical evidence, because the biblical authors did not have Benjamin to go by.

   3. The next is a wonky but important example of how Anidjar's book handles its evidence. Anidjar's Introduction makes much of a change in the Western translations of Acts 17:26, reading from the Reformation to the Revised Standard as "made one blood all nations" (25). The Vulgate had "made one all nations." One of Anidjar's more surprising hypotheses is that filiation in antiquity was not understood in terms of blood, but that the Spanish blood purity laws and Inquisition read blood back in. It suits Anidjar's purpose, therefore, for the conjunction of "blood" and "nation" to come very late. Anidjar's Introduction as it now reads suggests that the King James and the *Lutherbibel* unilaterally introduced the word "blood" into

APPENDIX

that verse, because the word "blood" did not appear in the Vulgate. His Introduction presents this fact with a tone of triumph, as if it would, later in the book, become a crux. (It turns out to be a hit-and-run.) The reader familiar with New Testament reference books becomes very uneasy at this point. Of course Anidjar knows that the New Testament was written in Greek, but the oldest source mentioned in the paragraph is the Vulgate. Anidjar must also know that the Protestant Reformers prided themselves on returning to the Greek to wrest the text from the Catholic magisterium, but the paragraph makes it sound as if he finds Reformation translations suspect for smuggling recent ideas into the "correct" Vulgate. The paragraph reminded me of students who compare translations without consulting the Greek. The contrast becomes ineffective because the presentation lacks authority, and it sounds, in Anidjar's Introduction, where many readers will begin, as if something important hangs on a faulty idea that early modern Christians slipped an extraneous but powerful word into a text established by the Vulgate rather than the Greek. "The more recent variant is attributed to 'ancient authorities,'" he notes (25), supplying scare quotes, as if research into earlier sources were illicit. The task is to clean up the contrast so that it introduces no further doubt into the mind of the reader. If you consult the critical Greek text in Nestle-Aland,[2] you see that the editors have chosen to exclude the word "blood," just as Anidjar would like. Surely that would carry more weight than quoting the Vulgate in Latin? Why would you quote the Latin when you could quote the Greek? I can think of reasons, but they would have to be explained.

But the reader, now having picked up Nestle-Aland, glances down at the apparatus to see what those dubious "ancient authorities" might be. You remember that you learned this stuff thirty years ago for just such an occasion; it's like finding algebra useful for once; and you go treasure-hunting among the sigla. For the reading *with* blood, not in the main text, but among the variants in the notes, what do we find? Anidjar needs it to be confined to the East and as late as possible. First we find D; that's the fifth-century Codex Bezae in Cambridge – the principal representative in Greek of the *Western* text-type. Furthermore, its Old Latin (pre-Vulgate) versions date to 250 or earlier. No Reformation invention, that one. Then a surprise: we see the gothic-font 𝕸 or M that stands for the Majority Text. This means that since the fifth century, the largest number of mss belong to this group, using "blood," including over fifty uncials, a papyrus, and over 80 percent of the

---

[2] Eberhard Nestle, Erwin Nestle, Kurt Aland, Barbara Aland, et al., *Novum Testamentum Graece*, 26th ed. (Stuttgart: Deutsche Bibelstiftung, 1979), s.v. Acts 17:26.

minuscules. (Often referred to as the "Byzantine" text, in recent editions of Nestle-Aland it simply contains *all* the mss not cited individually, including Alexandrian and eclectic ones.) The next abbreviation, gig, for Codex Gigas, is obscure; way in the back you find it means that the reading with "blood" continued to be copied, in Latin and against the Vulgate, into the thirteenth century. Then we find the abbreviation sy, which tells us the Syriac tradition is unanimous in preserving the reading with "blood," which is interesting if you are trying to distinguish in binary form between "Christian" and "Semitic" readings. Finally we come to the notation Ir^{Lat}, which tells us that the Latin version of Irenaeus quoted Acts with "blood"; he died in 202 CE. Between the Latin of the Codex Bezae and Irenaeus, we have good reason to think that the Vetus Latina (the reconstructed Latin Bible traditions before the Vulgate) contained the supposedly modern reading with "blood." Furthermore, it dominates the Greek tradition, received early unanimity in Syriac, and continued to be copied in the West through the thirteenth century. The Introduction as it stands, therefore, claims to present evidence in favor of its hypothesis that a connection of blood and nation "emerges in the momentous distance that separates the Vulgate from Luther and filiation from blood" (25). The suspicious reader finds evidence that instead it emerged by 202 at the latest and belongs to the short distance that separates the Vetus Latina and the Greek majority from Jerome. The Introduction raises instead an opposing question: Why did the Western church, in the form of Jerome's translation, *suppress* the reading with "blood"? So as not to undermine the contrast, a second edition should qualify its thesis, find another way to read the evidence, or remove the impression that anything important hangs on the translation of Acts.

4. Then one reads that "for Aristotle, semen has nothing to do with blood" (290, n. 81), which (however one reads Aristotle) seems to conflict with the more familiar view, presented later with approval that in Aristotle "blood ... is the source and origin of semen" (184). The apparent contradiction has to do with semen treated as spiritual spark versus ejaculated matter – a reading that imports into Aristotle a modern opposition of spirit and matter. On the contrary, the point ought to be that the father's *pneuma* travels in the blood and therefore in the semen. Because matter and spirit intermingle or vary on a continuum without modern ideas of transcendence, even *adopted* children could be said to resemble their (adoptive) *pater* through household contact with the paternal spirit. Blood and spirit belonged *more* closely together in antiquity, rather than less. Whatever the first edition of Anidjar means to say about Aristotle, it needs to be cleared up to persuade the

APPENDIX 223

reader that the association of blood with ancestry is a late, Christian invention that arrives *ex machina* around the time of the Inquisition.

5. The use of blood language in the Spanish era of *limpieza de sangre* gets full play, but why is that allowed to characterize Christianity without remainder, when the Vatican strongly *condemned* it? Anidjar mentions the condemnation, to be sure: but he does not allow it to complicate the aria.

6. You wonder anew about the choice and treatment of evidence in an entirely different field when Anidjar mentions blood in the U.S. Constitution. You would suppose he would write about the 3/5 compromise. Instead he writes of "the 'corruption of the blood' that sanctions treason in the US Constitution" (98). When, unfamiliar with that bit of the Constitution, you look it up, you read, in Article III, "The Congress shall have Power to declare the Punishment of Treason, but *no* Attainder of Treason shall work Corruption of Blood."[3] The sanction that Anidjar cites as evidence is not promulgated but prohibited. This sort of thing is hard to account for.

In all these cases, the treatment of the evidence blurs the contrast that Anidjar wishes to display.

Genealogy Biological and Cultural

In what follows, I'm not saying there was "race" before modernity. I'm saying that there were social uses of blood language before modernity, indeed before antiquity, *not* because there was "race," but because "blood" underwrites more conceptualities than one. Blood is (contingently and historically) a metalanguage in which people not only deploy but also *debate* conceptualities (and develop and subvert them). That's why blood can underwrite and undermine conceptualities at need. Anidjar insists that ancient Israel did not locate biological ancestry in the blood. That may or may not be. But even readers not specialized in ancient Israelite biology will wonder about *cultural* constructions of community. Cultural, in the sense of "cutting": they will want to know why circumcision, which cuts the penis and identifies male members of the community, does not count as connecting filiation and community-membership. They will want to know how the blood-prohibition of kashrut fits or does not fit among the hypotheses. They will want to know why blood-discourses and rituals of Dionysian and Mithraic mysteries are not allowed to influence Christianity either. And they will wonder why the work of Nancy Jay is footnoted but not dealt with in Anidjar's

---

[3] Constitution of the United States, Article III, § 3, clause 2.

224   APPENDIX

pages: since she is the great proponent that nations all over the world – Israelite, Greek, Roman, Nuer, Aztec, Ashanti, Hawaiian, Lefevrite Catholic – see sacrifice, when it cuts and bleeds an animal, as a figure of childbirth accomplished, culturally, by men. That is, the people present at a sacrifice belong to a community by cultural kinship, which is more secure than the kinship of childbirth, so that sacrifice is "birth done better" – done culturally. Jay's is a surprising and controversial thesis, but it opposes Anidjar's directly, because it says the theory of biological inheritance doesn't matter, but cultural practice trumps it. Circumcision? Kashrut? Sacrifice? Why are these topics not discussed – why are they not distinguished and reclaimed? To leave them untreated just raises questions that distract from Anidjar's hypotheses. A good model already exists, referred to but not absorbed by Anidjar, in David Biale's *Blood: The Circulation of a Metaphor.*[4] "Circulation" is a nonbinary, non-monolithic metaphor that works very well. In Christianity and Judaism we have to do not with agent and victim or with blood and no-blood. Rather we have two agents that *both* emerge from the destruction of the Second Temple and the end of animal sacrifice; who both use blood to disagree with and turn it to new purposes; who both trade the metaphors back and forth as they seek to differentiate and reclaim themselves from one another. The Gospel of Matthew and Mishnah Yoma both deal with the inability to sacrifice on Yom Kippur. The plausible thesis that Christianity comes to "own" the blood discourse that it has appropriated and developed, and that it projects it onto a Judaism that it invents, is made *less* plausible, not more, by the refusal of blood discourses to Judaism. The second edition must deal with those obvious objections.

Perhaps the reason that Anidjar fails to deal with Jay has to do with a bigger blind spot. He seems to ignore feminist readings of blood. This has to do, in turn, with the use of Walter Benjamin (*explication du texte sans texte*) in the first chapter to associate blood univocally with violence. Anidjar cites plenty of other scholars who themselves crudely or subtly gender the blood of violence as male and the blood of fertility (menstruation and childbirth) as female, but (whether or not the binary is justified) he seems not to take the life and fertility tropes seriously. Jay is the most sophisticated of those scholars. A related oversight is that he never mentions the extensive *internal* critique of Christianity by feminist Christians, who distinguish the blood of violence from the blood of solidarity. This is the integrity of a Gandhi or Martin Luther King, Jr. whose life is perseverance in solidarity to the end: Anidjar would find much grist for his mill in the fifty years of feminist

[4] Berkeley: University of California Press, 2007.

critique of Christian blood language, but it would require him to distinguish between some Christian theologies and others, upsetting the monolith; to acknowledge that blood functions to show fertility as well as violence, life as well as death; that gendering plays a role. Another book cited but unabsorbed by Anidjar is William Cavanaugh's *Torture and Eucharist*:[5] it would also require Anidjar to distinguish between blood rituals that promote and resist state violence. All of these things queer rather than reinforce the binaries according to which blood must mean only violence, be associated only with Christianity, arrive new on the scene at highly specific but shifting points; and can have nothing to do with life, peace, or Judaism. All this would be much more persuasive if it were less black and white and allowed to go gray: but shades of gray are not opera, so this may be help that Anidjar is displeased to receive.

In short: Anidjar's view depends on normative and phenomenological disciplines: philosophy of religion, the normative end of anthropology (even as he fights with it over blood), a neo-Freudian psychology applied to groups, the hermeneutics of suspicion, even Christian theology of Israel, turned on its head. In much of the book as written, history gets in the way. One option would be to drop the historical pose altogether. The book is brilliant at proposing hypotheses, but self-undermining at treating the evidence. Why not admit the genre and *start* with Freud's *Moses and Monotheism* and *Totem and Taboo*, which now come, belatedly, at the end? Those books are read, a century on, not because we think they are historically accurate, but because they open new possibilities.

Let me propose an alternative view, one that I have been developing independently from Anidjar for *The Analogy of Blood* [my private title for *Blood Theology*], though in dependence on some of the same figures – including Mary Douglas, Nancy Jay, and Bettina Bildhauer. This is a view with significant overlaps with Anidjar. It can take on board much of his critique, but it focuses on repair – which allows constructive reference to Christianity's ideals. It admits the power of binaries, but depends on queering them. It admits – it insists – on the danger, the pervasiveness, and the persistence of blood, but judges that, like gender, blood is not soon or easily going away. After we understand about blood, what shall we do next?

[The paragraphs that follow appear elsewhere in *Blood Theology*, mostly in the introduction. Readers who continue to be interested by Anidjar's book should not miss the review by David van Dusen, "Red Cells and Grey," *Times Literary Supplement*, no. 5818 (October 3, 2014), 32.]

[5] Oxford: Blackwell Publishers, 1998.

SOURCES CITED OR CONSULTED

Abelard, Peter. *Commentary on Romans*. In *A Scholastic Miscellany*, ed. and trans. Eugene Fairweather, 283–4. Library of Christian Classics 10. Philadelphia: Westminster Press, 1956.

Adams, Marilyn McCord. *Christ and Horrors: The Coherence of Christology*. Cambridge: Cambridge University Press, 2006.

Alison, James. *Raising Abel*. New York: Herder and Herder, 1996.

Alison, James. *The Joy of Being Wrong: Original Sin through Easter Eyes*. New York: Herder and Herder, 1998.

Allan, Lewis [Abel Meeropol]. "Bitter Fruit." In *The New York Teacher*, 1937.

American College of Obstetricians and Gynecologists, Committee Opinion No. 651 in *Obstet Gynecol* (2015);126:e143–6; accessed April 4, 2019 at www.acog.org/Clinical-Guidance-and-Publications/Committee-Opinions/Committee-on-Adolescent-Health-Care/Menstruation-in-Girls-and-Adolescents-Using-the-Menstrua-Cycle-as-a-Vital-Sign?IsMobileSet=false.

Anidjar, Gil. *Blood: A Critique of Christianity*. New York: Columbia University Press, 2015.

Anselm of Canterbury. *Oratio II*. In *Opera Omnia*, ed. F. S. Schmitt. Edinburgh: Thomas Nelson, 1951.

Anselm of Canterbury. *Meditation on Human Redemption*. In *Prayers and Meditations of St Anselm*, trans. Benedicta Ward, 230–7. New York: Penguin, 1973.

Baer, Fritz. *Die Juden im christlichen Spanien*. 2 vols. Berlin: Akademie-Verlag, 1936.

Baert, Barbara. "Touching the Hem: The Thread between Garment and Blood in the Story of the Woman with the Hemorrhage Mark 5:24b–34parr." *Textile: Journal of Cloth and Culture* 9 (2011): 308–59.

Balberg, Mira. *Blood for Thought: The Reinvention of Sacrifice in Early Rabbinic Literature*. Berkeley: University of California Press, 2017.

Barth, Karl. *Church Dogmatics*. 4 vols. in 13. vol. II/2. Edinburgh: T. and T. Clark, 1957.

Beeson, Ray. *Signed in His Blood: God's Ultimate Weapon for Spiritual Warfare*. Lake Mary, FL: Charism House Book Group, 2014.

Bennett, Jane. *Vibrant Matter: A Political Ecology of Things*. Durham, NC: Duke University Press, 2010.

SOURCES CITED OR CONSULTED

Biale, David. *Blood and Belief: The Circulation of a Symbol between Jews and Christians.* Berkeley, CA: University of California Press, 2008.

Bilby, Mark Glen. *As the Bandit Will I Confess You: Luke 23.39–43 in Early Christian Interpretation.* Cahiers de Biblia Patristica, 13. Turnhout: Brepols, 2014.

Bildhauer, Bettina. *Medieval Blood.* Cardiff: University of Wales Press, 2006.

Boggan, Steve. "Gold-Rush California Was Much More Expensive than Today's." *Smithsonian* (Sept. 20, 2015), www.smithsonianmag.com/history/gold-rush-california-was-much-more-expensive-todays-dot-com-boom-california-180956788/#J2MbopGZACucRz4

Bolman, Elizabeth. "The Enigmatic Coptic Galaktotrophousa and the Cult of the Virgin Mary in Egypt." In *Images of the Mother of God: Perceptions of the Theotokos in Byzantium,* ed. Maria Vassilaki. London: Ashgate Publishing, 2005.

Borowitz, Eugene. *The Talmud's Theological Language-Game: A Philosophical Discourse Analysis.* Albany: State University of New York Press, 2006.

Bowler, Peter J. *Evolution: The History of an Idea.* Berkeley: University of California Press, 2009.

Brown, Joanne Carlson, and Rebecca Parker. "For God So Loved the World?" In *Christianity, Patriarchy, and Abuse: A Feminist Critique,* ed. Joanne Carlson Brown and Carole R. Bohn, 1–30. New York: The Pilgrim Press, 1989.

Brown, Peter. *Augustine of Hippo.* Berkeley, CA: University of California Press, 1967.

Bryan, William Jennings. Closing speech for the Scopes Trial, 1925. Reprinted at www.wright.edu/~christopher.oldstone-moore/Bryan.htm.

Bryan, William Jennings. *The Menace of Darwinism,* 1922. Pamphlet reprinted at http://archive.org/stream/menaceofdarwinis00brya/menaceofdarwinis00brya_djvu.txt.

Bryan, William Jennings. *The Menace of Evolution,* 1920. Pamphlet reprinted at http://law2.umkc.edu/faculty/projects/ftrials/scopes/bryanonevol.html.

Bulgakov, Sergei. *Philosophy of Economy: The World as Household.* Trans. and ed. Catherine Evtuhov. New Haven, CT: Yale University Press, 2000.

Butler, Judith. "Contingent Foundations." In *Feminist Contentions: A Philosophical Exchange,* ed. Seyla Benhabib, et al., 35–57. London and New York: Routledge, 1995.

Butler, Judith. *Bodies That Matter: On the Discursive Limits of Sex.* London: Routledge, 2011.

Bynum, Caroline Walker. "The Blood of Christ in the Later Middle Ages," *Church History* 71 (2002): 685–714.

Bynum, Caroline Walker. *Jesus as Mother.* Berkeley: University of California Press, 1984.

Bynum, Caroline Walker. *Wonderful Blood: Theology and Practice in Late Medieval Northern Germany.* Philadelphia: University of Pennsylvania Press, 2007.

Byrd, A. Dean, Shirley E. Cox, and Jeffrey W. Robinson. "A Slippery Slope That Limits the Atonement." *FAIR Foundation for Apologetic Information and Research,* 2009, www.fairlds.org/Reviews/Rvw200505.html.

Camporesi, Piero. *Juice of Life: The Symbols and Magic Significance of Blood.* New York: Continuum, 1995.

Carbonell E., and M. Mosquera, "The Emergence of a Symbolic Behaviour: The Sepulchral Pit of Sima de los Huesos, Sierra de Atapuerca, Burgos, Spain." *Comptes Rendus Palevol* 5 (2006): 155–60.

Carrasco, Davíd. *The Aztecs: A Very Short Introduction.* Oxford: Oxford University Press, 2011.

228 SOURCES CITED OR CONSULTED

Carrasco, Davíd. *City of Sacrifice: The Aztec Empire and the Role of Violence in Civilization.* Boston: Beacon Press, 1999.

Cassell's Latin Dictionary. Ed. J. R. V. Marchant and Joseph F. Charles. Rev. ed. New York and London: Funk & Wagnall's, 1904–58.

Cavanaugh, William T. *Torture and Eucharist.* Oxford: Blackwell Publishers, 1998.

Chesterton, G. K. *The Man Who Was Thursday.* London and New York: Penguin Books, 1986.

Clancy, Joseph ed. *Twentieth Century Welsh Poems.* Llandyssul, Wales: Gwasg Gomer, 1982.

Coakley, Sarah. *Flesh and Blood: The Eucharist, Desire and Fragmentation.* The Hensley Henson Lectures, 2004–5, Oxford University. Typescript.

Coakley, Sarah. *Sacrifice Regained: Evolution, Cooperation and God.* Gifford Lectures. University of Edinburgh, 2012. Online at www.giffordlectures.org/lectures/sacrifice-regained-evolution-cooperation-and-god.

Cook, Charles. *The Scope's Trial [sic]: A Nation Deceived.* Grand Terrance, CA: Center for Creation Studies, 1986.

Coole, Diana. "Rethinking Agency: A Phenomenological Approach to Embodiment and Agentic Capacities." *Political Studies* 53 (2005): 124–42.

Coon, Linda. "What Is the Word If Not Semen?" In *Gender and the Transformation of the Roman World*, ed. Leslie Brubaker and Julia Smith, 278–300. Cambridge: Cambridge University Press, 2003.

Cowper, William, and John Newton. *Olney Hymns.* London: various publishers, 1779.

Crouch, Andraé. *"The Blood Will Never Lose Its Power."* Sony/ATV Music Publishing, 2005.

Diodorus. *Bibliotheca historica.* Ed. and trans. Francis R. Walton. Cambridge, MA: Harvard University Press, 1957.

Douglas, Mary. "The Bog Irish." In *Natural Symbols: Explorations in Cosmology*, 37–53. New York: Pantheon Books, 1982.

Douglas, Mary. *In the Wilderness: The Doctrine of Defilement in the Book of Numbers.* Oxford: Oxford University Press, 2004.

Douglas, Mary. *Leviticus as Literature.* Oxford: Oxford University Press, 2000.

Douglas, Mary. *Purity and Danger.* London: Routledge, 1984.

Durkheim, Emile. *The Elementary Forms of the Religious Life.* New York: Free Press, 1965.

Eckhardt, Benedikt. "'Bloodless Sacrifice': A Note on Greek Cultic Language in the Imperial Era." *Greek, Roman, and Byzantine Studies* 54 (2014): 255–73.

Eucharistic Devotions. London: Joseph Masters, 1870.

Finlan, Stephen. *Sacrifice and Atonement: Psychological Motives and Biblical Patterns.* Minneapolis, MN: Fortress Press, 2016.

Fonrobert, Charlotte Elisheva. *Menstrual Purity: Rabbinic and Christian Reconstructions of Biblical Gender.* Stanford, CA: Stanford University Press, 2000.

Frank, Frances Croake. "Did the Woman Say?" In *Celebrating Women*, ed. Hannah Ward, Jennifer Wild, and Janet Morley. Harrisburg, PA: Morehouse Publishing, 1986.

Frei, Hans W. "The 'Literal Reading' of Biblical Narrative in the Christian Tradition: Does It Stretch or Will It Break." In *The Bible and the Narrative Tradition*, ed. Frank McConnell, 36–77. Oxford: Oxford University Press, 1986.

Fuentes, Augustín. *Why We Believe: Evolution and the Human Way of Being.* New Haven: Yale University Press, 2019.

SOURCES CITED OR CONSULTED

Gellman, Jerome. *Abraham! Abraham! Kierkegaard and the Hasidim on the Binding of Isaac*. Burlington, VT: Ashgate Press, 2003.

George, Rose. *Nine Pints: A Journey through the Money, Medicine, and Mysteries of Blood*. New York: Metropolitan Books, 2018.

Gilders, William K. *Blood Ritual in the Hebrew Bible: Meaning and Power*. Baltimore: Johns Hopkins University Press, 2004.

Ginger, Ray. *Six Days or Forever? Tennessee v. John Thomas Scopes*. Boston: Beacon Press, 1958.

Good, Deirdre, Willis Jenkins, Cynthia Kittredge, and Eugene F. Rogers, Jr. "Liberal Response." *Anglican Theological Review* 93 (2011): 101–10.

Good, Deirdre, Willis Jenkins, Cynthia Kittredge, and Eugene F. Rogers, Jr. "A Theology of Marriage Including Same-Sex Couples." *Anglican Theological Review* 93 (Winter 2011): 51–87. Online at Same-Sex Relationships in the Life of the Church offered by the Theology Committee of the House of Bishops, www .collegeforbishops.org/s/ss_document_final.pdf.

Gorski, Phillip S. "Why Evangelicals Voted for Trump." *American Journal of Cultural Sociology* (2017), doi:10.1057/s41290-017-0043-9.

Gorski, Phillip S. "Why Do Evangelicals Vote for Trump?" *The Immanent Frame: Secularism, Religion, and the Public Sphere*, Oct. 4, 2016 at https://tif.ssrc.org/2016/10/04/why-do-evangelicals-vote-for-trump/, accessed Oct. 15, 2019.

Grahn, Judy. *Blood, Bread, and Roses: How Menstruation Created the World*. Boston: Beacon Press, 1994.

Gregory of Nyssa. *The Great Catechetical Oration* 37, ed. and trans. J. H. Strawley. In *The Eucharist*, ed. and rev. Daniel J. Sheerin. Message of the Fathers of the Church, vol. 7. Wilmington, DE: Michael Glazier, Inc., 1986.

Groopman, Jerome. "'Pumped: The Story of Blood.' Review of Nine Pints." *The New Yorker*, 94:44 (Jan. 14, 2019), 58–64.

Ham, Ken, and Charles Ware, *One Race, One Blood*. Green Forest, AZ: Master Books, 2007.

Ham, Ken, Carl Weiland, and Don Batten. *One Blood: The Biblical Answer to Racism*. Green Forest, AZ: Master Books, 1999.

Hamilton, Jill. "There Is No Role for Animal Sacrifice in Christianity." *The Guardian*, 15 December 2011, at www.theguardian.com/commentisfree/belief/2011/dec/15/no-role-animal-sacrifice-christianity.

Hand, John Raymond. *Why I Accept the Genesis Record*. Lincoln, NE: Back to the Bible, 1972.

Harvey, Susan. "Embodiment in Time and Eternity: A Syriac Perspective." In *Theology and Sexuality: Classic and Contemporary Readings*, ed. Eugene F. Rogers, Jr., 3–22. Oxford: Blackwell Publishers, 2002.

Haskell, Ellen. *Mystical Resistance: Uncovering the Zohar's Conversations with Christianity*. Oxford: Oxford University Press, 2016.

Hauerwas, Stanley. "Sacrificing the Sacrifices of War." *Criswell Theological Review* N.S. 4 (2007): 77–95.

Himmelfarb, Martha. "The Ordeals of Abraham: Circumcision and the Aqedah in Origen, the Mekhilta, and Genesis Rabah." *Henoch* 28 (2008): 289–310.

Hiscock, Peter. "Learning in Lithic Landscapes: A Reconsideration of the Hominid 'Toolmaking' Niche." *Biological Theory* 9 (2014): 27–41.

230 SOURCES CITED OR CONSULTED

Hoggard Creegan, Nicola. *Animal Suffering and the Problem of Evil*. New York: Oxford, 2013.

Hollander, Aaron T. *The Multimediation of Holiness*. Ph.D. dissertation. University of Chicago, 2018.

Huey, S. J., Jr. and J. R. Weisz. "Ego Control, Ego Resiliency," *J. Abnormal Psychology* 106 (1997): 404–15.

Hughes, Liz Rank. *Reviews of Creationist Books*. Berkeley, CA: National Center for Science Education, 1992.

Hughes, Robert, III. *Beloved Dust*. New York: Continuum, 2008.

Ignatius of Antioch. *Letter to the Philadelphians*. Trans. Alexander Roberts and James Donaldson. Ante-Nicene Fathers, vol. 1, Buffalo, NY: Christian Literature Publishing Co., 1885. Rev. and ed. for New Advent by Kevin Knight. www.newadvent.org/fathers/0108.htm.

Ignatius of Antioch. *Letter to the Romans*. In Ante-Nicene Fathers, vol. 1, trans. Alexander Roberts and James Donaldson. Buffalo, NY: Christian Literature Publishing Co., 1885. Rev. and ed. for New Advent by Kevin Knight at www.newadvent.org/fathers/0107.htm.

Irenaeus of Lyons. *Against Heresies*. Trans. Alexander Roberts and William Rambaut. Ante-Nicene Fathers, vol. 1. Buffalo, NY: Christian Literature Publishing Co., 1885.

Irenaeus of Lyons. *Against Heresies*. In *Theological Anthropology*, ed. and trans. Patout Burns, 23–8. Sources of Early Christian Thought. Philadelphia: Fortress, 1981.

Irwin, Terence. *Aristotle's First Principles*. Oxford: Clarendon, 1990.

Isaac of Nineveh. In *Mystical Treatises*, trans. A. J. Wensinck, 211–12. Amsterdam: Koninklijke Akademie von Wetenschapen, 1923. Reprinted in *The Holy Spirit: Classic and Contemporary Readings*, ed. Eugene F. Rogers, Jr., 111–212. Oxford: Wiley-Blackwell, 2009.

Jacob of Serugh, *Homily on the Veil of Moses*. In *Studies in Syriac Spirituality*, ed. and trans. Sebastian Brock, 177–209. Syrian Churches Series 13. Poonah, India: Anita Printers, 1988.

Jay, Nancy. *Throughout Your Generations Forever: Sacrifice, Religion, and Paternity*. Chicago: University of Chicago Press, 1992.

Jenson, Robert W. *Systematic Theology*. 2 vols. New York: Oxford University Press, 1997–99.

Jobe, Sarah. *Creating with God: The Holy Confusing Blessedness of Pregnancy*. Paraclete Press, 2011.

John of Damascus. *The Orthodox Faith*. Trans. E. W. Watson and L. Pullan in *Nicene and Post-Nicene Fathers*, Second Series, vol. 9, ed. Philip Schaff and Henry Wace. Buffalo, NY: Christian Literature Publishing Co., 1899.

Johnson Hodge, Caroline. *If Sons, then Heirs: A Study of Kinship and Ethnicity in the Letters of Paul*. Oxford: Oxford University Press, 2007.

Jones, David Gwenallt, "Pechod" ["Sin"], in *Cerddi Gwenallt: Y Casgliad Cyflawn* [Collected works], ed. Christine James. Llandyssul, Wales: Gwasg Gomer, 2001.

Joseph, Tyler. "Drown." The Early Years. New Albany Music, 2007.

Joynes, Christine E. "Still at the Margins?: Gospel Women and their Afterlives." In *Radical Christian Voices and Practice: Essays in Honour of Christopher Rowland*, ed. Zoë Bennett and David B. Gowler, 117–35. Oxford: Oxford University Press, 2012.

Julian of Norwich, *Showings*, trans. Edmund Colledge. New York: Paulist Press, 1978.

Kearns, Cleo McNelly. *The Virgin Mary, Monotheism, and Sacrifice*. New York: Cambridge University Press, 2008.

Kerr, Fergus. *Theology after Wittgenstein*. Oxford: Blackwell Publishers, 1986.

Kerr, R. S., and A. D. Weeks. "Postpartum Haemorrhage: A Single Definition Is No Longer Enough," *BJOG* 124 (2017): 723–6.

Kilby, Karen. "Perichoresis and Projection: Problems with Social Doctrines of the Trinity." *New Blackfriars* 81 (2000): 432–45.

Knohl, Israel. *Divine Symphony*. Philadelphia: Jewish Publication Society, 2003.

Kornreich, David. "Is Human Placenta Kosher?" at judaism.stackexchange.com/questions/50865/is-human-placenta-kosher.

Krueger, Derek. "Homoerotic Spectacle and the Monastic Body in Symeon the New Theologian." In *Towards a Theology of Eros*, ed. Virginia Burrus and Catherine Keller, 99–118. New York: Fordham University Press, 2006.

Lear, Jonathan. *Aristotle: The Desire to Understand*. Cambridge: Cambridge University Press, 1988.

LeMarquand, Grant. *An Issue of Relevance: A Comparative Study of the Story of the Bleeding Woman Mk 5: 25–34; Mt 9: 20–22; Lk 8: 43–48 in North Atlantic and African Contexts*. New York: Peter Lang, 2004.

Levenson, Jon D. *The Death and Resurrection of the Beloved Son: The Transformation of Child Sacrifice in Judaism and Christianity*. New Haven, CT: Yale University Press, 1995.

Lewis, Edna. *The Taste of Country Cooking*. 30th anniversary ed. with a Foreword by Alice Waters. New York: Alfred A. Knopf, 2006.

Lockhart, James, and Stuart B. Schwartz. *Early Latin America: A History of Colonial Spanish America and Brazil*. Cambridge: Cambridge University Press, 1983.

MacKinnon, Donald. "Evangelical Imagination." In *Religious Imagination*, ed. James McKay, 175–85. Edinburgh: University of Edinburgh Press, 1986.

Maori Dictionary at http://maoridictionary.co.nz/search?idiom=&phrase=&proverb=&loan=&histLoanWords=&keywords=TAPU.

Marks, Jonathan. *What It Means to Be 98% Chimpanzee: Apes, People, and Their Genes*. Berkeley: University of California Press, 2003.

Marshall, Bruce. "Absorbing the World." In *Theology and Dialogue: Essays in Conversation with George Lindbeck*, ed. Bruce Marshall, 90–7. Notre Dame, IN: University of Notre Dame Press, 1990.

Maximos the Confessor. *Ad Thalassium 35*. In *On Difficulties in Sacred Scripture: The Responses to Thalassios*, ed. and trans. Fr. Maximos [Nicholas] Constas, 212–14. Fathers of the Church Series 136. Washington, DC: Catholic University of America Press, 2018.

Maximos the Confessor. *Ambigua*. Trans. and ed. as *On Difficulties in the Church Fathers* by Nicholas Constas. English and Greek text on facing pages. Washington, DC: Dumbarton Oaks Press, 2014–15.

Maximus the Confessor. *Questiones et dubia*. In *St. Maximus the Confessor's Questions and Doubts*, trans. Despina Prassas. DeKalb: Illinois University Press, 2010.

McCarthy, David Matzko. "The Relationship of Bodies: The Nuptial Hermeneutics of Same-Sex Unions." *Theology and Sexuality* 8 (1998): 96–112.

McCracken, Peggy. *The Curse of Eve, the Wound of the Hero: Blood, Gender, and Medieval Literature*. Philadelphia: University of Pennsylvania Press, 2003.

232   Sources Cited or Consulted

McFarland, Ian A. "Microcosm and Mediator: Humanity and the Destiny of Creation." *Clergy Journal* 87 (2010), 9–11.

McIver, Tom. *Anti-Evolution: An Annotated Bibliography.* Jefferson, NC: McFarland, 1988.

McNabb, John, Francesca Binyon, and Lee Hazelwood. "The Large Cutting Tools from the South African Acheulean and the Question of Social Traditions." *Current Anthropology* 45 (2004): 653–77.

McPhee, John. *The Patch.* New York: Farrar, Straus and Giroux, 2018.

McPherron, Shannon, et al. "Evidence for Stone-Tool-Assisted Consumption of Animal Tissues Before 3.39 Million Years Ago at Dikika, Ethiopia." *Nature* 466 (2010): 857–60.

Meacham, Tirza. "Female Purity, Niddah." *Encyclopedia of the Jewish Women's Archive* at https://jwa.org/encyclopedia/author/meacham-tirzah accessed 5/10/2019.

Meszaros, Julia, and Johannes Zachhuber, *Sacrifice and Modern Thought.* Oxford: Oxford University Press, 2013.

Midrash Tanhuma: Genesis. Trans. and ed. John T. Townsend. Jersey City, NJ: KTAV, 1989.

Milgrom, Jacob. "Israel's Sanctuary: The Priestly 'Picture of Dorian Gray.'" *Révue Biblique* 83 (1976): 390–9.

Milgrom, Jacob. *Leviticus 1–16.* Anchor Yale Bible Commentaries. New Haven, CT: Yale University Press, 1998.

Milgrom, Jacob. *Leviticus.* Continental Commentaries. Minneapolis, MN: Augsburg Fortress, 2004.

Milgrom, Jacob, "Prolegomenon to Leviticus 17:11," *Journal of Biblical Literature* 90 (1971): 149–56.

Moore, Sebastian. "The Crisis of an Ethic Without Desire." In *Jesus the Liberator of Desire,* 89–107. San Francisco: Crossroad Publishing, 1989. Reprinted in *Theology and Sexuality: Classic and Contemporary Readings,* ed. Eugene F. Rogers, Jr., 157–69. Oxford: Blackwell Publishers, 2002.

Morris, Henry. *Creation and the Modern Christian.* El Cajon, CA: Master Books, 1987.

Morris, Henry. *King of Creation.* San Diego, CA: Creation-Life Publishers, 1970.

Morris, Julie. "A Story of Two Leaky Bodies: In Mark 5, a Hemorrhaging Woman Meets a Permeable Savior," *Christian Century* (Jan. 10, 2017), at www.christiancentury.org /article/story-two-leaky-bodies.

Moss, Candida. "The Man with the Flow of Power: Porous Bodies in Mark 5:25–34," *Journal of Biblical Literature* 129 (2010), 507–19.

Motolinía Benevente, Toribio de. *History of the Indians of New Spain,* ed. Elizabeth Andros Foster. Albuquerque: Cortés Society, 1950.

Murray, Michael. *Nature Red in Tooth and Claw: Theism and the Problem of Animal Suffering.* New York: Oxford University Press, 2008.

Nestle, Eberhard, Erwin Nestle, Kurt Aland, Barbara Aland, et al., eds. *Novum Testamentum Graece* 26th ed. Stuttgart: Deutsche Bibelstiftung, 1979.

Netanyahu, Benzion. "Did the Toledans in 1449 Rely on a Real Royal Privilege?" *Proceedings of the American Academy of Jewish Research* 44 (1977): 93–125.

Niditch, Susan. *Underdogs and Tricksters: A Prelude to Biblical Folklore.* San Francisco: Harper & Row, 1987.

Nirenberg, David. "Was There Race Before Modernity? The Example of 'Jewish Blood' in Late Medieval Spain." In *The Origins of Racism in the West,* ed. Ben Isaac,

SOURCES CITED OR CONSULTED

233

Yossi Ziegler, and Miriam Eliav-Feldon, 233–64. Cambridge: Cambridge University Press, 2010.

Norris, Richard. *God and World in Early Christian Theology: A Study in Justin Martyr, Irenaeus, Tertullian and Origen*. New York: Seabury, 1965.

Numbers, Ronald L. *The Creationists: From Scientific Creationism to Intelligent Design*. Cambridge, MA: Harvard University Press, 2006.

Ochs, Vanessa. "Publicizing the Miracle: Optimistic Discursive Practices and the Commodities of Passover." *Contemporary Jewry* 35 (2016): 187–202.

Olaweraju, Samuel. "The Efficacy of Prayer in the Blood of Christ in Contemporary African Christianity." *Africa Journal of Evangelical Theology* 22 (2003): 31–49.

Origen of Alexandria. *Commentary on the Epistle to the Romans*, trans. Thomas P. Scheck. The Fathers of the Church. Washington, DC: Catholic University of America Press, 1990.

Origen of Alexandria. *Homélies sur le Lévitique*. Latin and French text. Ed. and trans. Marcel Robert. *Sources Chrétiennes* vol. 286. Paris: Cerf, 1981. English translation: *Homilies on Leviticus*. Trans. Gary Wayne Barkley. The Fathers of the Church, vols. 83–4. Washington, DC: Catholic University of America Press, 1990.

Otten, Herman J. *Baal or God*. New Haven, MO: Leader, 1965.

Parker, Robert C. T. *Miasma: Pollution and Purification in Early Greek Religion*. Oxford: Clarendon Press, 1983.

Philoxenus of Mabbug. "Letter to Abba Symeon of Caesarea." In *Hebrews*, ed. Erik Heen and Phillip D. W. Krey, 142–3. Ancient Christian Commentary series, New Testament vol. 10. Downers Grove, IL: IVP Academic, 2005 = *Ascetical Homilies of St. Isaac the Syrian*. Trans. Holy Transfiguration Monastery [Dana Miller], 427–48. Boston: Holy Transfiguration Monastery, 1984.

Pieper, Joseph. *The Silence of St. Thomas*. New York: Pantheon, 1957.

Radcliffe, Timothy, O. P. "Christ in Hebrews: Cultic Irony." *New Blackfriars* 68 (1987): 494–504.

Radner, Ephraim. *Leviticus*. Brazos Theological Commentary on the Bible. Grand Rapids, MI: Brazos Press, 2008.

Ragir, Sonia. "Diet and Food Preparation: Rethinking Early Hominid Behavior." *Evolutionary Anthropology* 8 (2000): 153–55.

Rahner, Karl. "Christology within an Evolutionary View of the World." In *Theological Investigations* 5, trans. Karl-H. Kruger, 158–92. New York: Crossroad, 1983 (1966).

Ray, Stephen. "Black Lives Matter as Enfleshed Theology." In *Enfleshing Theology: Embodiment, Discipleship, and Politics in the Work of M. Shawn Copeland*, ed. Robert J. Rivera and Michele Saracino, 83–93. Minneapolis, MN: Fortress, 2018.

Rogers, Eugene F., Jr. *After the Spirit: A Constructive Pneumatology from Resources Outside the Modern West*. Grand Rapids, MI: Eerdmans Publishing, 2005.

Rogers, Eugene F., Jr. "The Fire in the Wine: How Does the Blood of Christ Carry the Holy Spirit?" In *Third Article Theology*, ed. Myk Habets, 251–64. Minneapolis, MN: Fortress, 2016.

Rogers, Eugene F., Jr. "The Genre of This [that is, Anidjar's] Book." *Syndicate: A New Forum for Theology* 2 (2015): 145–54. Online at https://syndicate.network/symposia/theology/blood/.

Rogers, Eugene F., Jr. "How the Semen of the Spirit Genders the Gentiles." In *Aquinas and the Supreme Court: Race, Gender, and the Failure of Natural Law in Thomas's Biblical Commentaries*, 289–97. Oxford: Blackwell Publishers, 2013.

234   SOURCES CITED OR CONSULTED

Rogers, Eugene F., Jr. "Isaac in the Eucharist," *Journal for Scriptural Reasoning* 2:3 September 2002 at etext.lib.virginia.edu/journals/ssr/.

Rogers, Eugene F., Jr. "Marriage as an Ascetic Practice." *INTAMS Review, The Journal of the International Academy of Marital Spirituality* 11 (2005): 28–36.

Rogers, Eugene F., Jr. "Nature with Water and the Spirit: A Response to Rowan Williams." *Scottish Journal of Theology* 56 (2003): 89–100.

Rogers, Eugene F., Jr. "Paul on Exceeding Nature: Queer Gentiles and the Giddy Gardener." In F. S. Roden, ed., *Jewish/Christian/Queer: Crossroads and Identities.* Aldershot, Hants: Ashgate, 2009.

Rogers, Eugene F., Jr. "Romans and the Gender of Gentiles." *Soundings: An Interdisciplinary Journal* 94 (2011): 359–74.

Rogers, Eugene F., Jr. "Same-Sex Complementarity." *Christian Century*, 128:10 (May 17, 2011): 26–9, 31.

Rogers, Eugene F., Jr. *Sexuality and the Christian Body: Their Way into the Triune God.* Oxford: Blackwell Publishers, 1999.

Rogers, Eugene F., Jr. "The Spirit Rests on the Son Paraphysically." In *The Lord and Giver of Life: Perspectives on Constructive Pneumatology*, ed. David H. Jensen, 87–95, 174–6. Philadelphia: Westminster/John Knox, 2008.

Rogers, Eugene F., Jr. *Thomas Aquinas and Karl Barth: Sacred Doctrine and the Natural Knowledge of God.* Notre Dame, IN: University of Notre Dame Press, 1995.

Romanos the Melodist. "On Baptism." In *Kontakia of Romanos, Byzantine Melodist*, trans. and ed. Marjorie Carpenter. 2 vols. Vol. 2, 227–36. Columbia, MO: University of Missouri Press, 1970.

Root-Bernstein, Robert. "On Defining a Scientific Theory: Creationism Considered." In *Science and Creationism*, ed. Ashley Montagu, 64–94. Oxford: Oxford University Press, 1984.

Saler, Michael. "Modernity, Disenchantment, and the Ironic Imagination." *Philosophy and Literature* 28 (2004): 137–49.

Sapolsky, Robert. *A Primate's Memoir: A Neuroscientist's Unconventional Life among the Baboons.* New York: Scribner, 2001.

Schiller, Gertrud. *Iconography of Christian Art.* 4 vols. New York: Graphic Art Society. 1971–2.

Schmemann, Alexander. *For the Life of the World.* New York: St. Vladimir's Seminary Press, 1998.

Sedgwick, Emma. *From Flow to Face: The Haemorrhoissa Motif Mark 5: 24b-34 parr between Anthropological Origin and Image Paradigm.* Leeuven: Peeters, 2015.

Sicroff, Albert A. *Los estatutos de limpieza de sangre: Controversias entre los siglos XV y XVII.* Trans. Mauro Armiño, revisada por el autor. Madrid: Taurus, 1979.

Sigal, Peter. *The Flower and the Scorpion: Sexuality and Ritual in Early Nahua Culture.* Durham, NC: Duke University Press, 2011.

Sigüenza, Fray José de. *Historia de la Orden de San Jerónimo.* 2nd ed. 2 vols. Madrid: Bailly-Bailliére é Hijos, 1907–9.

Singer, Peter. *Animal Liberation.* New York: HarperCollins, 2007.

Soskice, Janet Martin. "Blood and Defilement: Christology." In *The Kindness of God: Metaphor, Gender, and Religious Language*, 84–99. Oxford: Oxford University Press, 2007.

SOURCES CITED OR CONSULTED

Stibbs, Alan M. *The Meaning of the Word Blood in Scripture*. 3rd rev. ed. Oxford: Tyndale Press, 1963.

Stiegler, Bernard. *Technics and Time. Vol. 1, The Fault of Epimetheus*, trans. Richard Beardsworth and George Collins. Stanford: Stanford University Press, 1998.

Stökl Ben Ezra, Daniel. "Atonement. Judaism: Second Temple Period." In *Encyclopedia of the Bible and Its Reception. Vol. 3, Athena-Birkat ha-Minim*, ed. Hans-Josef Klauk *et al.* Berlin: de Gruyter, 2011.

Stout, Jeffrey. "Blood and Harmony." In *Blessed Are the Organized: Grassroots Democracy in America*, 181–5. Princeton, NJ: Princeton University Press, 2010.

Stowers, Stanley. "Greeks Who Sacrifice and Those Who Do Not: Toward an Anthropology of Greek Religion." In *The Social World of the Earliest Christians: Essays in Honor of Wayne A. Meeks*, ed. L. M. White and O. L. Yarborough, 293–333. Minneapolis, MN: Fortress Press, 1995.

Stowers, Stanley. "Matter and Spirit, or What Is Pauline Participation in Christ." In *The Holy Spirit: Classic & Contemporary Readings*, ed. Eugene F. Rogers, Jr., 92–105. Oxford: Wiley-Blackwell, 2009.

Straussman-Pflanzer, Eva. *Violence and Virtue: Artemisia Gentileschi's "Judith Slaying Holofernes."* Chicago: Art Institute of Chicago, 2013.

Stroumsa, Guy. *The End of Sacrifice: Religious Transformations in Late Antiquity*, trans. Susan Emanuel. Chicago: University of Chicago Press, 2009.

Sullivan, Shannon. *Living across and through Skins: Transactional Bodies, Pragmatism, and Feminism*. Bloomington: Indiana University Press, 2001.

Sykes, Stephen, ed. *Sacrifice and Redemption*. Cambridge: Cambridge University Press, 1991.

Symeon the New Theologian. The Ethical Discourses. In *On the Mystical Life: The Ethical Discourses*, trans. Alexander Golitzen, 3 vols. St. Vladimir's Seminary Press, 1995.

Tagliaferro, Eleonora. "Ἀναίμακτος θυσία – λογικὴ θυσία: a proposito della critica al sacrificio cruento." In *Sangue e antropologia nella liturgia III*, ed. Francesco Vattioni, 1573–95. Rome: Pia Unione Preziosissimo Sangue, 1984.

Tanner, Kathryn. *God and Creation: Tyranny or Empowerment*. Oxford: Basil Blackwell, 1985.

Tanner, Kathryn. *Jesus, Humanity and the Trinity*. Minneapolis, MN: Fortress, 2001.

Teilhard de Chardin, Pierre. "The Mass on the World." In *The Heart of Matter*, 119–34. New York: Houghton Mifflin, 2002.

Thomas Aquinas. *Commentary on the Gospel of John*. Trans. by Fabian Larcher and James Weisheipl. Washington, DC: Catholic University of America Press, 2010.

Thomas Aquinas. *De potentia*. In *Quaestiones disputatae de potentia Dei*, trans. English Dominican Friars. Westminster, MD: The Newman Press, 1952. Online edition ed. Joseph Kenney at isidore.co/aquinas/QDdePotentia.htm.

Thomas Aquinas. *Summa Theologiae*. Madrid: Biblioteca de autores cristianos, 5 vols., 1962–78. English: *Summa Theologica: First Complete American Edition, Literally Translated by Fathers of the English Dominican Province* [Laurence Shapcoate], rev. ed., 3 vols. New York: Benziger Brothers, 1920. Reprint in 5 vols. Allen, TX: Christian Classics, 1981.

Thomas Aquinas. *Super epistolas S. Pauli lectura*. Ed. Raphael Cai. 8 rev. ed. 2 vols. Truin: Marietti, 1953.

236   SOURCES CITED OR CONSULTED

Thomas Aquinas. *Super Evangelium s. Ioannis lectura.* Ed. Raphael Cai. Turin: Marietti, 1952. English translation: *Commentary on the Gospel of John,* trans. James A. Weisheipl and Fabian R. Larcher, with introduction and notes by Daniel Keating and Matthew Levering. 2 vols., with parallel Latin text and the Greek text of the gospel. Lander, WY: The Aquinas Institute, 2013 and online at aquinas.cc/la/en/~Ioan.

Thunberg, Lars. *Microcosm and Mediator: The Theological Anthropology of Maximus the Confessor.* Trans. A. M. Allchin. Chicago: Open Court, 1995.

Toumey, Christopher P. *God's Own Scientists: Creationism in a Secular World.* New Brunswick, NJ: Rutgers University Press, 1994.

Tregear, Edward. *Maori-Polynesian Comparative Dictionary.* Wellington, NZ: Lyon and Blair, 1891. Searchable facsimile: https://archive.org/details/maoripolynesian01treggoog/

Twain, Mark. *Adam's Diary.* New York and London: Harper Bros, 1904 [1893].

Ullucci, David. *The Christian Rejection of Animal Sacrifice.* Oxford: Oxford University Press, 2011.

van Dusen, David. "Red Cells and Grey." *Times Literary Supplement,* no. 5818 October 3, 2014, 32.

de Waal, Frans. *Chimpanzee Politics: Power and Sex among Apes.* Baltimore: Johns Hopkins University Press, 2007.

Wadley, Lyn. "Recognizing Complex Cognition through Innovative Technology in Stone Age and Palaeolithic Sites." *Cambridge Archaeological Journal* 23 (2013): 163–83.

Ward, Graham. "The Displaced Body of Jesus Christ," in *Radical Orthodoxy: A New Theology,* ed. John Milbank, Catherine Pickstock, and Graham Ward, 163–81. London: Routledge, 1999.

White, Heather. *Reforming Sodom: Protestants and the Rise of Gay Rights.* Chapel Hill, NC: University of North Carolina Press, 2015.

Williams, Rowan. *Headwaters.* Oxford: Perpetua Press, 2008.

Winner, Lauren. *The Dangers of Christian Practice: On Wayward Gifts, Characteristic Damage, and Sin.* New Haven, CT: Yale University Press, 2018.

Wittgenstein, Ludwig. *Bemerkungen über Frazers Golden Bough/Remarks on Frazer's Golden Bough.* German and English on facing pages. Ed. Rush Rees, trans. A. C. Miles. Atlantic Highlands, NJ: Humanities Press International, 1979.

Wyschogrod, Michael. *The Body of Faith: God in the People Israel.* San Francisco: Harper & Row, 1983.

SCRIPTURE INDEX

Genesis 1: 17, 172
  1:29, 24
  1:4–7, 70
Genesis 3:16–17, 113
Genesis 4:3–5, 203
  4:10, 136
Genesis 12:11–13, 43,
  46
Genesis 13:8, 43, 46
Genesis 15:9–18, 74
Genesis 18:27, 46
  18:30–32, 46
Genesis 19:2, 46
  19:7–8, 47
  19:18–20, 47
  19:30–34, 47
Genesis 22:2, 43
  22:10, 39
Genesis 24:1–6, 46
Genesis 27:2–3, 47
  27:9, 47
  27:21, 47
  27:26, 47
Genesis 30:15–17, 47
Genesis 31:11, 48
  34–35, 91
Genesis 32:11, 48
  32:29, 48
Genesis 35:16–18, 97
Genesis 49:11, 81

Exodus 4:25, 118
Exodus 29:12, 18

Exodus 30:10, 18

Leviticus 4:7, 18, 62
  4:18, 18
  4:25, 18
  4:30, 18
  4:34, 18
Leviticus 8:15, 18
Leviticus 9:9, 18
Leviticus 14:5–7, 174
Leviticus 15:19–24, 86
Leviticus 16:18, 18
Leviticus 17:11, 14, 9, 21, 24, 34,
  220
Leviticus 20:21, 89

Deuteronomy 12:23, 9, 34, 220
Deuteronomy 21:23, 20

Judges 13:4, 44
Judges 16:6, 44
  16:10, 44
  16:28, 44
Judges 19, 36

Ruth 2:2, 199
  2:7, 49
Ruth 3:4–7, 129
  3:9–15, 130

1 Samuel 15:22, 180
1 Samuel 18:4, 129
1 Samuel 20:41, 130

238 SCRIPTURE INDEX

2 Samuel 11:2–4, 86

Judith 10:10, 86
  10:11–13

Job 29:14, 176
Job 40:10, 43
Job 41:1, 77

Psalm 34:8, 31
Psalm 40:6–8, 180
Psalm 50:9–10, 180
Psalm 72:14, 34
Psalm 82:6, 124
Psalm 89:35, 44
Psalm 145:15, 199

Proverbs 15:8, 180
Proverbs 21:2–3, 180

Isaiah 1:11, 180
  11:18, 49
Isaiah 36:8, 49
  36:12–13, 49
Isaiah 43:3, 168
  43:27–44
Isaiah 47:12, 43
Isaiah 51:21, 49

Jeremiah 6:20–21, 181
Jeremiah 7:21–22, 181
  7:31, 43
Jeremiah 19:4–5, 43, 44

Ezekiel 7:19–20, 89
Ezekiel 22:3, 84

Hosea 6:6, 181

Amos 5:21–24, 93, 181

Malachi 1:10, 181

Matthew 3:9, 215
Matthew 5:23–24, 181
Matthew 9:13, 181
  9:20–22, 89
Matthew 12:7, 181

Matthew 23
  35–36, 136
Matthew 26:6–13, 88
  26:27–28, 62, 141

Mark 4:24, 62
Mark 5:25–34, 83, 88
Mark 7:28, 199
Mark 14:3–9, 88
  14:24, 175

Luke 7:8–9, 215
  7:36–50, 88
Luke 8:43–48, 89
Luke 9:17, 199
Luke 15:20–22, 129
Luke 19:40, 215
Luke 22:20, 62

John 1:13, 33
John 6:50–57, 35, 175, 185, 191,
  215
John 12:1–8, 88

Acts 5:30, 20
Acts 10:39, 20
Acts 13:29, 20
Acts 15:29, 141
Acts 17:26, 35, 152, 220,
  221

Romans 1, 110, 128
  1:4–9, 24
Romans 3:24–26, 16, 24
Romans 8:17, 128
Romans 11, 110, 128
  11:18, 168
Romans 12:1, 181
  12:6, 14
Romans 13:14, 176

1 Corinthians 3:9, 144
1 Corinthians 11:20, 138
  11:24, 23, 137
1 Corinthians 12:13, 79
  12:27, 79
1 Corinthians 15:28, 210
  15:57, 10

SCRIPTURE INDEX

Galatians 3:13, 20, 168, 176

Ephesians 1:10, 25
Ephesians 4:24, 176

Philippians 2:6–11, 124

Colossians 1:15, 175
Colossians 3:10, 176
 3:12, 176

Hebrews 2:14, 172
 2:17, 172

Hebrews 9:22, 3, 31, 40, 84, 112, 113, 152,
 179, 203
Hebrews 12:1, 172

1 Peter 1:19–20, 25,
1 Peter 2:24, 20

1 John 2:2, 197
1 John 3:9, 80, 129

Revelation 7:14, 84
Revelation 12:11, 118
Revelation 13:8, 25

SUBJECT INDEX

Abelard, Peter, 15–17, 36, 175, 176

Abraham, 39–50, 64, 74, 84, 215

Adam, 124, 143, 146–148, 151–153, 155, 156, 168, 194, 198, 201, 202

Adams, Marilyn, 61, 132, 155, 156, 226

adoption, 108, 109–111, 128

analogy, 13–15, 20, 65, 73, 120, 132, 157, 225

Anidjar, Gil, 7, 85, 213, 218–225

Anselm, 8, 15–17, 29, 125–126, 187–189

anthropocentrism, 30, 204, 212

Aquinas, 4, 14, 18, 20, 27, 31, 34, 65, 70, 104, 108, 128–129, 139, 145–146, 185–186, 189–193, 194–196, 206–210, 211–212

Aristotle, 102, 104, 108, 189, 190, 193, 194, 210, 222

ascetic, 28, 112, 113, 114

Athanasius, 29, 110, 131, 140, 143, 157, 195

atonement, 8, 14–16, 17, 20–22, 24, 25, 29, 65–66, 77, 95, 113, 115, 118–121, 123–124, 126, 127, 131–132, 134, 138, 139, 143, 145, 146–148, 155, 156, 188

Augustine, 77, 89, 159, 188, 190, 206

Aztec, 5, 162–163, 173, 176, 182, 224

baptism, 40, 79, 80, 98, 99, 105, 108, 110, 126, 152, 164, 167, 168, 197

Benjamin, Walter, 220, 224

Bennett, Jane, 30–31, 204–208

Bildhauer, Bettina, 6–7, 9, 10, 18, 19, 101, 102, 119, 148, 213, 225

Black Lives Matter, 36, 76–77, 78, 80

blood, *see other entries*

blood libel, 25, 173–174

Body of Christ, 12, 14–15, 72, 79, 104, 120–121, 138, 192–193, 195

body, social, 9, 12, 17, 29, 64, 75, 78, 79, 80, 121, 132, 145, 146, 148, 156

bonds, 12, 17, 75, 81, 87, 122–123, 135, 204, 212

boundary, 6, 7, 9, 10, 11, 36, 60, 68, 75, 78, 92, 99, 121–124, 128, 148, 156, 159, 171, 200

Bradford, Aminah, xi, 85, 95, 152

Brown, Michael, Jr., 36, 76, 77, 78

Bryan, William Jennings, 132, 147

Bulgakov, Sergei, 27, 69, 140, 142, 189, 198

Butler, Judith, 10, 26, 41, 102, 126, 136, 182, 207

Bynum, Caroline, 7, 12, 113, 213

Calvin, John, 4, 89

Cavanaugh, William, 199, 225

childbirth, 4, 15, 18, 28, 31, 60, 75, 79–81, 85, 93–100, 102, 103, 110, 112–114, 115, 121, 123, 203, 224

Christ, *see incarnation, atonement, body of Christ, etc.*

Coakley, Sarah, 5, 18, 124, 132

conquest of the Americas, 162, 174

covenant, 42, 44, 74, 118, 131–134, 141, 175, 197

COVID-19, 22–23

Cornelisz, Jacob, cover, 19

creationism, 15, 20, 22, 115, 134, 137–138, 139, 144–149, 150–151, 153, 159, 211

de Cartagena, Alonso, 168

de Waal, Frans, 188

Dismas, *see Thief on the Cross*

Douglas, Mary, 6, 15, 17–18, 26, 34, 56, 63–65, 73, 75, 119, 121–122, 140, 171, 219, 225

Durkheim, Emile, 6, 13, 15, 18, 33, 65, 92, 109, 119–122, 150, 157

SUBJECT INDEX

Eden, 23, 96, 111, 138, 141, 143, 203, 204

Eid al-Adha, 39, 40, 56

Eucharist, *see table of contents*, 12–14, 16–17, 23, 32–33, 35, 39, 51, 62–63, 65–66, 69, 71–72, 80, 85–86, 92, 98, 100–101, 108, 110–111, 118, 120, 123–124, 127, 138–140, 142, 155–156, 179, 181, 185–200, 211, 216, 225

evolution, ix, 15, 20–22, 23, 33, 68, 103, 115, 120, 131–132, 137–142, 143–149, 150, 153, 155, 156, 157, 179, 188, 197, 201, 202, 204, 211

felix culpa, 23, 78, 99, 138, 141

Ferrer, Vicente, 164

forgiveness, 18, 41, 60, 61, 68, 112, 129, 138, 141, 179, 188, 203

gender, 15, 21, 22, 28, 36, 54, 68, 84–89, 90, 92, 93, 97, 98, 101, 103, 110, 112, 113, 115, 118, 120, 121, 123, 124, 127, 129, 131, 178, 224

Gregory of Nyssa, 77, 186

Ham, Ken, 20, 131, 147, 150

hatta't offering, 57, 60

Hauerwas, Stanley, 180

heaven, 23, 72, 96, 138, 141, 143, 152, 176, 187, 197, 200

hecatomb, 56, 63, 95

Holiday, Billie, 19

Holy Spirit, 71, 101, 104, 108, 110, 112, 126, 129, 151, 190, 192, 194, 216, *see also* pneuma

homosexuality, *see sexuality*

Ignatius of Antioch, 12–13

incarnation, 15, 20, 25, 29, 32, 98, 101, 112, 121, 124, 128, 131, 132, 134, 139, 143, 154, 160, 185, 188, 195, 196, 211, 215, 216

Irenaeus, 35, 98, 110, 131, 136, 144, 157, 222

irony, 19, 23, 25, 41–44, 45, 49, 60, 139, 141, 153, 171, 190, 196

Isaac, 18–19, 24, 40–41, 42, 44, 46, 47, 48, 50, 51, 66, 154

Isaac of Nineveh, 112, 200

Islam, 39–40, 65, 162

Israel, 103, 154, 168, 223, 225

Jacob, 47–48

Jacob of Serugh, 21, 89, 126, 133

Jay, Nancy, 6, 15, 18, 81, 91, 93, 94, 109, 112, 113, 118, 119, 123, 219, 223, 224, 225

Jenson, Robert, 201–203, 215

Jews/Judaism, 4–5, 19, 24, 39, 41, 44–45, 50–51, 53–57, 60, 62, 163–171, 173–174, 199–200, 219–220

Jobe, Sarah, xi, 85, 88, 91, 94, 96, 97, 99, 100, 230

John of Damascus, 104, 193

Jonah, 77

Joseph, 48

Julian of Norwich, 67, 72, 135, 157

Kerr, Fergus, 177

kinship, 14, 21, 25, 73, 91, 100, 111, 120, 132, 148, 149, 150, 156, 173, 224

Last Supper, 10, 26, 29, 41, 62, 76, 80, 81, 99, 127, 172

limpieza de sangre, see purity

Lod, *see St. George Christians*

Logoi, 31–32, 35, 103, 212, 215

Logos, 31, 35, 39, 101–103, 104, 124, 135, 138, 156, 197, 199, 210–213, 215–216

Luther, Martin, 89, 222

lynching, 19

Maori, 92, 95, 106

marriage, same-sex, *see sexuality*

Martyrdom, 12, 22, 25, 36, 72, 75, 76, 120, 179

Mary (the mother of Jesus), 36, 85–86, 89, 98, 101, 104–105, 113–115, 165–6, 173, 216

Maximus the Confessor, 14, 20, 32–34, 36, 101–103, 120, 131, 138, 173, 189, 207, 210, 211–213, 216

McCracken, Peggy, 90, 96, 97

menstruation, xi, 10, 15, 22, 25, 28, 31, 81, 84, 88–90, 93–95, 96, 99–102, 103, 104–107, 113, 120, 121, 141, 194, 203, 224

Meshel, Naphtali, xi, 59, 62, 73

Milgrom, Jacob, 59–61, 73

Moore, Sebastian, 125, 127

mutability, 20, 70, 131, 133, 143, 153, 155

Nirenberg, David, 167, 182

nutritive theory of the Eucharist, 185, 190, 192, 195–197

Origen of Alexandria, 4, 24, 63–65, 68, 95

Orthodox Christianity, 86, 92, 118, 125, 157

para phusin, 110, 128

paraphysically, 110, 111, 128, 195

Subject Index

patriarchy, 126
permeability, 10, 11, 120
Peter, 42, 98, 157
Philoxenus of Mabbug, 4, 112, 113
Pirkei Avot, 24, 39
pneuma, 109–111, 128, 192, 194, 222, *see also* Holy Spirit
primatology, 3, 20, 100, 153, 185, 186, 188, 197, 199, 202
purity, 6, 11, 21, 62, 70, 104, 105, 133, 136, 159, 161–164, 166, 167–173, 178, 220

race, 11, 25, 30, 76, 146, 148, 150–151, 163, 164, 223
Rachel, 47, 48, 91, 97, 114
Radcliffe, Timothy, 171–173
Rahner, Karl, 22, 137, 188
rape, 124
Ray, Stephen, Jr., 77
recapitulation, 133, 135–136
Reconquista, 174
remission of sins, *see Hebrews 9:22*
Repentance, 60, 152
Romanos, 89, 187
Rotorua, 92, 95

sacrifice, *see table of contents*, 3, 6–9, 13, 17–20, 22–25, 27, 29, 32–35, 39–82, 84–85, 87, 94, 96–100, 104, 108–110, 112–115, 118, 123–124, 126, 136–137, 139–140, 142, 152–153, 161–163, 172–182, 186, 202–204, 213–214, 216–217, 224
Saint George Christians, 51, 56
Samaritans, 51, 52–54, 55–57
Satan, 42, 44, 50, 77, 78, 118, 119
Schmemann, Alexander, 71, 189, 197, 198
scripture, 132, 151, 156, 159–160, 163, 170
semen, 86, 96–97, 102, 104, 108, 110, 129, 188, 222
sexuality, x, 3, 15, 115, 117, 118, 119, 121, 122, 123, 124, 128

Sicroff, Albert, *see purity*
Stout, Jeff, 11
Stowers, Stan, 17
structuralism, 64, 65

Teilhard de Chardin, Pierre, 23, 132, 156
Teresa of Avila, 171
theodicy, 45, 61, 146, 149, 153
theology, 5, 21–22, 26, 31, 34, 64, 68, 69, 90, 115, 124, 132, 145, 164, 165, 167, 171, 173, 187, 190, 202, 206
thief on the cross, 118, 124, 125
thing theory, 30, 31, 204
Thomas Aquinas, 3, 14, 18, 20, 27, 31, 34, 65, 70, 104–105, 108, 128–129, 139, 145–146, 185–186, 189–193, 194–196, 206–210, 211–212, *see Aquinas*
tools, 30, 73, 203–207, 215
trickster, 41, 42, 43, 44, 48, 77

vegetarianism, 29, 140, 142
veins, *see bonds*
violence, 5, 7, 10, 25, 26, 31, 41, 72, 75, 76, 77, 78, 80, 81, 85–87, 127, 132, 136, 139, 145, 146, 149, 155, 160, 167, 182, 195, 199, 203, 219, 220, 224, 225
virgin birth, 85

de Waal, Frans, 188
Watts, Isaac, 40, 59
Wilgefortis, St., 99
Williams, Gregory S., xi, 20, 66, 77, 78, 80, 85, 94, 96, 100, 103, 111, 144, 166, 167, 168
Winner, Lauren, 26, 199, 200, 202
Wittgenstein, Ludwig, 4, 5, 17, 27, 29, 176, 177, 178, 203, 204
Woman with the Issue of Blood, 85–87, 90–93, 98, 100, 112
Wyschogrod, Michael, 3, 4, 5, 75